D0989631

HOW
TO FISH
FROM
TOP TO
BOTTOM

HOW TO FISH FROM TOP TO BOTTOM

By
Sid W.
Gordon

The
Stackpole
Company

•

Harrisburg
Pennsylvania

Printed in the U. S. A.

by

THE TELEGRAPH PRESS

Established 1831

HARRISBURG, PENNSYLVANIA

Contents

Photographs by Alan N. Miller; sketches by
Jennett Swanson and Les Farrow

HOW
TO FISH
FROM
TOP TO
BOTTOM

CHAPTER I

Water Can Be Read
Like a Book

LAKES AND STREAMS too often appear as strangers to a fisherman. It is not necessary to have this feeling of unfamiliarity about them when, by using only your eyes and common sense, you can go upon them with a spirit of confidence.

Then, in a very short time, you can regard them as intimately as an old friend with whom you may quickly enjoy pleasant and profitable fishing relations.

There is, of course, a knack in whipping a fly and casting a lure, but you can learn that in half an hour. If you really want to know what's what about fishing, by all means learn to read the water.

"How can a fisherman read water?" you ask.

Actually, water is quite simple to read. It is my hope that in this book you will find the inspiration to judge all waters you intend to fish, making intelligent decisions as to how they should be fished with fly or lure, thereby becoming what I regard as an "all around angler."

The fisherman who looks analytically at water, just as a good hunter appraises the land and knows what sort of game will be in the clearings and the hardwoods and what to hunt in the pine or spruce, will soon get out of the novice class.

You will discover that plants in the lakes and streams are like the words in a book, revealing whether the water is rich or poor, and indicating what kind of fishing you have a right to anticipate.

The lakes will often tell you whether they are in three layers, to be fished only on the surface and in the upper layer, or whether the water is so intermixed that the lake can be fished from top to bottom. You will learn the importance of air, water penetration of the sun, and the food shelf in telling you what tackle to use and HOW to use it.

You will find that river water speaks different words to a fisherman than lake water. While both have one thing in common—the water itself—a river is much more talkative. It is virtually a chatterbox with its riffles and rapids, a demure sort of person in its pools, mystifying in its eddies and intriguing in its reaches.

The novice will use all the knowledge he has acquired on lake water but will, in a brief time, learn to combine the more faithful tendencies of the "lady of the lake" with that "vixen of water," the river.

We fishermen speak of both lake and river in the feminine sense, yet a river needs a longer courtship before we can claim that "she" is ours.

In a river we sum up our fishing problems in just one word—current. It is an understanding of the current which will make a river angler an expert. Neglect to read current and you assuredly will remain a dub fisherman all your life. Observe current carefully, listen to the language it so clearly speaks and great benefits will come to you, for the current really tells you how to fish.

Brought up among loggers and lumberjacks in the Upper Peninsula of Michigan, I learned to call all running water a "crick." This word, however, will never do in discussing water in this book. Right here it is best that I tell the fisherman the various terms I shall use in discussing the streams.

A stream three to 10 feet wide I shall call a brook. A creek will mean a stream over 10 feet wide to 30 feet in width. A river will be any stream from 30 feet to the breadth of our greatest streams, such as the Mississippi.

Not in a study of the brook or the river will a beginning angler obtain his quickest schooling. It is the creek—10 to 30 feet wide—which will best enable him to learn how to read stream water. A good creek of about 25 feet in width will prove ideal. Here he will learn more in a shorter time than may seem possible if he will just sit down and observe current before he begins his fly fishing career. In fact, three hours spent studying creek current will give the beginner more knowledge of a stream than an entire summer of hit and miss angling.

I had an exceptional opportunity to see how fishermen worked the waters during the years I had charge of the lake and stream improvement projects in Wisconsin, from 1934 until 1941. I covered over 150,000 miles making water surveys and supervising several hundred men. From my observations of hundreds of anglers, I would say that the methods of most of those who fished with fly or plug were surprising indeed. I came to the conclusion that the vast majority could be rated only as "tackle" fishermen.

To me, the water comes first in my fishing thoughts, then the behavior of the fish, and last, the tackle with which I catch the fish. Most of the fishermen I saw reversed the process. To them, the be all and the end all apparently was their rods, lines, reels, flies and lures. They hoped they would be "lucky." A few little blue gills gave them much pleasure, while the water seemed to be just something to carry their boat while they worked the tackle from morning until night.

I saw fishermen come to a resort where there were at least 500 lakes within a two hours' drive. They would cruise around one of these lakes like a blind dog in a meat market, so confused that they did not know where to stop for a "bite." The next day, spurning the lake they had just fished, and ignoring the other good lakes in the immediate area, they would be off in their car to some other county which had no better water. Surely its lakes had no larger fish and probably the food and lodging was not as good as that of the resort they had just abandoned.

I maintain that an angler *should stay with a beautiful lake or a grand stream long enough to get acquainted with it.*

If the fisherman of our overcivilized Hydrogen Bomb age can't avoid being restless and insists upon moving from place to place, he should at least have a keener knowledge of water than he now seems to possess. We "old timers" had no such roving habits, for we were forced to study the fish and water. We had no automobiles or airplanes for quick and easy get-aways. The result was that we analyzed every bit of water we fished and tried to make every cast pay dividends.

It has always been an amazing thing to me that a fisherman will go along with his wife, son or daughter in the woods and discuss the trees, flowers, birds and animals, along with the soil and the formation of the land, but seldom points out anything to them in the water. Rather, when they come to a lake or stream, he will tell them where he caught a large fish, what he used to tempt it to strike, and what a ferocious battle the fish put up.

I have found that women and children generally are more interested in fishing than in killing a squirrel, duck, partridge or a deer. This probably is because they have no qualms about catching a fish, which is a cold-blooded animal, has no mercy

3

on other fish and often eats its own offspring, but can be returned to the water without harm, if you wish.

When you study the water and point out various facts about it to your family or fishing friends, you open a new and enjoyable field of thought to them. Surely an incessant talk of rods, reels and lines must be a sort of mumbo-jumbo to them. Discussion concerning the water will make them more observant of it, and as eager to read its "signs" as you are. Given the right information, and good tackle, women and children become excellent anglers.

Let me assure you that these "signs" of the water are easily interpreted when we learn the facts about them. In the next seven chapters I shall endeavor to show the short cuts you will be able to use in reading water, those which I have noted in more than 50 years of angling. If you will give careful attention to these early chapters before getting into those on fishing, I am confident you will eliminate much of the grief and many of the headaches I suffered because I did not recognize at once what nature tried so hard to tell me.

Had it not been for my continuous habit of reading the water, I know I never would have made an observation about insect behavior which later led me to try a new type of fishing. This I have called the wet-dry fly method, a term that I feel exactly describes it.

The insect behavior of which I speak is something that has prevailed for ages, yet no angler that I know of has ever discussed it in his writings. To me, the amazing thing is that we have been fly fishing for over 2,000 years, using the wet fly, the nymph and the dry fly, still we have overlooked this fourth possibility, the wet-dry fly.

This fly, let me hasten to explain, is not just a dreamed-up creation of tinsel and feathers. On the contrary, this fourth kind of fly is patterned to conform strictly with insect behavior.

Through the centuries we fishermen have thought that insects drop their eggs into lakes and streams solely from the surface. You can well imagine how surprising it was to me on a summer's day back in 1937 when I for the first time noticed on Wisconsin's Brule River that some insects were descending to the bottom to lay their eggs.

I had never heard nor read about that before, and after extensive research I came to the conclusion that here indeed was something new for the fisherman. Although my research dis-

4

closed that entomologists knew that some insects crawl or swim beneath the surface to deposit their eggs. I found none who had commented on the vast change in appearance which comes over the insects when so doing. It is this great change which had never been brought to the fisherman, and which is the basis for the entirely new method of fly fishing.

As I watched those insects descend to the bottom of the Brule River to lay eggs, I could but conclude that trout were accustomed to feed upon them as the insects struggled with the current so they could get down under to drop their eggs. I saw that these fast swimming insects were not inert, drowned flies. They were extremely lively creatures, their bodies displaying a great amount of flash, and undoubtedly very attractive to feeding fish.

If, through the centuries, it made sense to float an imitation dry fly on the surface to tempt rising fish, then it also made sense to sink certain types of dry flies toward the bottom to simulate those insects with the underwater egg-laying tendency. It was this reasoning, based upon my years of observation on lakes and streams, that prompted me to experiment with the wet-dry fly.

I have here only briefly sketched a general idea of the new fly. Later I devote an entire chapter to this discovery, with the thought that anglers the world over will study its possibilities themselves, and perhaps answer some of the questions which still are baffling me.

I am confident that the principle of the wet-dry fly, based as it is upon this little known behavior of water insects, is sound, but I have not yet succeeded in producing the "perfect" imitation fly which I feel adequately simulates the action of a living dry fly swimming so fast to the bottom of a lake or stream to deposit her eggs. It is my sincere hope that some other fisherman, from his experience in reading the water, will produce a fly which fully brings out the flash which the living fly exhibits so vividly to the fish on her egg-laying descent.

That fisherman may well be you.

CHAPTER II

Transparency Is a Guide
To Daytime Angling

IT GIVES ME tremendous satisfaction to look at the water of a strange lake for a moment or two and allow the effect of the sun's rays to tell me how it should be fished.

One lake tells me to use a diving, floating lure just a few feet underwater, while another says, "You have to fish me at 30 feet under the surface, with a sinking lure."

It is the rays of the sun that enables me to read the lakes in this manner. They reveal the transparency of the water, which has an effect upon the eyes of the fish and consequently upon my methods of fishing.

For the purposes of angling, I classify water transparency into five groups, or colors. These are: *dark brown, brown, tan, clear* and *very clear*. In each of these groups the fish may lie at a different depth between 9 A. M. and 4 P. M. therefore each calls for a different technique in angling.

You no doubt will agree with me that there is much pleasure fishing during these delightful daytime hours, but those who neglect to take transparency into account too often find this period frustrating. That is because they are casting futilely too near the surface when the fish are down under and do not even see the lures. Oddly enough, the bait fisherman does much better even though he may not know a thing about transparency. He sits in his boat dropping his baited hook at varying depths until by trial and error he catches a fish and discovers the level at which it was feeding or resting. Then he proceeds to catch more fish while the man who is casting lures at or near the surface gets nothing but a sore arm.

There are, of course, some other factors besides transparency that affect daytime fishing. The angler, if he reads the waters properly, will take into consideration cloudy days, ripples on the water, and waves and wavelets, all of which reduce sun glare and visibility of the fish. Warm or cold water, as well as inlets and outlets, also have effects on the behavior of fish in a lake.

A sure and reasonably quick way to ascertain the transparency of a lake is to attach an eight inch white enamel plate to a cord so that when the plate is lowered in the water its flat surface will be uppermost, just as it would appear lying on a table. See Figure 1. You lower the plate—flat side up—until you lose sight of it. Then you raise the plate slowly until you see its dim outlines in the water.

By measuring the distance of the cord from the surface to the dimly outlined plate you will have determined the transparency of the lake. The best time to do this is at high noon when the sun is highest and brightest, giving the lake its very greatest amount of sunshine.

On a sunny day in unruffled water, between the hours of 9 A. M. and 4 P. M., the largest fish will lie at or below the depth where the submerged plate is dimly visible. They seek this level to avoid the glaring rays of the sun which hurt their eyes just as glare does the eyes of a human.

Knowing the transparency of a lake you are about to fish is important because it tells you how far apart your casts should be between the hours of 9 A. M. and 4 P. M.

FIG. 1.—The eight or 10 inch white enamel plate for reading the transparency of lake or stream water. A five-ounce dipsey swivel sinker on a 45 pound test Cuttyhunk line is used for sounding to find bottom, reef, pocket and drop-off depths.

Although I do not know exactly how far a fish can see your red and white plug in the *dark brown* water, I give him credit for seeing as far as you can see the white enamel plate. In other words, your transparency reading tells you that your fly, lure or minnow will not be seen unless it is within 18 inches of either side of the fish. You probably are aware of the fact that fish can see with each eye separately.

Thus, when you fish in *dark brown* waters, close casting is required, regardless of whether you are fishing during the morning, afternoon or evening, whether with your casting, spinning or fly rod. My advice is, don't cast more than 50 feet from your boat, and space your casts *not over* five feet apart, with your lure under the surface but not lower than six feet. In this manner you will cover all the good water without running your boat over some that has not been searched thoroughly.

Before you try the white plate, however, let us sit down at the breakfast table with a pitcher of *clear water*, a pot of strong coffee, a quarter teaspoon of flour, a pepper shaker and a few drinking glasses. With these I believe I can simplify the explanation of transparency and show you how you can fish any waters you may meet in your travels.

By pouring the strongly boiled coffee into one of the glass tumblers you will immediately notice the dark brown color. The water in hundreds of lakes and streams is of that hue. As I have already pointed out, an eight inch white enamel plate lowered into a lake of that color would be vaguely discernible at a depth of about 18 inches. Your transparency reading, therefore, is 18 inches. While 100 per cent of the sun's rays is hitting the surface of this *dark brown* water, 80 per cent of its light is lost in the first one and one-half feet of water.

If the water in a lake is classed as *clear* in the early spring and late autumn, a fisherman must consider it in the *dark brown* group if it is full of "bloom" during July and August, and often through part of September. We have thousands of such "blooming" lakes in our country.

For a better understanding of the transparency of a lake in "bloom," let's fill one of those glasses with clear water from the pitcher, and mix that quarter teaspoon of flour and some pepper in it. The flour and pepper in the glass of water will give you a fair idea of the summer transparency of an ordinarily *clear* water lake full of the blue and green specks we fishermen call "bloom."

This "bloom" in reality is plankton, small particles of plant life

9

which multiply by cell division under the effect of the sun's rays, plus tiny animals which eat the plants. It is easy to comprehend why "bloom" clouds the water so intensively when a microscope reveals there are as many as 20 million of these tiny plants and animals to a gallon of lake water in "bloom."

As in actual *dark brown* water, you will lose sight of a white enamel plate in 18 inches of a lake whose water is clouded with plankton. Under such conditions it should be obvious that the lake must be fished as closely with your fly or lure as the lakes of *dark brown* water, although fish can lie much deeper in "bloom-filled" lakes than in *dark brown* water. This is because a high oxygen content is created at good depths by the plants of the plankton.

Let us now consider the *brown* water lakes which also are numerous in our country. If you will pour a little *clear* water into a glass half filled with your coffee you will note the mixture is somewhat clearer than the undiluted coffee. Your white plate lowered in a lake with waters of this *brown* hue would be visible to a depth of approximately five feet.

Here you can space your casts about 10 feet apart instead of the three to five feet in lakes of *dark brown* and "bloom-filled" water, all because the fish's range of vision is somewhat greater in the lighter colored water. Also, it is advisable to use a lure that sinks not over 10 to 12 feet.

If you now add a few more tablespoons of *clear* water to that glass of diluted coffee, the mixture will resemble the *tan* water so often encountered in our fishing. In *tan* water your plate should show a transparency of 10 feet. Here your casts can be spread as far apart as 15 or 20 feet because in *tan* waters the fish can see your lures at a distance of 10 feet from either eye. In this kind of water your lure should sink to a depth of not more than 10 to 15 feet. If it's too close to the surface the fish is not likely to see it.

Clear and *very clear* water lakes have much greater transparency than the *dark brown, brown* and *tan*. It is not wise, however, for an inexperienced person to conclude that a lake is *very clear* without first judging it with a white plate. The plate is apt to reveal it as a *clear* water lake rather than one that is *very clear*.

Clear water lakes allow about 60 per cent of the sunlight to penetrate the first three feet of water, but at a depth of 10 feet there are but 25 per cent of the rays. In other words, a *clear* water lake loses 95 per cent of its sunlight in its first 25 feet of water, the depth at which your white plate would be but indistinctly observable. These waters can be fished with your lures as far down as 25 feet.

Very clear water lakes, on the other hand, allow the sun's rays to penerate at least 10 feet deeper so that you can see the vague outlines of your plate at a depth of from 30 to 35 feet. Such lakes seem almost as clear as distilled water, so great is their transparency. Fish can lie as far down as 40 feet in such water. I have fished or surveyed thousands of lakes in this country and Canada, and regard any water with a summer transparency of 35 feet or over as outstanding.

After a season's use of the white plate, you can safely discard it. By that time you will have became so accustomed to appraising the transparency of water that you will be able to do it merely by cupping the palm of your hand 12 inches or so under the surface of the lake and looking at the water in it. Check this method with your plate at first. You will be delighted and surprised to see how soon you can classify each lake as *dark brown, brown, tan, clear* or *very clear*.

Based upon transparency of the water, a table I have prepared gives me a more or less unscientific but reliable method for my daytime fishing from June 10 until September 10. It shows the approximate depth at which a white plate is dimly visible in the various colored waters, and shows the fish's range of vision, which indicates how far apart my casts can be spaced. While transparency, as revealed by the white plate, measures the distance at which a fish can see your lures, it also shows you the upper limit at which fish can lie to escape the bright rays of the sun. They can, and often do, lie deeper, but never below a depth where there is not enough oxygen in the water for them to breathe. The table indicates the various depths below which fish will not be found.

In a lake of *very clear* water, for instance, a walleyed pike (pike perch) will often lie in 30 to 35 feet of water from 9 A. M. until 4 P. M. Bass lie higher than wall eyes as a general rule. I have often found northern pike at 35 feet in *very clear* water lakes.

One of the largest muskellunge I ever saw, a world's champion at the time, was caught by Gus Peterson, of Irma, Wis., at 2 p. m. after hitting his plug at a 30 foot depth in one of the *clear* water lakes of the Lac du Flambeau area.

Here, for the guidance of fishermen, is my transparency table:

Color of Water	Transparency and Distance a Fish Can See a Lure	Where Fish Can Range	Where Fish Do Not Have Enough Air to Live
		Down to	Not below
Dark Brown	1 to 2 feet	6 feet	7 feet
Brown	3 to 5 feet	10 feet	12 feet
Tan	5 to 10 feet	15 feet	16 feet
Clear	Up to 25 feet	25 feet	30 feet
Very Clear	Up to 40 feet	40 feet	50 feet*

*There are a few exceptions to this general rule. In Wisconsin, which has over 8,500 lakes, there are about a couple dozen where there is enough air in the water during the summer for fish to breathe at depths below 50 feet and down to 150 feet.

Although my casts with plugs, spoons or spinning lures are spaced about 20 feet apart in *clear* waters, they are spaced but 10 feet apart with flies or very small spinning lures, the same as in *tan* waters. The reason for this is that they are so much smaller and therefore are not as readily distinguishable at a greater distance.

Despite the fact that I know fish can see farther in *very clear* waters than *clear* waters, I employ the same casting techniques as in *clear* waters. I much prefer coaxing a fish to dash no more than 10 feet for any lure. I do not believe in giving him too much time to look critically at a lure that is definitely a fraud.

When we seek the deep lying fish of the *clear* and *very clear* lakes by casting 50 or 75 feet and begin to reel in our spoon or underwater plug as soon as it hits the surface, our lure does not get within the fish's vision. Who can expect a resting walleye

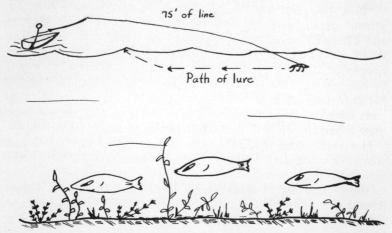

75' of line

Path of lure

Fig. 2.—Fishermen miss many fish by working the lure too high in the water.

12

or bass to come up out of the dark depths to seize a lure he doesn't even see?

Our angling literature, unfortunately, is full of conflicting statements such as "fishing fine and far off," or "make short casts and plenty of them." Many accept these as axioms but too often apply them in the wrong situation.

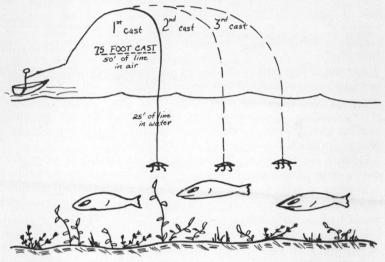

FIG. 3.—With a "lob cast" the lure searches the bottom waters effectively.

"Fish fine and far," is excellent advice for fishermen on a trout stream, given to us by those famous men, Izaak Walton and Charles Cotton. We definitely take a leaf from their book when we fish *clear* water streams. Nevertheless, we shouldn't overdo it. "Far off" to them was not as far as we might judge by today's standards. We must remember that Izaak Walton and his illustrious adopted son had no reels on their rods, so their casts with the fly probably were never over 35 feet, even though they fished the clear chalk and limestone streams in England.

How ridiculous it is to throw 50 feet of fly line and leader when we wade *dark brown, brown, tan* roiled or broken stream water in the United States or Canada. In such waters our methods must be "fish near and fish close" for there is little danger of trout seeing us with that kind of limited transparency. Fifteen to 35 foot casts under such circumstances are more sensible, with longer casts advisable only when we try for depth, hoping to get our wet fly or nymph well under.

13

On the other hand, knowing what we do about transparency, it is equally ridiculous to "make short casts and plenty of them" on lakes of *clear* or *very clear* water.

A good way to understand this is to have another fisherman cast a plug or spoon and observe the action of his lure from another boat. You will note that the plug starts back to the caster very quickly if he reels it in immediately. You will see that it gets nowhere near the deep lying fish as shown in Figure 2.

Only a lob cast such as shown in Figure 3 will allow your lure really to search the sunlit waters of a *clear* or *very clear* water lake. The idea is to cast 75 feet of line, in a high looping or "lob" cast, but to let the heavy underwater lure drop in the water 50 feet from the boat. When the plug strikes the water after traveling in the high arch or loop, it will go down to that 20 or 30 feet of depth you wish to work. Observe the plug's action for a few casts. This will teach you the exact moment to begin turning the handle of your casting or spinning reel. You'll get the hang of it in hardly any time at all.

A good sinking underwater lure has almost as much action while it is sinking as it has while being reeled in by the caster. There is but little difference, except that a strike on a sinking lure requires much firmer handling on the strike, a harder setting of the hook to take up the slack line, but this soon comes to one.

With a little practice you will learn how much time each particular lure in your tackle box requires to sink 15, 20 or 25 feet. Give the lure enough time to reach the proper depth, as indicated by your transparency reading, before you begin to turn the handle of the casting or spinning rod. Then, by reeling in slowly, starting and stopping, you can keep the lure at the level you wish for quite some distance. When you know that it is out of the fish's zone, too high in the water, reel rapidly and make another cast. This is where the spinning rod, with its almost invisible line and longer casts, has an advantage over the plug rod in *clear* and *very clear* waters.

The deeper the lure travels in lake water of good transparency the less distance the fish can see it. With 75 per cent of the sun's rays shut off down there, it is best to assume the fish cannot see it at a much greater distance than when they are surface feeding in the evening. Try to put your underwater lure right in front of their noses, if possible.

I have never understood just how far a fish can see an underwater lure at night. I believe that fish, by looking upwards, can see something moving on the surface quite plainly, for I know they often take a small natural or imitation fly at night. Yet I do not know how far underwater they will come up for it.

At night I try to drop my fly or floating lure as close as I possibly can to their night time swirls or rises. During the daytime I do not feel my reasoning is too far fetched when I work the deep waters of a lake with the belief that, while the surface is brilliant with sunlight, the depths are more like twilight, which means I must comb the water quite closely there. I judge this by the much better results, the many more fish I catch using these tactics which the transparency of the water, the little white plate, tells me to employ.

When I catch a fish at a good depth, I do not make my next cast to the same spot. He may be a "loner," but he is just as likely to be one of a school if he is a walleye. I let the school alone for a few moments before I try to drag another of its members through or around the school, so as not to make them wary. Knowing that I have found the right depth, I turn and cover another spot which I have not disturbed in the strike, the play and the landing of my first fish.

I do not worry overly much about fighting a fish in the upper waters in bright sunlight. It has been my experience that this does not disturb the fish in the lower waters—they can see but a few feet in the dark zone. Therefore, I try to bring them up towards the surface as fast as I can after the hook goes home, using all the strength the line will bear.

Transparency is not such a vital factor during the early morning fishing hours and during the later afternoon and evening hours. The shadows of the trees tell me plainly that the sun's rays slant quite sharply then, so they cannot penetrate the water as far as they do at noon. Each hour away from high noon, either way, means less visibility for the fish and less sun glare. Thus the northern pike, walleyes, bass, muskies and trout come much closer to the surface, enabling me to work my lures at or near the top of the water.

The surface caster who makes the mistake of using his light lures to get down to the fish in his daytime angling is apt to return to his cottage thinking he's been on a "fished out" lake. But let him stroll along the shore in the evening, contemplating his poor success, and let his thoughts be interrupted by the sound of fish breaking water. He'll rush back to the cottage and heave his tackle back into the boat. He'll catch fish, too, but alas, until he learns about transparency he'll regard the water as an "evening lake," useless to him during the wonderful daylight hours. Oh, well, if he likes mosquitoes, why worry about transparency?

CHAPTER III

Rich Water, Poor Water, It's All Good Water

THE OLD SAYING, "One man's meat is another man's poison," applies quite aptly to fishermen when they discuss the waters of the lakes and streams they fish.

The trout angler loves his waters, but the fisherman who prefers to battle the muskellunge, walleyed pike, northern pike and bass, shuns them. He considers the trout man's streams and lakes as "poor water," and devotes his attention to what he regards as "rich water."

A beginning fisherman, or a person who does no fishing at all, is more or less mystified by the varying opinions about the merits of the waters. He sees absolutely no difference between the waters of one lake or stream compared with another.

Yet there is a vast variation for there are five different *qualities* of water. These qualities are designated as *very soft, soft, medium, medium hard* and *hard*. Each quality has its own inherent characteristics, and each body of water has its individual color.

To me, all waters are good if they have fish in them. I like to consider myself an "all around fisherman" and as such it is my thought that not one lake in a thousand deserves to be rated in the "pauper" class. I fish them with due regard to their limitations and potentialities, as determined by their individual qualities.

I rely upon two methods to have a body of water tell me, in 15 minutes or so, just what kind of water I am about to fish. One is to test the water with a simple chemical kit. The other is to look at the underwater plants and allow them to tell me the quality of the water in which they are growing.

Either way, my aim is to judge the lime content of the water. Knowing this, I have a good idea how abundant the food supply

17

is, which in turn determines what kind of fish, how many and what size the water will support.

It is more fun to judge the water by the plants and then to verify your "guesses" chemically. A weed washed ashore, a quick glance at the underwater plants from shore, a look over the side of the boat, or observations made while wading give you such obvious clues. They back your judgment almost immediately concerning the "character" of the lake or stream and the fishing of it. Then comes the chore of filling a pint bottle with the water, testing it chemically at home and finding that your judgment by means of the underwater plant clues is positively verified.

Combine the easy knowledge of the chemistry of water with a quick reading of the weeds described in the next chapter, and most assuredly you will then know how to fish any waters, any place you go.

Once you have determined definitely whether the water is *very soft, soft, medium, medium hard* or *hard*, no longer does your fishing become a shell game, betting on the pea under the walnut. You know just where the "vegetables" are and you wager your skill and your fishing tackle against the fish every time, knowing you are going to get a run for your money.

A little chemical kit such as I carried around the United States and through Canada to give me a quick knowledge of the waters will allow any angler to test every lake and stream he may meet up with. The kit can be assembled for about $7.00.

Learning how to make a chemical test of water will require scarcely 10 minutes. If you are as slow as I am in learning something new, it will require 15 minutes. Should you be color blind, it will be impossible to make the tests. But if you can take a piece of ribbon to the thread counter and match its color with a spool of thread, the water tests will be easy for you.

A chemical analysis will give you a quicker, surer knowledge of the water you are fishing than anything else you can do to obtain it. It will reveal what sort of fish should be stocked there, what kind of fish food and fish cover are suited to it. The results of your fishing will let you know whether you are getting the kind of fishing that water is capable of producing. Moreover, the test will almost inform you what tackle to use, and it may influence your decision as to whether you want to buy frontage and build a summer home there. The test is also ideal for duck hunters because it indicates what duck food and cover will grow in that water.

18

In my opinion, every Conservation Club should have one of these chemical kits, along with an eight inch white plate and a water thermometer. By using this equipment to evaluate the waters, the club members who wish to get their own facts will know how those in their own territory should be handled, thereby ending much pointless arguing with the Conservation Departments. Backed by irrefutable facts pertaining to their area needs, their requests will be most convincing.

When you take a chemical test of water you are determining how many parts per million of bound carbon dioxide (ppm CO_2) it contains. Or to put it more simply, you are measuring its lime content. The more lime it contains, the more fish food the water will grow.

The *very soft* waters are acid and are the poorest, containing not more than five parts per million of bound carbon dioxide (5pmm CO_2). Since these waters have little lime content they can grow but a limited supply of fish food, and are suitable only for bass and blue gills.

The *soft* waters are somewhat richer in lime content, with from five to 10 parts per million of bound carbon dioxide. This water is still suitable for only bass and blue gills, but it will support twice as many pounds of fish and fish food to the acre compared with the *very soft* waters.

Medium waters are neutral and are sufficiently rich in food to nourish crappies, muskies, walleyes, and northern pike in addition to bass and blue gills. Since they contain from 10 to 20 parts per million of bound carbon dioxide they will grow up to four times as many pounds of fish and fish food per acre as the *very soft waters*.

The *medium hard* waters are alkaline, still richer, and are excellent for all species of fish. Their readings show from 20 to 30 parts per million of lime, which means there will be an abundance of crayfish and thousands of minnows. Nymphs of the mayflies, caddis flies, dragon flies, midges and damsel flies all add up to a wonderful natural supply of food for the fish.

With all that food the fish of all species will grow fast, and that water should never become "fished out." This bountiful water tells me I can troll here, fish with bait, with light and heavy spinning lures and almost every type of plug or spoon made for a casting rod or spinning rod.

If that water were from a stream of the same test, cold enough for brook, brown or rainbow trout, I could have a grand time with the fly rod. I could work it with dry fly, wet fly, nymph or

19

wet-dry fly and have thrills all day long. In fact, this water can be expected to contain as high as six times as many pounds of fish and fish food per acre as the *very soft waters*.

Richest of all are the *hard* waters, alkaline, with a lime content of from 30 to 100 parts per million. These, too, are ideal for all species of fish, and in vastly greater numbers because they will support up to 20 times as many pounds of fish and fish food to the acre as the *very soft* waters.

The angler must be careful not to confuse the word alkaline with the word alkali. Alkaline lakes are of fair to excellent lime content (fixed CO_2) but alkali waters will kill fish and fish food. When referring to *very soft* or *soft* waters, chemists say "acid" water. When they refer to *medium hard* to *hard* waters they say "alkaline."

I must emphasize here that transparency is a vital factor in the food supply and fish content of a lake. The figures I have just presented are for *clear* water lakes, those with a transparency of about 20 feet. In darker waters the pounds of fish and fish food per acre will be less. If the sun's rays cannot penetrate as deeply as in the *clear* water lakes, food just cannot grow in as great amounts even if the water is rich in lime content, from *medium* to *hard*.

When your white plate indicates *dark brown* water, the poundage of fish and fish food to the acre will be cut possibly 60 per cent from that of the *clear* water. For *brown* water, the poundage is reduced by 40 per cent and for *tan* water it is cut by about one third.

To simplify the interpretations of the readings I make with my chemical tests, I have prepared a table for *clear* water lakes that I find extremely useful. I consider it of value to both the fisherman and the duck hunter. The table indicates at a glance how chemical readings of parts per million of bound carbon dioxide (ppm CO_2) classify the waters as *very soft, soft, medium, medium hard* or *hard*.

Since the quality of water governs its food producing potential, I have arranged the table so it also indicates at a glance my own estimate of the pounds of fish and fish food per acre and what kinds of fish are suitable for stocking. For the benefit of duck hunters it shows whether the planting of duck food is feasible in the different types of water, as well as cover for the fish.

The table for bound carbon dioxide and pH was given to me by Dr. Edward A. Birge and Dr. Chauncey Juday at the University of Wisconsin during the early 1930's. They were rated the outstanding limnologists in the world, and I deeply appreciate the great help and advice they gave me in my lake and stream improvement work. Dr. Villiers W. Meloche, a noted chemist of the same University, showed me how to make tests for oxygen, carbon dioxide and potential hydrogen-ion which aided me so much in my surveys.

The pounds of fish and fish food to the acre which I have added to the table would probably bring a hearty laugh from Doctors Birge and Juday if they were living. I make absolutely no claim to any scientific exactness concerning this part of the table. Nevertheless, as a fisherman seeking to adapt scientific facts to the needs of fishermen, I feel there just has to be some sort of rule of thumb so the angler may realize what a great difference there is in the various qualities of water and how this affects his fishing.

WATER TABLE FOR THE FISHERMAN AND HUNTER

Bound CO_2 ppm	pH	Stocking Lake Fish	Pounds Fish & Fish Food Per Acre	Planting Duck Food
0-5	V.S.	Bass, blue gills	0-250	Wasting money
5-10	S.	Bass, blue gills	250-500	Some chance here. Consult nursery.
10-20	M.	Bass, blue gills, Above 15 ppm, crappies, muskies, walleyes northern pike	500-1000	All good plants will grow in water from 15 ppm upwards. Consult nursery.
20-30	M.H.	All species, bass, blue gills, crappies, muskies, walleyes, northern pike	1000-1500	
30-100	H.	All species	1500-5000	

V.S. means very soft water, S. is soft water, M. is medium or neutral water, M.H. is medium hard water and H. is hard water.

Whenever your test shows over 36 ppm CO_2 it is wise to suspect a marl influence instead of a limestone influence if you are not in limestone country. I do not know enough about the marl influence to recommend just what fish should be stocked, nor does anyone else whom I know.

From my fishing experience and from observing the stocking of fish with our failures and successes, I am inclined to believe that a lake of heavy marl influence should be handled as if it were *medium* water—neutral water—neither *hard* nor *soft* and testing 15 to 20 ppm CO_2.

Brook, brown and rainbow trout will live in all water from

21

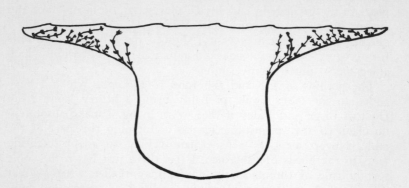

FIG. 4.–The ideal lake. A long, gradually sloping underwater shore with a minimum depth of 25 feet. Maximum food production.

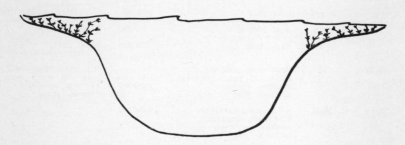

FIG. 5.–A good lake but a less productive food shelf than Fig. 4.

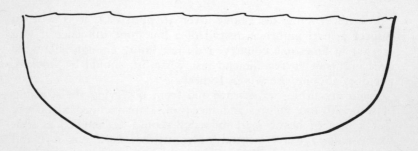

FIG. 6.–A much less productive lake than either 4 or 5.

22

very soft to *hard*, but they are limited by many factors, such as temperature and predatory fish.

From the qualitative and quantitative analyses I have made of lake and stream water I am satisfied that I am not very far off in contending that the *clear* water lake shown in Figure 4 can be regarded as the ideal standard. If a lake is of the shape in Figure 5 it does not have much of a food shelf, therefore its fish food would be much reduced. If it did not have the long sloping shoreline as in Figure 4, or the shorter food shelf as in Figure 5, but had a quick drop off such as in Figure 6, this would cut the fish and fish food per acre considerably.

As all good fishermen have an analytical mind, I shall unashamedly leave it to their common sense to size up shorelines and color of the water to decide for themselves how much to discount the poundage in each lake they fish.

I do not believe that muskies and walleyes do as well in marl lakes as in those of limestone influence, but northern pike, large and smallmouth bass, and panfish show excellent growth. If the marl lakes are of colder waters than the average run of lakes, brook trout, browns and rainbows grow to be real "lunkers," as is the case in the Waupaca chain of lakes in Wisconsin. The waters of marl lakes so often are unusually clear, and the lush bushy pondweeds and musk grass grow like mats of carpet on their bottoms.

I should point out here that the chemical kit I use in analyzing the quality of waters is not the only method that science provides. Also available is what is known as the pH, potential hydrogen-ion concentration test. It has been my experience that the use of the Birge and Juday symbols of V.S. to H. for the pH, is a much better arrangement for the fisherman when tests are being made in late June, July, August and early September. The hydrochloric acid in the CO_2 tests consistently will cut right through the plankton so abundant during these months and tell me what sort of fish to ask for from the hatcheries and what sort of duck foods if any, I should plant in that water. The pH test, on the other hand, will not give me a true reading during the summer months because the plankton which we fishermen call "bloom" is an impediment.

Imagine my requesting wall eyed pike and crappies for stocking in a lake in which they would not be suited! The pH tests shouted, "go ahead and put them in here, they'll be fine in this water." The trusty CO_2, however, contradicted by saying, "only large and smallmouth bass will do well here. You can ask for blue gills and a few northerns to keep the blue gills down to their proper numbers. The bass and northerns will then grow well and offer the fishermen a little variety."

As the fisherman's table indicates, some good bass lakes are of *soft* water, but those of *very soft* water should be fished hard for undersized fish. The large bass you catch should be returned to the water to keep the blue gill population down or soon there will be all blue gills—stunted at that—and but few bass for the angler. Eventually there will not be enough food for all the fish. Not until it is balanced again will there be nourishment for all. Walleyes, crappies and muskies should never be planted in such waters for they will never have enough food to grow to even fair size in any appreciable number.

When your test shows a lake of *medium* water—10 to 20 ppm CO_2—such water will not "bloom" as heavily as those of the hard water lakes if the water is of good depth, 30 feet or more. Yet if the *medium* lake is shallow in most of its acreage, there will be a heavy "bloom" there.

While lakes of *medium* waters are not as full of fish as the lakes of greater lime content—higher CO_2—they offer good fishing all year long. For all around satisfaction I would prefer a

Fig. 7.—Plankton, the beginning of all fish food.
All greatly enlarged.

Reading from left to right: *Polyphemus, Daphnia, Rotifer* and *Nostoc*.
Polyphemus, a soft shell water flea upon which muskie fry live. (Zooplankton).
Daphnia, a hard shelled water flea. (Zooplankton).
Rotifer, a voracious eater of the zooplankton but it eats both plant and animal plankton.
Nostoc, one of the blue-green algae of the *phytoplankton*, (plants). Responsible for much of the green "bloom" in our lakes. There are several hundred species of fresh water algae and many millions of some species in one quart of water. It is contact with the *phytoplankton* which give the fish a "fishy" taste.

24

medium water drainage lake in the 16 to 20 ppm CO_2 range for building my cottage for bathing and fishing off my "front yard." The bloom would not be excessive in July and August.

Plankton is a very necessary food element in our waters. Figure 7. It is, in fact, the very beginning of fish food. All lakes have it, but in varying degree according to the richness of the water.

Plankton is composed of tiny plants and animals, some so small they have to be magnified from 500 to 1500 times to be seen. The animals are known as zooplankton and the plants are called phytoplankton. Thousands can be squeezed through the mesh of your finest linen handkerchief. The tiniest are called nannoplankton while those which we can just barely see in the water without the aid of a magnifying glass to those almost as large as the head of a pin are all called plankton. Sometimes there will be 20 million to a quart of water. I have seen as high as 25 zooplankton feeding upon one speck of bloom and when the phytoplankton was magnified 300 times they were like cattle around a hay stack.

In *very clear soft* water lakes, plankton causes a possible hazard for small game fish in late June, July and August. Much of the animal part of the plankton, the zooplankton, goes down to 20 feet and below to escape the sun's rays and to feed upon the tiny plants, the phytoplankton. This brings the small game fish down there to feed upon the zooplankton. The large fish, living there during the day, eat the small fish in great numbers. Naturally they do not hit our lures then with much enthusiasm for they are not very hungry. The enormous amount of plankton strained through their gill rakers is also rich food. Rather than starve, I'd eat it myself.

The *very soft* water lakes of the Eastern states, as soft as rain or snowwater, need the brush, saplings and other cover provided in lake improvement projects. In such rehabilitated lakes the young game fish will use the refuges for cover and will feed around the shoals and on the food the refuges create. In this manner their numbers are not diminished heavily by the large game fish, with the result that the lake stocks itself.

Snails and clams, the nymphs of underwater insects, the fry which become fish and the minnows which feed the fish, all owe their existence to the plankton for food, for plankton is an all year around crop.

Since we find less plankton in *very soft* water lakes, more in the *soft* water lakes and millions more in the richer lakes, it is easy to understand why the richer waters can support more and greater varieties of fish. All lakes, however, are devoid of excessive "bloom" in early spring and late fall.

The fish are hungrier in the late spring and late fall, and lakes of good lime content grow muskies fast and of great size. They would be stunted in the poorer lakes because, like the walleyes and northern pike, they are enormous feeders, eating many pounds of fish to gain a single pound of weight.

Rich lakes can really never be fished out with fly rods, spinning rods and casting rods. The variety of flies and lures that can be used is amazing. Bait fishing, casting, trolling and fly fishing all yield great sport for children and adults, even when they become octogenarians. One never knows what will hit his lure. I have had many muskies strike my size 1 fly when I was fishing for bass. You use your best walleye spoon and a big northern hits it. Your spinning lure for northerns finds a small perch gobbling it. Time and again a fisherman returns from a trip to the lakes of *medium* to *hard* water with everything but that which he said he went fishing for.

After many years of fishing and studying the lakes and streams of the Midwest, portions of the Pacific Coast and parts of Central Ontario, it was only natural that I should be curious about the waters in other parts of the two countries. I had read many accounts of exploits on the well-known lakes and streams of the East, West, North and South, but nowhere had I ever read anything that gave me the real picture as far as the quality and transparency of these waters was concerned. Without that information I had no way of gauging their real potentialities. I knew I could obtain this knowledge by traveling about with my CO_2 chemistry kit, white plate and thermometer.

Early in 1946 I decided to make up for my ignorance. To my great joy, my wife thought it was a good idea to embark upon such travels, although I think she was dreaming of hats, not fish. I needed a secretary and a driver to spell me off now and then, so I hired her to go along. We left our incorrigible little Willie and a straight jacket with a neighbor who thought he was "so cute." When we returned, the neighbor was in the straight jacket and Willie was in the pink of condition—after I got through with him.

Through Michigan, Ohio, Western New York and the Eastern part of the province of Ontario and Western Quebec my chemical tests revealed rich water, ranging from *medium* to *hard*.

26

When I began testing the waters of Eastern Quebec I encountered acid waters, *very soft* and *soft*. I found the same situation in Maine all the way down to Bar Harbor and up again to Sebago Lake and the Rangely chain.

The waters continued to be *very soft* and *soft* in New Hampshire, Vermont, Massachusetts and Connecticut and in the streams of the Catskill and Adirondack Mountains of eastern New York. The same situation prevailed in Eastern Pennsylvania, New Jersey, Maryland, West Virginia and Virginia. I took the ocean highway in the Carolinas, turning off in Georgia to go through the Okefeenokee Swamp to test the Suwanee River at its source. The Suwanee in the Swamp was *very soft* water.

In Florida, Alabama, Mississippi, Kentucky, Tennessee, Louisiana, Missouri, Texas, New Mexico, Arizona and the entire West and Northwest I noted much richer water than in the East. On the Pacific Coast the waters rich in lime content extended far into British Columbia from the source of the Columbia to the Frazier, except on Vancouver Island—from the Campbell River to Victoria—where the waters ran from *very soft* to *soft* with one or two instances of *medium* water.

In Alberta and Ontario few waters tested as low in lime content as those of Eastern Quebec and our East Coast states.

The 32,000 miles I traveled, plus the 150,000 miles in my Wisconsin lake and stream improvement work gave me 182,000 miles of stimulating and educational moments which I shall never forget. Through these travels came much new knowledge of the waters and fishing, and convincing corroboration of the ideas I had formulated during my previous fishing experience on Midwestern waters, particularly those of my home territory in Northern Michigan.

But don't feel too sorry for the fishermen of the predominately *very soft* and *soft* waters of our eastern areas. Remember that there are "rich waters and poor waters, but all are good waters." There's plankton in all of them, few snails but plenty of nymphs, smelt and some minnows to sustain fish in many of their waters, and where there are fish, there you will find fun.

Also, bear in mind that the millions of anglers in the more or less crowded East see to it that their Conservation Departments keep the lakes and streams continually stocked. The time has come in all states where much of our water needs all the help possible for such intense fishing as many waters are receiving. We are far from knowing all the answers yet. Our hopes must

27

lie with the young biologists now coming along and the cooperation of every fisherman, together with decent salaries to their profession.

HOW TO TEST THE WATER CHEMICALLY

You don't have to be a chemist to test the lime content of water. Neither do you need complicated and expensive equipment to assemble a small kit that you can conveniently carry with you during travels to various lakes and streams.

Here are the simple "tools" you will need for the kit:

1 Erlenmeyer flask, capacity 125 cc.	$ .34
1 volumetric flask, capacity 100 cc.	1.32
1 burette, capacity 25 cc.	4.74
1 eye dropper	.05
1 pint distilled water	.10
	$ 6.55

1 quart of a 44th Normal Hydrochloric Acid. This
44N/HCL can be made up for you by your
city or school chemist.

The ¼ gram of Methyl Orange is to be mixed well in the pint of distilled water. This mixture will serve as the "indicator" in your tests and will be enough to make several hundred of them.

Before making tests of fishing waters, it is a good idea to experiment at home with the water from your kitchen faucet. When you succeed in making several tests that give you the same readings you can feel that you have a good understanding of the proper procedure.

Always, when making tests, your first step is to rinse the two flasks several times with the water you are about to analyze. Turn the rinsed flasks upside down for about a half minute so all the water drains out. This removes the influence of any chemicals and water from a previous test.

Fill the burette with the 44N/HCL for titrating, and fill the volumetric flask with the water you are testing. See that the water stops on the little ring, which is the volume mark around the tube of the flask. The bottom of the top film of water in the tube—the bubble called the meniscus—must rest exactly on the 100 cc. mark, the ring.

Pour this water slowly in the Erlenmyer flask so that ALL the water drains into the flask. Now put exactly three drops of

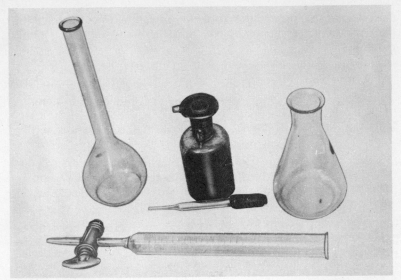

FIG. 8.—Materials For Testing Bound, Or Fixed, Carbon Dioxide (CO-2) Content of Lakes and Streams.

Bottom—25 cc. burette, graduated in two tenths of a cc.

Left—100 cc. volumetric flask.

Center—TK dropping bottle filled with methyl orange indicator. Handy when one makes hundreds of tests because the slotted stopper pours one drop at a time. The medicine dropper serves just as well for single tests.

Right—125 cc. Enlenmyer Flask.

the "indicator"—the Methyl Orange—in the flask with the eye dropper.

Before you titrate, take the reading of the burette, which is either graduated in tenths or in two tenths of a cubic centimeter, depending upon what type of burette you happen to have. Let us assume that the HCL is at the 2.2 cc. mark, and let us call the water Lake Doris.

With the water sample and the "indicator" in it, give the flask a gentle twist of the wrist until you get the water twirling in the flask. This is to help the HCL spread through the sample quickly, as you titrate.

While the water is twirling, turn the stop cock so that the HCL in the burette will flow slowly into the flask. When you see the *very first* faint pink color showing in the water sample, turn the stop cock off immediately.

Now that you have finished titrating, take another reading from the burette. The cc. mark now shows that you have used the HCL in the burette down to the 9.2 mark. Since you started with the HCL at the 2.2 mark, you make the following computation:

9.2 (the reading when you finished)

Subtract 2.2 (amount of acid in burette when you started)
___

7.0 (amount HCL used to get the "end" point)

Multiply by 5 (this is the *factor* you will always use with a 44th normal HCL)
___

35.0 (the final reading, which means that your mythical Lake Doris tests 35 ppm CO_2, or 35 parts per million of bound or fixed carbon dioxide)

The figuring should always be done on a card or in a notebook to be saved for future checking. Be sure that you identify the lake or stream by its name and location.

When you make your first experimental tests with water from the kitchen faucet you may have a little trouble seeing the first faint pink shade. You probably will get too much of the HCL into the water in the flask because you are so intent on watching for the first faint pink color that you forget to turn the stop cock *immediately*. A pink color that shows too vividly means that you have titrated too long—gotten beyond the "end point," the first trace of pink, and have a false reading. When you get so good that you can beat the Missus in detecting the *first* faint pink showing, you're in!

If you test water that is rich in lime, a large amount of HCL is used. You may see traces of pink and conclude that you are through. Satisfy yourself, however, by giving the flask a little more twirling. If the pink disappears then you know you must titrate some more until every drop of that water sample is so diffused that it shows the very faint pink color.

At the other extreme there is the water that is very low in lime. *Very soft* water will require so little HCL that the "end point" will appear immediately. Just one cc., a quarter teaspoonful, of the HCL will show you that there are but four parts of bound carbon dioxide to the million parts of water.

Lake or stream water which is to be tested should be obtained about a foot under the surface. If a bottle is used for this purpose, it must be clean and so must its cork. Rinse the bottle and the cork at least twice right there in the lake or stream before filling it to take home. To prevent contamination,

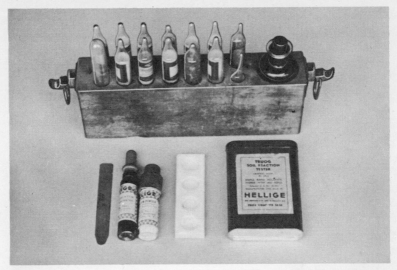

Fig. 9.—One of six pH sets I carried for testing hydrogen-ion content of the waters in Wisconsin. Below, a compact soil testing kit used to learn which shrubs and trees to plant along each stream bank or around a lake shore.

do not let your hands touch either the mouth of the bottle or the bottom of the cork that fits into the mouth. Use a quart bottle at first so you will have plenty of water to rinse the flasks if you make a mistake while testing at home. This saves going back for another sample.

Knowing from your computations that your mythical Lake Doris tests 35 ppm CO_2, I can close my eyes and tell you just what your little 10 or 15 minute test reveals.

Lake Doris is of *hard* water, rich in lime. If its transparency is *clear* I estimate its fish and fish food per acre at 1750 pounds. To get that figure I multiply each ppm CO_2 by 50 pounds. Simple, isn't it—35 x 50 equals 1750?

You can't be sure, however, that Lake Doris is that bountiful until you first sink that white plate and determine definitely that it is *clear* water. If the plate indicates it is a *dark brown* lake there will be much less food, fish cover, duck food and duck cover. If the water is *brown* there will be a little more than in the *dark brown*, and if *tan* a still heavier amount.

31

CHAPTER IV

Waters Can Be Analyzed
By Their Plants

UNDERWATER PLANTS fairly shout the secrets of water, if the angler will but listen.

If you know your plants you can walk along the shore of any lake for 50 or 100 feet in the summer and determine closely enough for any fisherman whether it is a *soft* or *hard* water lake, whether it should be a fair bass and panfish lake or one which will raise and support walleyes, northern pike, muskies and good forage fish to the point of keeping them fat and healthy.

The underwater weeds will tell you whether there is a light or good supply of snails, clams, crayfish and insect life, enabling you to estimate quite closely how many pounds of fish and fish food are to be found to the acre of water.

And, should you have a CO_2 chemical kit along, or at home, you can verify your reading of the plants against the infallible reading of your kit. You will be delighted to find that your analysis by means of the plants is as accurate as it needs to be for fishing success.

In reading a lake by its plants, surely an angler should be as good as the average farmer who evaluates his soil. If a practical farmer can stoop down, pick up a handful of soil, squeeze it through his fingers to judge the crops it will produce, so can you stoop down, look at the underwater plants and judge the production of fish food and fish that water might have.

I have already discussed the five different qualities of water: the *very soft*, *soft*, *medium*, *medium hard* and *hard*. Actually, for the purposes of the fisherman, the five classes can be reduced to three, including *soft*, *medium* and *hard*. It would be still more convenient to place all waters into two classes, just *soft* and *hard*, but *medium* water is an obstacle, a sort of fence which divides them, so we must recognize it.

With the reduced grouping in mind, we rate *soft* waters as poorest in fish food and cover. Similarly, these acid waters are poorest for duck food and cover. The *medium* waters are substantially richer in food and cover. They are neutral, neither acid nor alkaline. The *hard* waters are of good lime content—alkaline water—and are richest in fish food and cover. The same is true with regard to duck food and cover.

It is a simple matter to learn to judge waters and fishing by the vegetation in the lakes and streams.

As fishermen, we are not overly concerned by the names of the plants, although it is good to know them. We are more interested in knowing that stunted plants grow in *soft* water and that the *medium* and *hard* waters produce larger plants as well as those of "skimpy" variety. Also, a great many large plants in a body of water tells us plainly there must be a good lime content and we need not concern ourselves with the fact that some have long slender leaves or others are wide-leaved.

In determining the quality of the water, you must pay no attention to the lily pads or the reeds and rushes standing above the surface, nor the cattails along the border of the lake. They grow in all waters from *soft* to *hard*. It is the underwater plants only that make it possible for you to analyze the waters.

When you have learned to judge the quality of the water by means of the plants, you will realize they have also told you where to fish, how to fish, and what bait, spoon, plug, lure or fly to use, assuming you have taken the factors of transparency, oxygen, temperature and three layer lakes into consideration. You would know that the fish grow better in water of good underwater weed content, since there is more food for them, as well as more cover.

This being so, I am sure you will agree that we fishermen pay too much attention to our tackle and casting methods and not enough to the main subjects, fish and water.

If you plan to fish a lake during June, July or August, walk 50 feet or so along the edge of the shoreline before you get into your boat. You will find that you can read the lake by picking up wave-washed plants on the beach.

Should you see only plants with small leaves—like the grass which falls from your lawn mower—some thinner and some a trifle longer—and see none of the larger plants, you can safely say, "It's my guess this is a soft water lake."

Figure 10 shows how the lack of lime in *soft* water results in growth of only stunted plants. The following photographs 10,

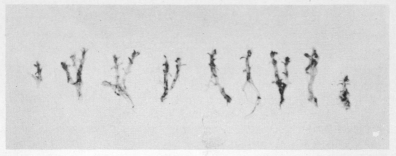

FIG. 10.—Waterwort *(Elatine minima)*. About one inch.

FIG. 11.—Needle Rush *(Elocharis sp.)*. About 3 inches.

11, 12 and 13 identify these *soft* water plants as waterwort, pipe-wort, quillwort, needle rush or creeping buttercup. But don't let the names get you down. Just call them, "*soft* water indicators." That will suit your fishing requirements just as well.

After visiting several lakes of this general type you may become so good in judging water that you can distinguish a *very soft* water lake from one of *soft* water. This will require some time, however, for you will have to let your eyes tell you that where the skimpy plants are the most sparse, there will be the *very soft* water. Your chemical tests for CO_2 will prove whether your judgment is right.

In *very soft* and *soft* waters there is one underwater plant—the only large one which will grow in such waters—which can delude you into judging a lake or stream to be of *hard* water.

35

This is the bladderwort. (*Utricularia vulgaris L.*, var. americana Gray, as the botanists call it.) See Figure 13.

The bladderwort looks much like some of the *hard* water plants, such as coontail, foxtail and other large water weeds. It is easily recognized, though, by the tiny green and black bladders all over it, hence its name. These plants take plankton from the water and trap them through hairs in their bladders just as pitcher plants trap and hold insects on land.

The bladderwort is a great asset to the *soft* water lakes, furnishing fish cover that these waters need so badly. I do not think the plant supplies food for ducks.

When you begin your appraisal of plants in *hard* waters, it may seem like leaping from poverty to riches. A *hard* water lake is indeed richly dressed, except in the wave-pounded shore-line food shelves of large lakes. In such lakes we must do our analyzing in the quiet bays where the plants have a chance to maintain themselves. Judging *hard* water is like deserting the lawn and its clippings for the garden and its choice vegetables.

Let us first look at corn in a garden. It is by all odds the

FIG. 12.—Rush Family *(Juncus pelocarpus sp.)*. About 3 inches.

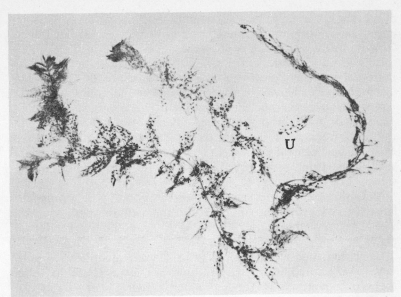

FIG. 13.—Bladderwort *(Utricularia sp.)* About three inch leaf. Note the small bladders shown more sharply in the insert (U). Otherwise, it might confuse you into thinking it to be a *hard* water indicator. While all of the above plants will grow in *medium* to *hard* water, absence of the *hard* water indicators will allow you to know that water to be a *soft* water lake.

FIG. 14.—Our Largest Bass Weed *(Potamogeton amplifolious)*. Leaves grow to a length of six inches in the hardest water.

37

tallest plant there. Reduce its height, shorten its leaves, thin its stems, but notice the prominent veins which run in its leaves. This will give you a fair idea of the largest underwater plant of the *hard* waters, commonly referred to as large bass weed. Its botanical name is *Potamogeton amplifolious*.

There are well over 50 species in this single family of water weeds. Some run from the almost hair-like leaves such as that good duck food, sago pondweed *(Potamogeton pectinatus)* to the largest leaves of the bass weed. The familiar muskie weed with its boat-shaped tip, bright green leaves and crooked white stem is the true muskie weed, *Potomogeton praelongus*. All are shown in the pictures of the water weeds, Figures 14 to 20.

No fisherman, however, will sneer at you if you group the larger-leaved plants into one family and call them all "muskie weeds," using the name "bass weeds" for the smaller-leaved plants.

If, at first, you are too timid to back your identification until you have learned many species, you are always safe in using the word pondweeds for all water weeds. With the word pondweed one can move in the best society of fishermen and botanists.

Now that we have looked at the corn in the garden—the larger pond-weeds—let us turn to the leaves of the carrots and all other plants which grow in masses. These masses, or beds, of garden plants—some high, some low—have their counterparts on the bottoms of *hard* waters. If the masses are lush and exceedingly thick, the water is *hard*. Where the beds are more open, less luxuriant in their growth, not so wide-leaved or so thick in their stems and probably not as long as their sister plants, you can judge that water to be *medium*.

The ducks eat every one of the *hard* water plants, including their seeds, buds and tubers. Like the fish, the ducks also eat the small clams, snails and insects which cling to or feed among the plants of the *hard* waters. The deer, moose, muskrat, beaver and shore-birds likewise find rich nourishment in the various plant species in both *soft* and *hard* water.

The color of the water, you will recall, does not determine its quality, but does affect its transparency. Since water plants must have sunlight for growth, just as your vegetable garden must have it, *dark brown* and *brown* waters kill the sunlight in water and make it impossible for plants to grow beyond the depth of the sun's rays. As a fisherman, you may be sure that when plants are brought up with your anchor, in that part

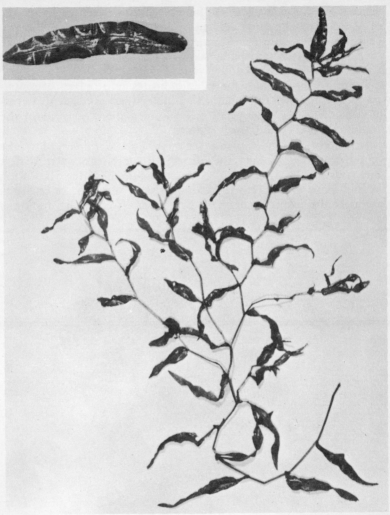

FIG. 15.—The True Muskie Weed *(Potamogeton praelongus)*. Bright green leaves on the crooked white stems. Note boat shaped leaf.

of the lake you will find fish even during the hottest days of the summer and in the deepest lakes, for plants make oxygen in the water.

For those who are interested in both fish and ducks I submit a table of "Most Useful and Common Water Plants," which John H. Steenis and I drew up many years ago. I am much indebted to him as well as to John S. Bordner, who had charge of Wisconsin's Division of Land Economic Inventory for many years. Bordner is the most capable authority in his field I have ever known. Wisconsin lost two good men when Steenis left the Lake Inventory and Bordner retired.

Among other things, the table indicates what plants are especially adapted for the creation of underwater oxygen so necessary for fish life. The good air-making plants are listed in the column "GO," good oxygenators.

In purchasing your plants from an aquatic nursery for lake or pond waters, be sure the nurseryman tests the water with a 44th normal HCL method as described in Chapter III, "Rich Water, Poor Water, It's All Good Water." Buying water plants through the litmus paper test is a great gamble. Buying them

FIG. 16.—Sago Pondweed (*Potamogeton pectinatus*). (Leaves about three inches).

Fig. 17.—Bushy Pondweed *(Najas flexilis)*. Grows like a carpet on the bottom. (Leaves about one-half inch).

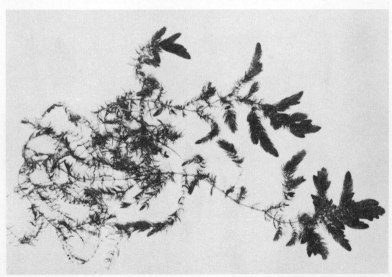

Fig. 18.—Coontail *(Ceratophyllum demersum)*. A floating plant, usually in masses. (Leaves about one inch).

THE FISHERMAN'S AND HUNTER'S MOST USEFUL AND COMMON WATER PLANTS

COMPILED BY JOHN H. STEENIS AND SID W. GORDON

These plants may be purchased from any good aquatic nursery. History and pictures through pamphlets available at U. S. Department of Agriculture, Washington, D. C.

Use
Good Oxygenator (GO)
Good Fish Food (GFF)
Good Fish Cover (GFC)
Good Duck Food (GDF)
Good Duck Cover (GDC)
(x) good. (f) only fair. (o) of little value.

pH
Very Soft Water (VS)
Soft Water (S)
Medium Water (M)
Medium Hard Water (MH)
Hard Water (H)

CO₂
0 to 5 ppm CO_2
5 to 10 ppm CO_2
10 to 20 ppm CO_2
20 to 30 ppm CO_2
30 and up ppm CO_2

	(GO)	(GFF)	(GFC)	(GDF)	(GDC)	Grows in Water
I. LONG LAX STEM AND LEAF TYPE PLANTS. Numbers 1 to 7 are (P) Potamogetons.						
1. Bass weed, *P. amplifolious*. Largest submerged plant with floating leaf.	x	x	x	x	o	M to H
2. Bass weed, *P. Richardsonii*. No floating leaf.	x	x	x	x	o	MH to H
3. True muskie weed, *P. praelongus*. White stem. Leaf boat-shaped tip.	x	x	x	x	o	MH to H
II. RIBBON LEAF PONDWEEDS.						
4. Floating leaf pondweed, *P. epihydrous*.	x	x	x	x	o	H, but if silty, S
5. Eel grass, *P. zosterifolius*. Delicate flat stem.	x	x	x	x	o	H
6. Narrow-leaf weed, *P. pusillus*.	x	x	x	x	o	M to H
7. Sago pondweed, *P. pectinatus*.	x	x	x	x	o	M to H

III. Compound and Filimentous Plants. Thread Leaf.

8. Coontail or hornwort, *Ceratophyllum demersum.* Not good in streams.	x	x	x	o	M to H
9. Muskgrass or stonewort. *Chara.* Good in trout streams. STR	x	x	x	o	S to H
10. Foxtail or water milfoil, *Myriophyllum spicatum.*	x	x	x	o	M to H
11. Bushy pondweed, *Najas flexilis.* STR	x	x	x	o	M to H
12. Water weed, *Elodea canadensis. Never* plant in a trout stream.	x	x	x	o	M to H

IV. Pad and ribbon leaf types.

13. White water lily, *Castalia odorata.*	o	f	x	o	S to H
14. Yellow pond lily, *Nymphaea variegata.*	o	f	x	o	S to H
15. Wild celery, *Vallisneria spiralis.* An outstanding duck food.	x	x	x	o	M to H

V. Upright emersed types.

16. Pickerel weed, *Pontederia cordata.*	f	f	x	x	S to H
17. Bulrush, *Scirpus spp.*	f	f	x	x	S to H
18. Cattail, *Typha latifolia.*	o	f	x	x	VS to H
19. Wild rice, *Zizania aquatica.* To thrive lake must have an exchange of water, preferably an inlet and outlet.	o	f	x	x	M to H

VI. SHORT STIFF LEAF AND ROSETTE TYPE, GROWING FROM ONE-HALF INCH TO SIX INCHES. THEY GROW IN ALL LAKES. It is of little importance to the fisherman. Plants such as needle rush, waterwort, quillwort, water grass, creeping buttercup, etc., will harbor some insects but are not good oxygenators or good cover. Fassett's *Manual of Aquatic Plants* is a good book to use for detailed information about water plants. It is published by McGraw-Hill.

Fig. 19.—The Waterweed (*Elodea canadensis* or *Anacharis canadensis spp.*) Good in lakes but a pest in streams and drainage ditches. Clogs and warms the water.

through the use of pH, the hydrogen-ion test, is just as bad in my opinion, if the tests are made in late June, July or August. Do not take a chance on throwing away your money when you can ask for and get water tests with the 44th Normal HCL method. Better yet, make the tests yourself.

In a public trout stream I do not advise setting out ANY plants. If you insist upon planting them in your own private stream, then plant only those which are marked "STR" on the chart. I cannot emphasize too strongly that the wrong plants can and will choke a trout stream. They either pile up great silt beds around them, or, through their dense growth in the stream beds form large and ever increasing stagnant pools which kill the fish in their warming of waters to the temperature border-line.

I recommend that you carefully read the chapter on "Lake and Stream Improvement" to decide how to handle a trout stream for best results.

As you study the table on plants, have in mind that neither Steenis nor I can gain by your purchase of plants, since we are not in the plant business. But you may have much to lose if you do not choose wisely.

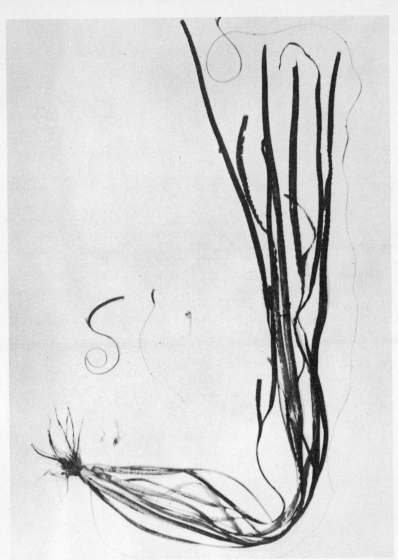

FIG. 20.—Wild Celery *(Vallisnera sp.)*. An interesting plant. Note male bud near roots which comes to surface only after female flower has formed at tip of long curled stem and is floating on the surface. After fertilization, the seed pod grows to maturity as shown at top. Above the roots are shown the female flower, next the forming seed pod and finally the mature seed pod. Diving ducks dig up the plant and the tip-up ducks "steal" it from them when they get the opportunity. A great food of the canvasback ducks.

45

CHAPTER V

Oxygen in Water Tells Much,
Temperature Little

WHEN BILL SAYS he has found a new lake and gives me just a few moments to gulp down my breakfast, I ask no questions. Throwing the tackle and packsack in the car, I kiss Momma and little Willie goodbye and we are on our way.

A "new" lake is always a challenge to a fisherman. True, it has been there since the glacial age, a mere youngster of about 10,000 years, and has only been fished hard since the first white man settled near it. Yet every lake I have never fished is a "new" one to me and I'm curious about it.

"What kind of fish are in the lake, Bill?"

"Walleyes," says Bill.

"Big ones?" I ask.

"Well, Jim came home with three that went over six pounds apiece."

"Where is the lake?"

"It's in 16-41-14 West."

I reach for my little plat book showing the counties of Wisconsin, find Township 41 North, Range 14 West and note that Bill's "new" lake covers Section 16, about 640 acres. We are in for a long ride, so I mentally begin to fish the big lake right there in the car.

I always carry a plat book to guide me on my fishing trips, and firmly believe that every fisherman should possess one for the state in which he fishes. No angler need ever be lost if he knows how to read one. With the aid of his car compass, and a pocket compass when he is afoot, he need never ask anyone to show him the way to any waters. A plat book ordinarily costs but $1.50, and most any local surveyor will show you within 15 minutes how it should be read. It is my opinion that every pupil in our elementary schools should be taught how to interpret a plat book. Two half-hour sessions will do it.

47

My plat book shows that the lake Bill and I are driving to has an inlet and an outlet. That tells me we are going to fish a drainage lake. I hope the inlet has good cold water. Then we can fish for trout in the stream as well as for walleyed pike in the lake.

It is also my desire that the lake will be of *medium hard* or *hard* water so it will be rich enough to grow many walleyed pike to a good size, and be deep enough for three layers of water.

To my great delight, we find upon arrival at the lake shortly before noon that it is everything I had wished for. A quick survey of the underwater plants along the shoreline food shelf assures me the water is *hard*, and we soon learn the lake is very deep.

Knowing this *clear* water is rich enough with lime to grow many fish of good size, and that its abundance of underwater plants is positive indication of an excellent supply of oxygen, our immediate problem is where to find the fish and how to catch them.

Since it is approaching noon on a hot, bright day in August, the matter of oxygen is of prime importance. It is our main clue in locating the fish in this large body of water.

Bill and I know that we will find oxygen spilling into the lake at the inlet. We prefer, however, to fish the waters near the inlet during the late afternoon and early morning. We are aware that when the fish go "on the feed" there they will strike our lures with zest because they will be invigorated by both the oxygen and the food brought by the stream flowing into the lake. We also know that the channel through which the incoming water follows as it works its way through the lake towards the outlet is oxygenated by the current, and that we can look for some exciting encounters with fish there, too.

Many anglers use a thermometer to determine the temperature of the water in different areas of the lake with the thought that finding colder water helps them to search out the fish. I am not one of them. I am afraid there is a great misunderstanding among fishermen concerning the use of a thermometer to find where lake fish lie during hot summer days.

Bass, muskies, northern pike and walleyed pike never dread water temperatures of 75 degrees. It is the oxygen and transparency of water which really matters in our endeavor to find where these fish lie during the daytime.

Hundreds of tests with a maximum-minimum thermometer

48

show me that fairly deep lakes seldom go over 75 degrees a foot or two below the surface of our Wisconsin lakes. They will average around 72 degrees in August.

Contrary to general belief, this temperature does not vary much over two degrees in the first 20 feet of water.

When my sounding line shows that a lake is over 50 feet in depth, I assume an average of 46 degrees for the bottom temperature of such lakes. I am seldom off more than three or four degrees and this is of little moment to any fisherman.

The lake may have surface temperatures of 70 to 75 degrees, but the bottom readings run from 42 to 50 in most all the deep lakes. This means absolutely nothing when we know that fish cannot live where there is not enough air in the water.

My oxygen tests show that only in a very few lakes over 50 feet in depth is there enough air for the fish to breathe at or anywhere near the bottom. The chapter on three layer lakes will show the fisherman this quite plainly, I am sure.

Where the factors of transparency, three layer lakes and underwater plants are favorable, there you will find plenty of oxygen and you can be sure fish are at hand to breathe it.

On a trout stream, though, a thermometer is worth carrying in your fishing jacket during July and August. The stream temperature reveals, to a great extent, what species of trout will do well in that water and gives you a good idea of where to search for them with fly or lure.

Cold, unpolluted stream water which runs from 50 to 70 degrees tells you that brook trout will thrive in that part of the stream. When the waters shows a maximum of 72 to 78 degrees brown trout can live there. The brook trout will get out of such water or die during the long periods of summer heat. Rainbows will abound in water cold enough for brook trout—50 to 70 degrees—but will also do favorably in waters which will go as high as 78 degrees for long periods, providing there is plenty of oxygen such as in riffles, rapids, fast runs and swirling eddies. Invariably though, the majority of large rainbows will swim to colder river water or run to large lakes if they can find them. Rainbows are by far the widest rangers of the three trout.

For an accurate reading of oxygen in water, I use an oxygen kit somewhat in the manner that I can accurately ascertain the quality of water with a CO_2 kit. The oxygen kit, however, is a heavy complicated affair so I rely upon transparency, underwater plants and the current caused by inlets and outlets to tell me how deep down in the lake the oxygen limit extends, and, incidentally, how far down I must send my lure to reach the fish on hot summer days.

I hope for about eight parts per million of dissolved oxygen in waters I fish, or, as the chemists put it, 8 ppm O_2. With that much air in the water, every fish should hit hard at feeding time. Who knows, I might even tie into a muskie or two, besides picking up a few nice walleyes?

The ideal oxygen reading is about 8½ parts of air to a million parts of water. Such a reading indicates the water is saturated with air. Anything over that reading I term super-saturated water. I have learned from many hundreds of tests that most lakes and streams are either "short" or "over" the ideal.

Cold water in a stream tumbling fast over riffles and rapids will give trout super-saturated water, from 12 to 14 parts per million. River water in the quiet stretches does not hold its oxygen as well during hot spells and it becomes "thin" there. It is then that the trout seek out the well-mixed waters of the rapids, eddies and fast runs to find sufficient air.

I realize that some chemists will tell me they have seen trout in water which runs as low as 3 parts of oxygen. From the standpoint of catching trout, this does not enthuse me one whit. Trout in a stream which warms up and becomes so "thin" that it can hold only 3 parts of air are almost dead. I'd just be tiring my wrist casting flies at trout too sluggish to be interested in fly, worm or minnow.

In "thin" waters fish work their gills so hard trying to extract air that they have no appetite for food. This is also true in winter in the "thick" water of some lakes. Without abundant oxygen they simply cannot breathe comfortably.

Fortunately, fish are not "tied down" any more than we are when we sit outdoors visiting with a friend. If we're uncomfortable with the heat, we find relief by moving our chairs around the corner of the house where we'll get a breeze and be in the shade away from the bright sun. It is the same with a fish. He will move out of water which does not have "breeze." One flick of the tail and he is off to cooler and more oxygenated waters where he does not have to work his gills half as hard to breathe. Why should he "pant" and suffer under the glaring rays of the sun? If he didn't move away he would soon die.

As Bill and I look over the lake we have come so far to fish, we make no attempt to work our spoons and plugs until we have thoroughly analyzed the situation. We have no intention of blindly plumbing the depths with various weights of lures, not when the oxygen will tell us where the fish are.

We have good reason to conclude this lake is saturated with oxygen because the plants we already have observed indicate its water is *hard*, lush with underwater growth that creates oxygen, and partly because we see the water is slightly clouded with "bloom."

Anyone who gazes intently at the large underwater weeds can actually see them creating great quantities of air, or "breeze" in the water. As the sun shines brightly over the surface, its rays penetrating as deeply as the transparency permits, small air bubbles rise continually from the plants and mix in the water, adding to its oxygen supply.

The "bloom," made up of both plant and animal life called plankton, also gives off oxygen under the rays of the sun. The plants of the plankton are manufacturing starch and sugar from the rays penetrating the water just as do our largest oaks and smallest shrubs from the rays hitting them on land. In this process they give off much oxygen in the water while the animals of the plankton give off carbon dioxide.

Yet this is a hot, bright day, and even though we know there is oxygen all over the lake, we depend solely upon our vision. Now is the time I apply my general rule for fishing lakes during hot weather.

The rule: *The clearer the water during bright summer days, the deeper the fish will lie. The darker the waters, the higher the fish will lie.*

Were there a moderate or fresh breeze breaking the sun's rays and churning up a generous amount of oxygen through wave action, we could expect the fish to be up and possibly hitting a lure wobbling a few feet under the surface, just beneath the wave troughs. But since there is not even as much as a gentle breeze riffling the surface and helping the water extract oxygen from the air above, we must conclude the fish are down under. It is up to us to "go out and get 'em where they ain't."

Although the "bloom" creates oxygen for our lake, the fish don't like the plankton when it becomes too excessive. Also, it is too close to the surface where the sun's rays are so unpleasant that the fish have only one place to go for comfort. That is down at the bottom of the *top* layer of the lake, just about where the *middle* layer of the three layer lake begins.

Down there the water is darker—about as obscure as twilight—

51

the water is slightly colder and there is just enough air—over 5 parts of oxygen—so that the fish are comfortable if they do not exert themselves. Many of the zooplankton, the tiny animals that feed upon the phytoplankton, leave the surface waters at dawn and go deeper, for some will not tolerate the sun's bright rays either.

Walleyes, northern pike, bass and muskies drop down to a lower level at about 9 or 10 o'clock in the morning and remain there while the sun's rays strike the surface quite sharply. They do not move towards the surface water of some 75 degrees until late afternoon. The largest fish may not shift position until 5 o'clock or later.

This situation tells us that temperature is of very little influence. Figure 21 plainly shows the fisherman how lake water becomes progressively darker in the depths through the loss of the sun's rays. The darkness actually offers protection for the fish.

Had there been a heavy rain to thin out the "bloom" and chill the surface water of our lake a little, the fish would work towards the surface and could see the plugs Bill and I would cast near the top water. Right now, in the brightness, if we used surface plugs they would not come within 20 feet of the fish's present resting place. So first off, Bill and I decide to locate some water plants growing deep under. Since we have already made a transparency reading and have decided this is a lake of *clear* water, we conclude that on this day we can expect fish to be living at a depth of about 20 feet.

We start the kicker of the boat and go out from shore quite a distance because this is a lake with a gradually sloping shoreline. We bring the boat to a stop and drop the anchor with 35 feet of rope attached to it. When the boat has lost way we pull up the slack rope, make mention of its length, and then pull up the anchor. An informative little "note" comes up with it and we read it happily. The "note" is in water language, a strand of waterweed. It says plainly, "Here is where fish can live now. Where I grow on a lake bottom there is always enough air for the fish to breathe." We measure the anchor rope from the point where the slack terminates and find the waterweeds are growing down there at a depth of 20 feet.

To make sure the plants aren't growing still deeper, we maneuver the boat farther off shore and let the anchor drop to full length of the 35-foot rope. As our transparency reading told us, we pull up no weeds with the anchor at this depth. We

FIG. 21.–The Viewpoint"
Of A Fish.

We look down but fish look
up. With our little white plate,
which I stress so greatly to
help judge the water, we can
find the shaded depths where
the majority of the big fish lie.
From 9 in the morning until
after four in the afternoon,
they seek shade. Drop that
lure at the "apartment" they
may move into with each
change of light from dawn to
dark. You'll find transparency
to be very important in your
fishing.

53

know from the Transparency Table on page 12, Chapter II, that in a *clear* water lake there is no oxygen below 30 feet, and no plants and no fish below that depth.

Were this a *very clear* water lake, however, we could expect the anchor to bring up a "plant note" because the Transparency Table tells us there is oxygen down as far as 50 feet in this kind of water. Were it a *dark brown* lake, there would be no oxygen for fish to breathe below seven feet. In a *brown* water lake the oxygen limit would be 12 feet and in a *tan* water lake it would be 16 feet.

Encouraged by our discovery of the weed, we each look over our tackle boxes to select deep sinking lures. I pick out a heavy spoon for my casting rod and Bill chooses a quick sinking lure for his spinning rod. We care not who made the lures nor what they are called in the tackle shops. All we ask now is that they will be heavy enough to sink deeply and of good action so we can place them right in front of the noses of fish down by the weeds and be able to set the hook firmly if they hit.

Bill takes a hefty walleye almost immediately, and when he catches another shortly after, we are sure we have a good spot. We take our landmarks—a tree on the east shore, a cottage on the west—knowing that if we row out here on future occasions and line the two up with a mark on the north shore, we'll be in good fishing territory again.

What Bill and I have done, other anglers can do, too. But when you get back to your resort dragging those big fish before all and sundry, even the guides will admit that you are a fisherman when you've caught fish during the sunny daytime hours. The next day you will find a dozen or more boats surrounding you when you go back to the spot you've located, and you will tangle lines and language with the fishermen.

Don't get angry. This is a big lake, so merely start the kicker and locate another 20 foot depth with weeds at the bottom and drag some more nice fish past the gallery on the veranda.

On the third day of such happenings every one of the girls at the resort will try to flirt with you. They have their orders from the "old man" who is jealous of you, but only as a fisherman who knows how to find fish. Somehow he is going to find out your secret.

But don't tell the girls it is the air that does it. They'll only think you are handing them the hot variety. Then the jealous "old man" will never take the women off your neck and you'll have no time for fishing.

A stream fisherman will never become a true expert without a full understanding of the three layers of a stream. Neither will a lake fisherman get into the expert class without an understanding of the three layers of his lake in the summer.

The three layers of a stream are discussed in chapter 11, The Wet Fly Is Intriguing. It is in the next chapter that the lake fisherman should combine his summary of water and the things in it. I feel that he then can use his water sense and common sense to a degree that will surprise him in his ability to secure more strikes.

CHAPTER VI

Three Layer Lakes
Concentrate The Fish

A DIVER WHO DESCENDS to the bottom of a deep lake in the summer shakes his body vigorously as he returns to the surface and often exclaims, "Boy, it's cold down there!"

He may not know it, but he has cut through three different layers of water in his descent, and each layer has become progressively colder.

He wouldn't notice it during his dive, yet the abundant supply of oxygen in the warmer upper layer thins out vastly in the middle layer, and in the third there is practically none.

Aside from the fact that he may shiver in the bottom waters, this information about the three layers is of absolutely no value to the diver. With a fisherman, however, it's a different story. Until he realizes the significance of three layer waters, he cannot expect to fish deep lakes intelligently.

Most deep water lakes acquire their layers early in the summer and retain them until about mid-September. The division into layers is caused by a warming of the upper waters, with a resulting concentration of most of the lake's oxygen there. During other seasons of the year there are no separate layers, and the oxygen is then distributed from top to bottom.

The top layer is known as the Epilimnion, Figure 22. Its depth in late spring may be but eight feet, increasing to as much as 20 or 25 feet as the water becomes warmer. Since practically all the lake's summer-time oxygen is confined there, that's where the fish are.

The middle layer generally is called the Thermocline, but sometimes is referred to as the Mesolimnion. The water in this layer is colder than the first, and its oxygen content is so low that the fish do not care to linger there. In *very clear* lakes the Thermocline may be as deep as 40 feet or more. The Thermo-

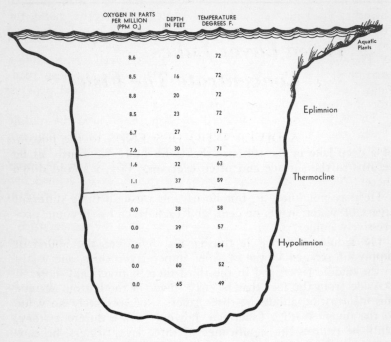

OXYGEN IN PARTS PER MILLION (PPM O₂)	DEPTH IN FEET	TEMPERATURE DEGREES F.	
8.6	0	72	
8.5	16	72	
8.8	20	72	
8.5	23	72	Eplimnion
6.7	27	71	
7.6	30	71	
1.6	32	63	
1.1	37	59	Thermocline
0.0	38	58	
0.0	39	57	
0.0	50	54	Hypolimnion
0.0	60	52	
0.0	65	49	

FIG. 22.—Judging An Average *Clear* Water Lake.

This drawing should give every fisherman a lifetime pattern for his fishing from the middle of June to the middle of September. The average *clear water* lake, over 40 feet in depth, all the way across from Maine to Washington will run about like this.

Farther north, in Canada the dates may run later before they go into a three layer condition. In this drawing, my tests of a Wisconsin lake plainly show that temperature has little consequence in our lake fishing. It is the air in the water that is of real significance.

We know that our game fish must have at least five parts per million of oxygen in the water (5ppm O_2) to live comfortably. The diagram proves that this amount of air does not exist below the first layer in the average *clear water* lake.

The middle layer, the thermocline, has not nearly enough air for fish to live. They will not linger there. Getting into the third layer, the hypolimnion, with our lures or bait would be useless for there is no air in the water, from 38 feet down to 65 feet in the summer time.

For *dark brown, tan* and *very clear* water lakes you will have a sound basis to judge any lake you may fish, if you glance at the chart on page 12, Chapter 2.

58

cline is not stable for it is forced lower and lower as the upper layer increases its depth by the warming of the sun.

The bottom layer, the Hypolimnion, is the lake's coldest water in summer. It does not hold enough air there for a minnow to breathe, let alone a game fish. In winter, on the other hand, the bottom layer is the warmest water, has ample air and is favored as a haunt by the fish.

The middle layer can be determined fairly well by lowering a maximum and minimum thermometer and taking various readings, but it is a very long drawn out and complicated process, too much for any fisherman.

Dr. Birge and Juday showed me how they found the middle layer, the thermocline, by using a maximum and minimum Centigrade thermometer. When the water temperature fell less than one degree Centigrade per meter they were still in the upper layer, the Epilimnion. As soon as the temperature declined one degree Centigrade per meter by further lowering they were in the middle layer, the Thermocline.

Lowering the thermometer, when the drop in temperature became less than one degree for each meter they were in the bottom layer, the Hypolimnion.

A simple formula for remembering the three layers of the average deep lake is: *Upper layer, much air, most of the fish. Middle layer, not much air, few fish. Bottom layer, no air, no fish.*

With this much information about three layer lakes already at your command, you can readily see how useless it is for an angler to "go way down to China" with his fly, spinning or casting lures in such waters. How absurd it would be to troll or sink live bait in the "dead" water—the bottom layer and the middle layer, too—when fish cannot live there until the lake "overturns" about the middle of September and diffuses oxygen at all levels.

I would say that in approximately 95 per cent of the deep water lakes in the United States and Canada the three layers begin forming about June 10 when the warmth of the sun really makes its influence felt. The layers in these lakes remain intact at least until the middle of September. I do not know if this would apply South of Kentucky. You can secure this information.

In mountainous areas of much higher altitude, the deep lakes are not warmed as quickly, so the three-layer period undoubtedly is briefer. Having made no first-hand observations of this one per cent of high altitude lakes, I can give no data for them.

There are a few *very clear* deep water lakes with no layers whatsoever. Some of these may be as deep as 100 feet or more. Your thermometer will show that such lakes usually have a temperature of 42 to 50 degrees at the bottom. I have never found any higher temperatures at such depths in my Wisconsin lake surveys.

The three layers in a lake during summer are in marked contrast to the condition of its waters during other seasons.

When the waters of the top layer begin to cool about the middle of September, the chilled water sinks down and down through the thermocline and into the Hypolimnion. This, together with an almost daily stirring of the waters by the wind, brings about a complete mix of oxygen. Soon the oxygen is distributed in equal proportions in all layers instead of being concentrated in the upper strata. The entire lake is then supersaturated with oxygen, 12 parts to the million parts of water, (12 ppm O_2).

With that much air, the fish take on new life, seeming to sense they now must build up their bodies for the long "winter of discontent." All game fish from muskies to northern pike, and all species of panfish hit hard and quickly. We can fool many of them with the lures they disdained during the hot weather.

When ice seals the lake for winter, very little oxygen can be added if the lake is in the seepage category. What little is added comes from underwater plants which the faint winter sunlight, through the snow and ice, causes them to produce. The holes we fishermen cut in the ice for winter angling contribute nothing to the air in any lake.

In a drainage lake, if there is a good flow at its inlet and outlet the current brings new air all through the winter.

We ice fishermen have our best luck on most lakes by lowering our bait within a foot or two of the bottom. The water is warmest there in winter. In the summer the opposite is true, it's coolest there then.

Since the temperature has to be 32 degrees or under to freeze a solid coating over the lake, the water directly under the ice is about 33 degrees and each three or four feet it becomes a trifle warmer. It usually runs around 39 degrees at the bottom.

Though that is very cold water, it's the warmest the fish can find. Only when they go in search of food or want a change from darkness to light do they cruise away from it. They sort of "just go out for a walk," coming near the surface now and then.

By December, the 12 parts of air in the lake may have declined to 9 parts. Fish, nymphs and other animal life are continually drawing on the available supply. Decaying plants and plankton give off free carbon dioxide which further reduces the oxygen content of the water. In January so much air may have been consumed that only six parts will be left and in early February the supply sometimes is reduced to but four parts.

Fish are still comfortable at five parts, but at four they begin to work their gills faster to extract the oxygen from the water. At three parts they are uncomfortable and some will die. If the water in March has only one and one-half parts, they will all die. Dogfish, bullheads and mud minnows, though, can live "in a heavy dew." I have never found one winter-killed.

We can be thankful that we have so many good lakes that do not reach this precarious situation. These are of the three-layer variety, so deep and full of oxygen that there is no danger of fish suffocating. We have many borderline cases, however, where fish gasping for what little air remains are saved only because the ice leaves the lake and a fresh supply of oxygen becomes available.

In a state like Wisconsin, which has thousands of inland lakes, hundreds can be classed as borderline. Usually it is the shallower lakes, rich in lime, that winter-kill the fish. If the winter is unusually severe, the ice gets thicker and the water depth shrinks accordingly, with the result there is less oxygen than in winters of less ice. Also, in the rich lakes there is greater decay of vegetation and plankton, another serious drain on an already limited oxygen supply.

Fish likewise die in the summer if a lake is too shallow and is so rich in lime that its plants grow at such a rapid rate that they rot and give off free carbon dioxide at night and very dull days, instead of the oxygen they would give off if growing in a deeper lake.

When I made the rounds of the lakes in Wisconsin during the years I was engaged in lake and stream improvement work, I always felt a deep pang of regret when we came across a lake in the early spring whose beach was filled with dead fish. Each season, after the break-up of the ice, my crews would haul away tons of decaying game, forage and rough fish. Oddly enough, people of the area viewing the sight would often exclaim: "I never knew there were so many fish in this lake." To me this meant they had not read their waters properly, otherwise they would have known the lake was excellent for angling.

61

When a certain lake will winter-kill is quite unpredictable. How, for example, could anyone foretell the experience of Town Corner Lake in Marinette County, Wisconsin, during the winter of 1935-36? When I tested its waters on October 23 I found it contained eight parts of oxygen. My survey card, which I still have in my files, shows the water tested 39 parts of lime to the million parts of water (39 ppm CO_2) telling me that it was a *hard* water lake, should grow many plants and should run about 2,000 pounds of fish and fish food to the acre of water. My card shows further that it was of *clear* water, 190 acres, and that we had built and sunk many lake improvement structures there. I marked the vegetation as "abundant" on my card, and indicated it was a seepage lake, spring fed, with a maximum depth of 20 feet.

I figured that lake had a good chance of pulling through the winter without disaster to the fish, but how could anyone know that the winter of '36 was to have one of the longest periods of sustained sub-zero cold in Wisconsin's history, and how could I know what the impact of such a continued cold spell would be?

Nevertheless, when I returned in the spring to "feel the pulse" of the lake with my oxygen kit, I approached it with vague misgivings. To my dismay, all along the shore I saw thousands of dead largemouth bass and many more thousands of perch. As a fisherman I almost cried to think of the wonderful bass fishing that would be lost to the fishermen coming to Marinette County each season to fish the lake.

I dispatched a note to B. O. Webster, head of the fisheries department of the Wisconsin Conservation Department, asking whether he would please restore the lake with more fish. When I met him later he laughed and said, "Don't worry, we'll give you plenty of fish, but I wish I knew just when these confounded lakes will winter-kill and when they won't. On some it happens every few years."

I could understand his feeling of frustration, trying to keep lakes stocked only to have the fish lost by an unpredictable winter-kill. I knew, too, that he was deeply concerned because both he and his assistant, Wendell Anderson, continually strove to keep the death loss of their hatchery-grown fish to the lowest possible level. These men raised more hatchery fish for Wisconsin waters with less disease loss in the hatcheries than was raised in any other state. I pay tribute to their great skill.

Although the angler often gets a gnawing sensation in his

stomach while fishing through the ice, and has tantalizing visions of a big fish fry, the fish themselves aren't hungry. True, the waters may have just as much oxygen at the bottom of the lake as at the top, but 39 degrees is a little too cold to stimulate their appetites. Their gastric juices flow best above 50 degrees.

The fish's lack of appetite during winter is probably a good thing, though. While the ice fisherman doesn't get as big a catch, more fish are spared for summer-time angling. For example, a northern pike might eat a two pound fish in June at 5 o'clock in the morning and eat another at 5 o'clock that afternoon. In the winter the same kind of two pound fish will probably last him for three days or more, and only small minnows will tempt him then.

During the very hot weather of summer, the fish in shallow lakes eat much the same as in winter. Water too cold slows their digestion, water too warm destroys their appetite.

In Wisconsin, Michigan and Minnesota the ice is out of the lakes at varying dates, but by April 15 the waters in these states usually are exposed once more. Farther north, in Canada, the ice may leave a bit later.

It is then that our three layer lakes gradually undergo the transformation that finally brings about the division of their waters early in June.

At the time the ice has melted, the water at the bottom still retains its winter temperature of approximately 39 degrees. The sun now warms the top water to 40 degrees and this water sinks just a little deeper through the lower water. Each day more surface water gets warmed, sinks and pushes the previously warmed water lower. Meanwhile the bottom water rises to the top and this in turn is warmed by the sun until all the water, from top to bottom, is about 40 degrees. We call this the "spring overturn."

In April the first moderate breeze—18 to 23 miles an hour—blows over the surface. Like a giant spoon, the breeze mixes the top waters with air. This it accomplishes with the waves that take oxygen from the atmosphere. The lake which contained possibly four parts of oxygen is churned until it has five parts. Another day a fresh breeze—23 to 28 miles an hour—mixes the water still more and now there are six parts of air. Next a strong breeze—28 to 34 miles an hour—helps to diffuse eight and nine parts all through the lake. Every gentle and moderate breeze throughout the summer likewise helps mix air in the water unless it is a small lake in a pocket.

In May the sun warms the shoreline waters substantially. The snails, clams and nymphs leave their winter quarters in the deep water and come to the warming shallow water of the beach. The minnows and crayfish move in from the depths to take up their summer residence, too. In scarcely no time at all there is tremendous activity all around the shallow water which was lifeless in the winter.

With but few exceptions lake fish spawn in the spring. From muskies to panfish, they are all on the move. The water is still too cold for active feeding, so the chances for the fishermen are better in the warmer waters near shore.

The sun now has a job to do that will change the entire lake to an extent that the average fisherman does not realize. It is about to "separate the men from the boys," to make it tougher for the angler to take fish, and to compel us to use all our understanding of water if we are to catch many.

While the sun is bright, the nights are still cool. This makes it impossible for the sun to have its way immediately. The surface of the water warms in the daytime but chills at night. All the fish except the bass have spawned, but the game fish are not as voracious as they will be later in this month of May or early June. But both male and female recover quickly after spawning.

Each day finds them a little hungrier as the water continues to get warmer. Now the fisherman does not know where to look for the fish, nor can I tell him where to fish as they are scattered all over the lake. There is some hope for the angler in that they soon begin to cruise around the bars and reefs. But for the most part, any spot may be their home. If we want to catch them we've got to work the waters hard with our spinning, casting and fly rods, with the warmed inshore waters having the edge.

Soon the waters are warmed for a few feet beneath the entire surface, thanks to the relentless rays of the sun. The muskies, which ate seldom and little during the winter, now have a quickened appetite. They turn from eating minnows to devouring larger fish. Now they are the wolves in the water. No fish is safe from them except those which are too large to swallow.

The bass congregate in hundreds during early June. It is now that the fisherman can get a good estimate of the lake he fishes, for he will see them lying ever so still in the shallow water. They are waiting until their bodies become warm enough for milt and eggs to "rise" in their bodies like dough in a pan by the stove. Then they will mate and spawn.

The bass will not strike now to any great extent. They move away from a lure, and I have seen them utterly ignore the nymphs which come up out of the water to hatch. The bass fishing season is not open yet, and no conservation-minded angler would take them if he could, except if the law allowed in overcrowded lakes.

Some minnows are spawning, too, each in the territory for which nature best fitted them. Those minnows which make their home over the sand spawned there sooner, for their grounds are warmed earliest by the sun. Those which live around silt, spawn earlier, too, for black silt warms the water quickly through the sun's effect. Minnows which live over gravel and among the plants spawn a little later, for the plants have not shown much growth yet.

As the time approaches for the lakes to divide into three layers, the waters become a great food factory. Every *drop* of water now fairly teems with plankton, working to furnish nourishment for the minnows and fish. We would not have one muskie, walleyed pike, trout or any other kind of fish if nature did not furnish plankton in our waters. The fry are hardly hatched out of their eggs before they begin drawing this essential food through their gill rakers. Without this all year around food, the fry would soon die.

The bigger fish, too, dine on plankton. You have heard it said that "he drinks like a fish." What a poor simile! Fish drink but little. When they open their mouths repeatedly they are not supping water, they are extracting air from the water as it passes over their gills, and straining the plankton for food at the same time.

Now that the spawning period is over and all growing things are well underway, the sun, too, is making progress. It is just about ready to divide the deep lakes into three layers.

The surface water that is warmed by the sun cannot sink to the colder water underneath. Rather, it floats over the cold water. In effect, it forms a sort of lid, which by about the 10th of June virtually prevents oxygen from passing through it to the middle and bottom layers which have also developed at this time.

It is now that the summer fisherman sees why he is so often out of luck. This three layer change has much to do with his tackle and the amount of fish he can catch if he understands and takes full advantage of this great change in many waters.

To me, this is a happy time of the year, for I consider it a great advantage to have our deep waters acquire three layers in summer. The concentration of oxygen in the upper waters certainly makes it much easier to find the fish, since they, too, are more concentrated than at other periods of the year. All you have to do to catch them is apply your knowledge of transparency, temperature and oxygen during daytime fishing, and your knowledge of the food shelves for the early morning and late afternoon fishing.

Incidentally, if you ever get a limnologist, one of these scientists of water, in your fishing camp, make a casual remark to one of your other companions that you caught a nice smallmouth bass in a four layer lake.

If the limnologist rises up on his hind feet and vigorously denies there is any such thing as a four layer lake, bet him a couple good cigars that there is and that you can prove it. When he takes the bet, start naming the layers.

"First, there is the bottom layer, the Hypolimnion, isn't there?"

He'll agree to that.

"Then there is the middle layer, the Thermocline, isn't there?" He'll say, "Yes."

"Then there is the Epilimnion, isn't there?"

"Sure," he'll say, "but that is all. I knew you were bluffing." Then he'll reach out for the cigars.

Just as the stakeholder is about to hand them over, you interrupt, "How about the top layer, the fourth layer where you float your fly on a lake or stream? You call it the Meniscus, but you do give it a name and do recognize it as existing. As for me, I use it in my fishing."

Surely the fisherman jury will award you the cigars, for isn't a three layer lake like a three layer cake, topped off with frosting? And isn't that fourth layer, the Meniscus, every bit as inviting to you as the cake frosting, inasmuch as it floats the dry fly or bass bug that catches the big fish that tops off those mealy potatoes you are preparing for your dinner?

I presume that, if I interviewed a fish about the three layers, he'd reply: "Three layers bosh! All of a sudden there is one big wall through which I cannot go and live as I used to. You can divide it into ten layers if you wish, I can't breathe in any of them, so why bother me with foolish questions? I'm more concerned about you animals who drag us up into the layer above this lake; we can't breathe there either. Don't you know that we can't even swim in it?"

CHAPTER VII

The Food Shelf Tells You Which Lure to Use

WHEN AN ANGLER looks at the vast display of spoons, plugs, lures and flies in the tackle shops, he realizes there is no tackle box in the shop large enough to carry specimens of all of them on a fishing trip.

His problem is to select the right kind and number of lures to take care of his fishing needs. If he has never studied the food shelf of lakes, he is inclined to load himself down with a fantastic assortment and becomes what is known in the angling fraternity as a "bait changer," so busy is he trying out his numerous lures.

On the other hand, if he makes it a point to study the food shelf of the lake he intends to fish, the shelf will tell him he can cut down the number of lures and learn to catch fish with almost any plug, from black all through the color ranges to a plain white lure, which is not a color but lack of it.

Often I have seen a fisherman reach into his well-filled tackle box to select a half dozen different plugs to hook in the rib or gunwale of the boat so they will be handy for quick changing. It isn't that I consider it ridiculous to hook six plugs in such a manner. The difficulty is that usually those half dozen lures are all of the same type, generally floating plugs, although they may be greatly varied in their color schemes. To make good fishing sense, the half dozen lures should consist of three different types, two floating plugs, two spoons and two sinking plugs.

In my tacklebox I carry but nine lures for bait casting, including three floating plugs, three spoons and three sinking plugs, and about the same number for the spinning rod. One of each would be sufficient under ordinary circumstances, but there's nothing like carrying some spares. A spoon which at the moment is taking fish might be lost, and without an extra I would be compelled to fish with my floating or sinking plug.

With these I would be unable to work the waters as they should be at that given time.

The food shelf of a lake is just what its name implies, the part of the lake where the food on which the fish feed is to be found. Since our angling technique is based primarily on the feeding habits of fish, it is essential that we have a thorough understanding of the food shelf if we expect to be using the right lures at the right time in the right place.

During the fishing season, with which we are mainly concerned, the beginning of the food shelf of all good lakes is the immediate sloping shoreline. As the water deepens the great mass of visible fish food begins to dwindle. The shelf ends when the water becomes so deep that the rays of the sun cannot penetrate to supply the growing power for plants and fish food. This is at the point where a white plate lowered by a cord into the water becomes invisible.

We must not, however, regard the shoal waters of the shorelines as the only food shelf during the fishing season. Reefs, bars, drop-offs and floor-pockets are food shelves, too, and often attract more large sized fish per square yard than the shoreline food shelf.

Before the first snowfall, weeks before the ice covers the lake, almost all the animal life which comprises the fish food leaves the shoreline shallows, swimming to deeper water. Just as the chipmunk, the woodchuck or the bear has a natural instinct to "den up" for the winter, so does nature in her fall chilling of the lake waters warn the animals of the shoreline to seek the comfort and safety of the deeper waters. By May they all return to their spring and summer homes, their breeding places. There is then no danger of ice freezing to the bottom of the shallow water to kill them as would be the case during winter, or an ice push during the early spring melting period when they would be lifted off the bottom and crushed ashore.

A natural question arises: "What kind of fish food is to be found on the food shelf?"

By looking into the water in the first foot or two offshore you will see many snails and clams. Here also you will note the caddis cases of the sedge or caddis flies and the nymphs of the mayflies, shown in Chapter IX. On the waterweeds growing there you will find the nymphs of damsel flies. Below them, on the floor of the lake, will lie their relatives, the dragon fly nymphs. You will see minnows swimming in schools and crayfish will be hidden among the rubble stones or the underwater

Fig. 23.—Snails and Clams *(Mollusca)*.

Mollusks furnish much food for fish. The snails (univalves) are as eagerly eaten as the small clams (bivalves). Two bivalves are shown in the first row at left. Fishermen call them "fingernail" clams. The four in the last two rows are snails or univalves.

plants. By digging the lake bottom with a shovel you will turn up considerably more fish food, mainly snails and clams, and even aquatic worms.

Sandy, wave-swept underwater shorelines have but little animal food or plants. You will find the largest percentage of food on underwater gravel, in the silt and on the rubble stones. True, certain species of minnows do live and spawn only upon sandy shores, but most minnows use the plants or rubble stones for cover.

This does not imply that the fisherman must disregard the sandy beach. He need but wade just beyond the wave action to find barren sand that often is covered with dead plankton. Here both plants and animals find food enough to grow, and where this fish food is found, there also will be fish, but the time must be right. In large wind-swept lakes, however, the sandy bottom cannot retain such rich silt covering.

"When and how should the shoreline food shelf be fished?"

Your knowledge of transparency gives you the answer to that question.

You know it is useless to fish the shoreline shelf on a sunny day in July and August between the hours of 9 a.m. and 4 p.m. because the fish aren't there. You know that during this period they are out in deeper water, at a level where a white plate lowered in the water is but dimly visible, although now and then a fish will hide under the protecting shelter of plants in a good weed bed near the shore, or in other cover.

You also know that in the early morning hours and when evening approaches, the sun's rays are not so penetrating. The fish then lose their daytime caution and cruise along the shallows feeding freely upon the animal life or devouring any smaller fish their hungry mouths can grab. The fish are to be found even on what seems to be barren sandy bottom, for they are in quest of those minnows which make that *clear* water their homes and spawning grounds.

Fig. 24—Crayfish *(Decapoda)*

Crayfish (crawfish, crawdads, crabs). Trout pack their stomachs with crayfish when they are this size, about one-fourth grown. Large fish eat them in lakes even when they are full size, three to four inches in length.

70

10 ft   15 ft   10 ft

FIG. 25.—Hole or Pocket.

During the ice age, some 10,000 years ago, large and small areas were dug by glaciers and lakes were formed. Where the erosion gouged out a large or small hole in an otherwise shallow part of the lake, away from the deep center, "pockets" were formed. They bring rich reward to the fisherman who discovers them by sounding shallow parts of a lake. Large fish lie here and find easy prey around the pocket.

It is when the fish are "on the feed" on the shoreline shelf that you can expect good luck with your flies or surface lures worked with your casting or spinning rod. Whether you cast from shore, from a boat, or while wading, you never know when you are going to tie into a walleyed pike, northern pike or a bass. The panfish, too, are likely prospects for your creel.

You must remember, though, that it is a floating plug you must use. Its design and color is of little consequence.

When twilight comes, or when dawn is turning into daylight, the floating lure should be the kind which dives a little below the surface. When it is dark, use any kind of surface plug which wobbles but does not dive. In kicking up the surface waters, a wobbling plug invariably will get those fish which are then surface feeding.

If the day is rather dark or if a brisk wind is ruffling the waters, it is a good idea to try some shoreline casting during the daytime hours. This is especially true along the shoreline weed beds where fish, free from bright rays of the sun, take advantage of this opportunity to rest and perhaps feed if they are so inclined. Again it is the floating lure you must use, making your casts parallel with the weed bed, but not at right angles toward the weed bed. As your lure is slowly retrieved along the edge of the weeds, a fish may come out to grab it.

It is when we fish the other food shelves in the lake—the reefs, bars or pockets—that we have an opportunity to use our other lures, the spoons and the sinking plugs, in addition to the floaters. See Figure 25. (When I refer to a pocket I mean a flat piece of underwater bottom with a hole, or pocket, which a glacier dug there.)

As fish are more concentrated around a good reef, bar or in a pocket, it is apparent that if fished properly, any such crowded feeding place will produce more fish with lesser casts than the more extensive shoreline shelf. For this reason these areas should be searched out. They are ideal for daytime fishing, and also during the early morning, afternoon and evening hours. Again, the secret in fishing these areas is in allowing the water to tell you how.

Before we set out in our boat for a good reef, let's select six good lures and hook them on the boat rib, or better still, have them handy in a small covered box where a boated fish will not scatter them. From my tacklebox let's remove a light colored floating plug and a darker one. For spoons, a thick-metaled silver model and a red and white one with copper lining look good. That black and green faced spoon with a silver lining might do just as well, but we are trying to equip ourselves with a small, balanced outfit on the rib of the boat. Next we select a pair of underwater plugs which will sink quickly and deeply. We choose one with a dark back, an imitation of a chub minnow, and another with a lighter back, a perch finish.

That will be the sum total of our ammunition, six lures— two floaters, two spoons and two sinking plugs for plug rods or spinning rods. With these we can fish all day and evening, unless we should lose some. One way to avoid such loss is to check for line fray from time to time as we are fishing.

Your reel can be a level wind, a self-caster or anything else you can handle with ease and accuracy. Your line can run from a 10 pound test to an 18 pound test if you aren't after fish which will weigh over 20 pounds. For spinning in weedy or cluttered waters a six pound test line will do.

Your casting or your spinning rod can be split bamboo, steel or glass. Regardless of the type of rod you employ, the same methods of fishing and types of lures will be used.

With the less important matter of tackle settled, let us now get into the boat and have to do with that far more essential

72

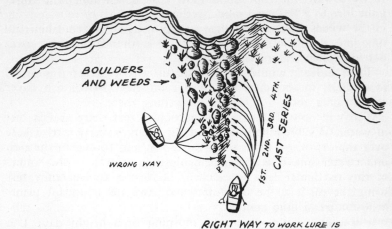

BOULDERS AND WEEDS →

1ST. 2ND. 3RD. 4TH. CAST SERIES

WRONG WAY

RIGHT WAY TO WORK LURE IS ALONG SIDE OF REEF, WEED BED, DROP-OFF OR BAR.

FIG. 26.—Fishing a Reef. (See Text).

part of angling, the water and the fish. Some may tell us that "all of fishing is not in catching fish." That may be sweet and nice, and often a good alibi for poor success, but when I go fishing I want to catch fish.

I think I return them to the water far oftener than the average angler, nevertheless I try my best to engage them in battle. I crave the strike, the play, and the satisfaction of feeling that the old "bean" and the old rod arm aren't slipping.

Who was it that shoveled tons of snow and coal all winter, and with every shovelful of the stuff counted the days (and his bank roll) until the opening of the season? Who tied flies, varnished rods, touched up plugs and fought fish mentally in lake or stream, all winter long, planning his tactics and their capture while drying the skis and snowshoes?

So sit on your cushion lad, but do not close your eyes to the grand waters while you work this reef in a manner befitting its true worth. Here IS a treasure house, probably laid down by a glacier some 10,000 years ago. Notice that the reef is shaped like a wedge of pie. That's because the glacier shoved the gravel, rubble stones and boulders high and wide at the north end, and the push tapered off at the south end.

Let us not make the common mistake of dropping our anchor 50 feet or more from the reef and casting a floating lure directly toward the edge of it. How absurd it would be to offer your lure to a walleyed pike, northern pike, bass or muskie lying in the weeds on the reef, then snatching it away from him and dragging it on the surface farther and farther from good cover out into open water. See Figure 26.

That, indeed, would be a shameful way to treat this grand food shelf, so abundant with fish food, heavy with fish cover and many a good fish resting or feeding there.

You will note that over this particular reef there are six feet of water. Wave-washed silt and dying plankton have settled here over the centuries. Plant seeds drifted in and rooted in the rich underwater soil. It is understandable that growth in the waters of this particular lake is excellent because a transparency test would reveal it to be of *clear* water, and the abundant plants denote a good lime content.

It is now 10 o'clock in the morning of a bright day. The fish fed last night and early this morning and will not feed heavily again until evening. On this bright day they are lying among the weeds growing on the reef. They get protection and cover from the plants and boulders. The plants shade the fish, and in effect cause a "breeze" in the water by exuding oxygen. Right now the fish resting in this ideal area might be tempted to strike at easy prey, even though they are not very hungry.

We know that lake fish, like other animals, do not like to race for their food. They depend upon ambush, if possible. A quick flirt of body and tail and the unsuspecting victim—usually a smaller fish—is seized and held before he can overcome the sudden rush of the predator.

Here, then, is no place to cast a floating lure towards the weed bed and reeling it towards us the moment it hits the water. We cannot expect a resting, not very hungry fish, to come to the surface for a floater at this time of day, nor to rush out from weedbed to open water.

If a fish should leave his cover to chase our floating lure as it is being reeled away from him towards open water, we'd be most apt to have a "following" fish, one which half-heartedly pursues the retreating lure, finds it is a fake and turns away. "Followers" are the result of wrong casting at the right spots.

Fish have no hands. A quick grasp with their mouth is the only way they can hold and examine an object coming suddenly past their cover. So let us take advantage of this trait and ignore those floating lures on the rib of the boat and choose an underwater spoon or plug. You want something that will sink rapidly as soon as it hits the water so the fish will see it for but a moment, and in his surprise will involuntarily make a short, quick lunge. That will give you an opportunity to hook him before he has time to react. See Figure 26.

You select a sinking plug—a spoon would do just as well—snap it on your leader and judge its action by working it in open water on the other side of the boat. Satisfied that it will function well at the depth you wish it to go, six feet underwater, you decide to use it.

The reef, you will recall, runs like a piece of pie, wedge shaped. Before you do any casting, we'll row the boat down to the south end, the tip. You'll be aided by the south breeze as you cast while working the edge of the reef.

As is the case with a shoreline weed bed, it is poor fishing technique to cast toward this bed at right angles. The correct way is to cast parallel with the reef, just about a foot or two from the edge of the weeds. Your first cast is a relatively short one, approximately 30 feet. On the retrieve you try to bring your lure back along every foot of the weed bed, past a fish which may be in the cover. In this fashion you are working your sinking plug alongside his home, not taking it away to the open water where the fish can see that it is a fraud.

Every action of that lure is in the fish's home territory. He is quite likely to grab it quickly as it goes past him. Aware of this possibility, you are alert and set the hook before he discovers his mistake. If there is no strike, you extend your next cast by throwing 40 feet of line instead of 30. Your next cast is about 60 feet and the last cast, before we move the boat farther along the weed bed, covers up to 85 feet of water. This is about the limit of line you can handle nicely.

If the fish are hitting you may be lucky enough to take one at every cast. Should you make the mistake of casting a long line on your first try instead of a short one you would be a poor fisherman. Your first long cast, say 85 feet, might hook a fish but it would be folly to drag one from that distance past all the good cover which you hadn't first fished with shorter casts. The fight and play would frighten all the fish you might otherwise have had by working UP to the 85 foot casting. When the edge of the reef has been covered for 85 feet we turn and fish the main body of the reef before moving farther along the edge. See Figure 26.

I do not know why it is that so many fishermen persist in making long casts first and short ones later. It must be that

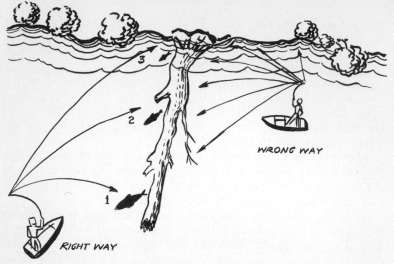

FIG. 27.—A Log In The Water.

A down log, tree or deadhead at the shore line finds the largest fish in cover nearest open water. The smaller fish will lie nearer shore. Dropping the lure alongside the log—at the shoreline—results in one small fish but the fight puts the larger fish down. Surprising the largest fish and forcing him to fight in the open water, may result in taking all three fish. These tactics apply in either lake or stream.

they are water chasers, preferring to dash all over a lake for the scenery instead of the fish. The same wrong tactics often are used in fishing around a sunken log or a windfall in a lake or stream, as in Figure 27.

My experience in fishing reefs is that you can stay with a good one such as this from morning until late afternoon and on into the evening if you choose. Combing both edges and the entire body of the reef is the only way to do it justice. By experimenting with the lures in the boat you will soon learn just what to do.

Since this is a *clear* water lake, try a dark lure, then a light one. You will find that action is everything and color really has little to do with your success. It's how you fish the lure that matters. By observing the action of lures in the water, an angler soon learns that one lure can be a "peach" at certain depths but a "lemon" at others. What great latitude the lake fisherman has, lures of all sizes, shapes and colors, providing he uses each intelligently!

Using your landmarks during the course of the day, it is a

good plan to sound the reef all over. Measure the varying depths with a heavy dipsey swivel sinker tied on a light cord. Once you learn almost every foot of a good reef you have a "gold mine" which you can go to month after month and remove treasure. No longer need you chase aimlessly all around a lake in a desperate search for fish when you can continually go to a good area such as this and have the satisfaction of knowing your every cast is working over reliable, familiar water. It makes for calm, restful and productive fishing.

When evening comes you can still stay with your reef or shift your activities to the shoreline shelf because the fish will really go "on the feed" at either place. They will be feeding up near the surface, so now you can switch to your floating, popping or wobbling plugs. Your bass bugs, large dry flies or wet flies will also be effective, taking the surface feeding fish and those which are chasing top minnows.

If a lake has no reefs, the fisherman uses the same tactics of working along the edges of weed beds he can see down there in the *clear* water. If a 20 foot depth shows weed growth in a lake of *clear* water, a heavy lure will bring good results if it is worked just *over* the tops of the weeds. It is darker down there and the fish do not need the shade of the weed bed as over a shallow reef, but they do like the cover and the oxygen which the plants give off, a good reason why they are there.

If you decide to use a spoon rather than a sinking plug to get down to these fish, the spoon must not be of the light dime store quality. It can be small but it must be of thick metal, heavy enough to keep it on the floor of that food shelf with your looping casts and a "jerky" style of retrieving.

In this deep water, *steady reeling of the spoon will not do the business*. Your style must be one turn of the handle and a pause for the same length of time. Then reel and pause again. This will raise the spoon, give it movement and action. It must rise and sink, rise and sink, so it will cover the bottom waters as evenly as you can possibly cause it to work.

In this way you can search the bottom water as thoroughly as the worm or minnow fisherman who sits in his boat and gets his bait right down there in the fish's daylight home. But you will cover 10 times more water than any bait fisherman with your casting or spinning rod.

A good drop-off or a deep hole lying in the flat floor of a lake harbors large fish during the daytime. It pays to locate

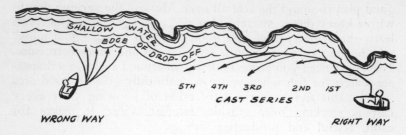

FIG. 28.—A Drop Off.

Whether the drop off occurs far from shore or begins immediately at rocky cliffs or canyons, fishing towards the edge means a following fish. Fishing alongside the edge brings far greater results.

such a pocket with a sounding line and then use your best skill in trying to catch them. Figure 28.

My advice is to learn every bit of the shoreline. The underwater cover such as down trees or waterlogged material of every sort yield good fish and many of them. If you draw a map of the shoreline, you'll probably pay closer attention to the bays, each of which has its individual characteristics. Some parts of a bay are great producers while other parts of the same bay are worthless.

For instance, if the prevailing winds are south, southwest, the bay which gets the benefit of the ripples, wavelets and waves will always have good fishing. The shoreline of that same bay which does not get the effect of the prevailing winds may be useless if the lake is of *hard* water. There floating algae mats may grow so thick in that persistently calm water that the fish will not live there during July and August. They will be on the wind-swept shore of the bay.

This calls for careful study of the lake you may fish constantly. One lake may be 700 acres and have but five miles of shoreline, while another of half that size will have more bays, giving it as much as seven miles of shoreline.

Find the productive shores of a lake and you will save much time in not fishing the spots where fish cannot be comfortable in the summer.

I seldom drag my feet nor little Willie, either, when Momma says "dinner is ready." I may find only hash from yesterday on my food shelf, but the fish have a cafeteria. Locate that cafeteria, offer them a "dessert" spoon and you'll have no more hash for a day or two at your home food shelf.

CHAPTER VIII

Drainage and Seepage
Lakes Differ

"HAS THIS LAKE AN INLET or outlet?"

That is a question I invariably ask when a fisherman invites me to his favorite lake, or to try a new one which he has just heard about. I suppose that sometimes it must sound rude, interrupting that way, but if you'll pardon the four dollar words, it retards my anticipatory thought process about the forthcoming fishing trip unless I know immediately whether we are going to fish a drainage or a seepage lake. Each calls for a different approach in angling. I do not take just any lure from my tackle box and drop it hither and yon in the water.

All lakes, ponds and springholes are classed as either drainage or seepage.

A drainage lake simply means what the name signifies—there must be water running into or out of it, or in and out of it. At the inlet, water drains into the lake from a brook, creek or river, and at the outlet the water drains out in a stream of various widths.

A seepage lake, on the other hand, is landlocked, with neither inlet nor outlet. It contains only the water which oozes into it from underground springs or water seeping into it from springs above the shoreline, plus rain and snow water which falls upon or seeps into it.

Wherever a dam backs up river water for several acres, or several hundred acres or more, it is a "flowage," and the residents of the area so term it. The maps and the tourists often call it a lake. In effect it is a lake, of the drainage variety.

When nature, through log jams or any other obstruction in a river holds back a considerable amount of lowland water before spilling it again through a narrows, I call it a "widewater," the same as my lumberjack friends did in the "old days."

Today such water is usually given the name of a lake, although it is really but a wide spot in the river. If regarded as a lake, it, too, is in the drainage class.

A fisherman must be prepared to encounter most anything in the way of fish if a drainage lake is part of a chain of lakes to which the fish have spawning access by stream or thoroughfare, or if the lake has a shoreline favorable to spawning, See illustration. Such a lake, if it is not in the *soft* water class, is almost certain to have a wide variety of game fish, including wall-eyed pike, northern pike, and bass, as well as the smaller panfish.

In *medium* and *hard* water drainage lakes there may even be muskies which may pounce upon large spoons, bucktails, lures of most every other description, and big suckers. Muskie fry, just out of the egg, might not do well in the drainage lake you are fishing, still you may find his parents thriving there. They do their spawning in the suitable kind of waters connected with that lake. The newly hatched fry of the muskie must have a certain soft water bug—*polyphemus*—which grows in water, or he dies.

No angler or ichthyologist can look at a drainage lake and say with certainty just what fish will be found in that lake. That is why we fishermen have a tackle kit with a varied assortment of lures so that we are expectantly prepared for anything and everything in a lake of that kind.

Who knows, except by long observation, how far the muskies in drainage waters go to spawn?

Where do the smallmouth bass spawn if the lake in which we catch them contains none of the essential gravel? They may have to travel through two or more lakes to find the marl or gravel which will allow them to fan out nests, deposit their eggs and produce a hatch. Their offspring eventually may, and usually do, range far from the original nest.

Walleyed pike and perch are great travelers, too, and one may find them in any good drainage lake. The crappies, blue gills and rock bass likewise spread through the waters of the drainage district, often in countless numbers.

All fish have their cycles. In drainage lakes there may be a scarcity of crappies, northerns or walleyes for several years, but an abundance of fish during the same period when one or the other species become dominant.

Even if a drainage lake is of *soft* water, poor in fish food but possessing good fish cover in the form of logs, stumps and other down stuff, the angler must always be alert. Here is no place for weak lines or a weak heart, either.

Many years ago I would look at the water for "sign" in a drainage lake, and if I decided it was poor water, would fish it only when there was nothing else to do. I'm afraid I was guilty of careless casting, especially on *soft* water drainage lakes of *brown* to *tan* waters. Because of the poor transparency I had to make 10 fruitless casts here to one on better waters, so I did not always guard against the surprise that a large fish gave me when he hit from his vantage point by a fallen tree, a stump or a reef which I did not see in the dark water. The line would break, or the fish would throw the hook or wrap the line around a snag, leaving me with my mouth wide open, wondering why I was fishing, but not fishing.

This experience, repeated all too frequently, finally led me to study the waters of drainage lakes more intently.

I learned to observe the waters of the inlets and outlets in my efforts to locate the fish. I discovered, to my great joy, that the current, or lanes, where the inlets poured into the lakes were ideal homes for them. When I caught crappies 30 feet below the surface of *dark brown* water, where crappies ordinarily could not live because of the poor transparency, I knew the reason. I had hit the channel of a good inlet which still retained the oxygen, and food spilled into it from the stream pouring into the inlet, carrying it along to the outlet, causing a "stream" through the lake.

On one occasion when I fished an inlet channel for crappies I hooked two muskies. I landed the first, but the hook of the small white bucktail pulled out of the other as I tried to get the net under him. I have profited ever since from the knowledge those two muskies gave me.

Current means movement, movement means oxygen and oxygen means more breathing comfort for the fish. He who searches the waters of flowage or drainage lakes until he finds the stream flow, or the current which each good rain causes an inlet to pour along through a lake, will take fish on hot days when the shallower, thinner upper waters yield little.

A seepage lake, sometimes called "landlocked," is also a challenge to my fishing ability, requiring me to use all my knowledge of fish, water and tackle. While both the drainage and seepage lakes are food factories in the sense that they are continually manufacturing fish food, a seepage lake has no natural outside help to bring up its fertility or to change the types of fish to be found in it.

In Wisconsin you can leave many a drainage lake, walk a

81

very short distance across the land and find a seepage lake so different in its physical aspects that you would think you were in another part of the country. The drainage lake, thanks to its inlets and outlets, will harbor everything from muskies to crappies, and, in all situations but *soft* water, will abound with a luxuriant growth of water weeds. In the seepage lake of *soft* water you are likely to find only bass, blue gills and skimpy water plants. In the richer lakes there will be a wider variety of species.

On the trip which I made around the United States and through Canada to get a cross section of the waters, I tested the Suwanee River at its headwaters in the Okefinokee Swamp in Georgia. My readings at that point showed *very soft* water, *dark brown* in color. I gave it a rating of but 100 pounds of fish food to the acre of water.

One hundred fifty miles downstream, above the mouth where the Suwanee empties into the Gulf of Mexico in Florida, my river tests showed *clear* water and about 3200 pounds of fish food to the acre of water! Thus can drainage waters be enriched through their inlets, while a seepage lake must depend solely upon its individual characteristics to make its water rich or poor, good or not so good for the fisherman.

A seepage lake is not necessarily of *soft water* Figure 29. It

FIG. 29.—A Seepage Lake.

Soundings and reading the water will soon make any local fisherman an expert on such water.

82

can just as well, though not as often, be of *medium* to *hard* water, with enough lime to manufacture substantial supplies of fish food. Such seepage lakes can raise great numbers of fish, although the varieties will be limited for lack of inlets or outlets to provide a gateway for other species.

Seepage lakes can easily be managed by the Conservation Department in each state. For this reason an angler cannot always be sure just what he will find in such a lake. It may originally have been a poor bass lake or one with northern pike or walleyes, but the Conservation Department may have poisoned the lake, killed everything in it and stocked it with just one species of fish such as trout. That is why it is always advisable to ask the local fishermen about a seepage lake if you want to be sure just what kind of fish are to be had.

A case in point was my experience in the state of Washington where I was making a survey of Liberty Lake. The Conservation Department crossed up my readings completely. The lake indicated bass water to me, but the Department had poisoned the water to make a rainbow trout lake out of it.

Fish which must have running water to oxygenate their eggs cannot renew themselves in a seepage lake. Brook, brown and rainbow trout are among the fish that cannot multiply in a lake or pond which has no outlet or inlet. All seepage lakes must be continually stocked by man if we wish to have trout permanently in such waters, unless underground springs of good flow oxygenate the gravel there. But this seldom happens.

An angler who fishes a seepage lake has a right to expect largemouth bass, northern pike and panfish there. The size and condition will depend greatly upon what sort of water the lake contains. If it falls into the *soft* water class it will be lacking in food. Should the lake be fished hard, the large, legal size fish will be few.

There may be thousands of stunted fish, blue gills and undersized bass in such *soft* water. They are so hungry for lack of natural food that each will eat the other if he is not too large to swallow. Yet the stunted fish will keep on spawning with the result that the lake is often a mass of small fish, with but few growing to any appreciable size. Northern pike should be planted there to keep the lake "balanced."

The fisherman should never take the limit of larger fish in small ponds or medium size seepage lakes of *soft* water. Better that he should keep every small fish he catches to thin out the stunted population, leaving as much natural food as

83

possible to those which manage to attain larger size. There should be no minimum size or possession limit in such waters. By returning the large fish and keeping the small ones, anglers by intensive fishing tend to balance the lake in a few years. Fortunately, many states now advocate this idea.

The only other remedies for seepage lakes with an over-crowding of stunted fish are to fertilize the water, or to net the lake or poison all the fish and to stock lightly with the sort which will propagate themselves or to stock with hatchery trout each and every year.

FIG. 30.—A Thoroughfare.

Connections such as this between two or more lakes find fish spawning where conditions are best. After spawning they cruise and select homes where the habitat is to their liking.

Seepage lakes of *soft* water offer much sport with a fly rod and a bass bug. Small spinning lures and casting rods with light lines will take everything from panfish to northern pike. Wall-eyed pike seldom grow to legal size in these lakes. Crappies should not be stocked in *soft* waters either as they are deadly to small game minnows.

In *medium* to *hard* water seepage lakes of *clear* and *very clear* water, much good fishing can be had, for it is easier to learn the waters of landlocked lakes. Spinning and casting rods need larger lures in these waters, and if the lake is deep, long casts with close combing of the water is the best procedure during July and August.

The fly rod along the shore in the evening will catch splendid bass with either flies or bass bugs. When there is a light to moderate daytime breeze—from five to 18 miles an hour—a short leader and a large fly, size six or four, brings results here too. A bass bug rides along the waves in a tempting manner and almost any fish is apt to hit it.

In Wisconsin, if your plate shows a transparency of over 25 feet, the chances are very good that it is a seepage lake. What's more, the shore is probably sandy. The sand beach sifts the silt run-off from the land, no matter how hard it rains, and keeps the water *clear*.

It is a handicap to wade or fish from a boat in such *clear* seepage lakes with a fly rod because the fish can see an angler a long, long way. Such waters require fishing "fine and far off." The spinning rod or the casting rod does the business, especially on bright days. Dull or windy days reduce the handicap greatly.

I always feel I must fish harder and more cautiously when I work a seepage lake of *clear* water. Drainage lakes are easier to fish because the fish roam around more and seem willing to smash at a lure quicker than the fish in seepage lakes. We cannot expect the fish in a seepage lake to be a rover, for, like the canary in a cage, he has no place to go.

We all try to catch the largest fish because the hazard of hooking, playing and landing him allows us to prove our skill to ourselves. It helps us to know that in a seepage lake each large fish seems to have an exclusive home which he deliberately chooses and will allow no other fish to use it.

When I am convinced that a weed bed, a deadhead, a reef or a sunken spot in the floor of a lake should be the home of a large fish, I use my best strategy in that spot. I "sneak" right

85

back there if I do not take him the first time. I fix such spots firmly in my mind by landmarks and watermarks.

If I have taken a good fish from there, I feel that another will move in and he, too, will be a good sized fish or he wouldn't be able to hold that spot. Trout always do this in a stream. When I fail to take a fish from a likely place of this kind, I blame only myself.

Either I did not discover the spot until I was well over it and the boat frightened the fish, or my shadow or the flash of the reel, or the waving rod scared him. Also, I may have created too much disturbance pawing over my tackle box, or I may have given him too much time to look over the lure after I had cast it down into the hole. Should I make any of these, or other mistakes, I return in an hour or two to work the place properly. I consider myself a sociable sort of fellow and like to "go calling" around a seepage lake after I have fished it once. I present my card—a spoon, plug or a large bucktail fly with a dipsey swivel sinker—at the front door of a fish. I return most of the fish who accept my card to the water, but first I snip a small piece off their tail fin. It is surprising how often the same fish accepts my card, as indicated by the snipped tail.

Never one who likes to be in a rut, I try to offer the fish a different card each time. The peculiar thing about it is that the fish will hit them all—spoon, plug, fly or lure—if only I get them to their front door in the approved manner, right in front of their nose.

I have another firm belief about the large fish of a seepage lake in the early morning or just before or after dark. But don't get me wrong—I'm not puffed up about having discovered this for myself, for it was forced upon me by a big walleye.

My belief is that the largest fish come on to feed very early in the morning. Just about everyone knows that, too, but not everyone knows where they feed in the early morning, or at dusk. Those bigger fish have a "feeding trough" of their own, but let me tell you how I found it.

I had anchored my boat about 100 feet from shore just before dawn one July morning. The undershore had a gentle slope and the boat was in four feet of water. I was waiting for the first splash of a fish at the shore minnows.

I intended to work over each splash with what we then called a Dowagiac. It was made by Heddon in Dowagiac, Michigan, but now we call these lures "plugs." The light that morning enabled me to see the bottom very clearly. To my right, in about four feet of water, I saw a small walleyed pike, about 15 inches long, swimming leisurely towards shore. A "whale" of a fish came suddenly into sight, swimming much faster than the walleye. The large fish lunged at him with tremendous speed, but the walleye dashed quickly to one side and I did not see the outcome.

I had worked that shoreline many times. My procedure always had been, "watch for a splash, drop the Dowagiac a little nearer the shore than the splash and work it around the spot where the fish is chasing minnows." Almost every third cast meant a walleye. Then I'd go home for some shut-eye.

That morning when I saw the huge fish make for the smaller walleye, I wondered if I had not been fishing improperly when I worked those shoreline splashes. It dawned on me that by trolling or casting in the deeper waters during the daytime I had often caught some large walleyes and northerns from the bay, but by casting at the shoreline in the morning and evening I had taken smaller ones, with only now and then a large black bass.

I asked myself, "Can it be that the large fish camp right out here in the four or five foot depths during the shoreline feeding time to pick off the smaller fish when they are heading for the shore?"

My boat had its nose pointing directly toward the beach. Wondering what the answer to my question might be, I cast my plug from the side of the boat. It looped for a distance of 75 feet, parallel with the shore. Maybe I would have forgotten what I had been observing and thinking if I had not had a grand strike about 60 feet from the side of the boat. A 9 pound walleye hit the plug so hard he scraped the paint down to the wood.

It was a seepage lake that revealed how I could take large fish consistently in the "feeding trough" on midwater plugs early in the morning and in the evening. I found later that the same rule applies in drainage lakes, even more so than in the seepage lakes.

Early morning fishing, however, definitely seems to be twice as productive as the dusk to night fishing. I am puzzled as to why this is. The only explanation I can offer is that the fish must be twice as hungry in the morning. It may well be that the only reason they hit our lures in the daytime is that they are just tempted by "snacks" between meals.

Unfortunately, a seepage lake "dies" a little each year. There is no steady flow of water emptying into it, consequently over the centuries it gets shallower through evaporation and lowered

FIG. 31.—An Ice Push on Lake Winnebago.

In smaller lakes an ice push can change a drainage lake to a seepage lake by blocking a lightly flowing outlet. I have seen several instances where it has changed a good lake to a partly bog lake by dividing it into two lakes, one deep, the other shallow.

water tables. It may have been a drainage lake as recently as 200 years ago, but the water level dropped over a period of years so that a once fair flow of water into it, or out of it, no longer exists.

As the level dropped and the flow out of the lake became blocked by some kind of obstruction, possibly an ice-push piling up the sand and the silt across a feeble outlet, it became a seepage lake. See Figure 31. Meanwhile, the plankton dropped to the bottom along with the washed-in silt from rains, filling the lake ever so slowly but inexorably. Only returning high water levels or man-made inlets can bring such a lake back to its original condition, a drainage lake.

A seepage lake without good underground springs, or one with a lowering water table, dies rapidly as the geologist reckons time. Our many bog lakes, our dwindling kettle holes, all show this as we get around the country and observe them carefully. That is why, in some areas, I dislike to see artesian wells uncapped. The continuous flow of water helps lower our water table, and the seepage lake, with its heavy evaporation of water all summer long, slowly dies.

Seepage lakes, through dwindling, are not likely to vanish in your lifetime, so let the geologists worry about that. Go out and fish your favorite lake and hope it's there for many future generations to enjoy.

CHAPTER IX

Nymphs Will Make a Fly Fisherman an Expert

NYMPHS ARE THE FOUNDATION of all fly fishing. Just as you think first of the foundation when you build a house, so should you first concern yourself with nymphs if you want to get the most out of fly fishing.

As surely as the sun rises and sets, but not as regularly, the time comes to a fisherman when he stands there in the stream with the trout churning the water all around him, yet the fisherman cannot catch even one. There comes a hopeless, agonizing period of frustration. Unless he knows why the trout are behaving like this the angler futilely offers both wet and dry flies, in all sizes and patterns. He wonders how trout can suddenly make him feel so thwarted, so utterly dumb.

The trout in this exasperating situation are simply taking advantage of nature to enjoy a sumptuous banquet. They are feeding greedily upon mayfly nymphs about to say farewell to their underwater homes, to rise from the bottom of the stream to hatch into flies upon coming to the surface of the water. These hatches have no set time table. They may occur any time of the day or evening.

Such an experience with nymphing trout can be a challenging revelation. It not only opens a fisherman's eyes to the opportunity of catching trout under these conditions, but it can lead to a thorough understanding of all phases of the intriguing life cycle of our water bred flies. And once an angler knows his nymphs he has an intelligent grasp of the basic principle of successful fly fishing.

Usually a beginning fisherman has only a vague knowledge of the insects he sees flying above the stream. If you ask him where they come from he gives you a puzzled look and says, "I never gave it a thought." Like a city child who never sus-

91

Fig. 32.—Two Mayfly Nymphs and a Typical Mayfly, body one-half inch. The Nymph shown live under water for a year, then come to the surface to hatch into the fly.

pects a cow is the source of the bottles of milk on the doorstep each morning, the angler's impression is that the flies are "just there."

This same angler, however, knows that every butterfly comes from a caterpillar's cocoon. He also knows that the cycle of this familiar land fly is the egg, the caterpillar, the cocoon and finally the butterfly. It should be no great surprise to him, therefore, that the water bred insects also have a life cycle.

But if you lift a rock or a stick out of the water and show him the nymphs crawling about he will exclaim in amazement, "Do those things live under water like that?" He is also astounded to learn they represent a stage in the life cycle of a water insect corresponding somewhat to the caterpillar and cocoon stage of a butterfly. It is now that the beginning angler

92

should get a new outlook on his fly fishing. He should suddenly realize that nymphs are a major source of food for fish, and as a result of this discovery he must seek how best to apply this knowledge to his fishing methods.

The life cycle of a water insect is quite simple. As a general rule, female flies hovering over the water lay eggs on the surface, although some swim and some climb down toward the bottom to deposit them on an underwater object. The eggs, which drift with the current, eventually fasten upon some underwater log, rock or similar object. In a week or two tiny animals hatch from the eggs. Scientists call these animals nymphs and larvae. In this book, however, all such animals will be called nymphs for purposes of simplification. These nymphs begin to grow underwater so that the next year's flies can hatch from them. During the growing process the nymphs shed their outer skin—really their skeleton—as many as 20 times before they are mature. Some species do not mature and hatch into flies until they are three years old.

It was a 10-inch brook trout which taught me how to fish the nymph while the hatching period of the mayfly nymphs

Fig. 33.—A full grown year-old Mayfly nymph and a 60-day-old nymph of the same species, *Heptagenia*. (Body five-eighths of an inch).

93

is on. Had it not been for this particular brookie I might still have gone through many years of doubt, indecision and frustration before I learned how to catch trout during their "nymphing sprees." Sometimes these feeding periods would come at sun-up. Sometimes the trout would be feeding fast around me at nine, at 11 or during the afternoon or at twilight.

I was eating lunch on a limestone shelf which hung over the rich waters of my favorite stream near Gladstone, my hometown in the Upper Peninsula of Michigan. It didn't surprise me when the same old swirls and "boils" I had so often seen were again forming on the surface of the water, all about me.

"They are doing *that* again," I thought dejectedly. But this time I decided not to hurry as before. I did not excitedly grab my rod, rush into the river and begin throwing flies over the trout. True, the usual whipped, defeated feeling came over me as I gloomily watched from the shelf. My lunch was anything but tasteful. But as I continued to stare down at the water I saw that 10-inch brook trout come up, go down, turn to the right, turn to the left, go down and come up again. He did not cover a space in the water over four or five feet square. "What's this?" I pondered.

Now and then I saw a bug struggling from the bottom of the stream to the surface. This wasn't new to me. I knew it was the nymph of a mayfly coming to the surface in its slow, easy turning and twisting, to break out of the bug to become a dainty mayfly, resting upon the water film for a moment, drying its wings and flying off the water. What *was* new to me was the action of that trout!

Then and there I realized what was happening. How wrong I had been when I had switched from wet to dry flies when those swirls and "boils" began to form on the water. No, under these conditions the trout weren't taking dry flies off the surface. That 10 inch brookie showed me this swirling was caused by *underwater* action of the trout, not surface action. He was creating those swirls while devouring the rising nymphs in great numbers. He wasn't down at the bottom, stirring up the silt in his feeding. He was right up there where he had a field of clear water.

So this was the secret of those frenzied feeding periods which up to this time had driven me all but frantic! From then on I used nymph flies instead of the dry fly and soon was able to catch dozens of nymph feeding trout in our limestone streams and ponds.

94

It is easy to distinguish between a trout feeding on floating flies off the surface and one which is dining on rising nymphs. You have only to read the water.

When a trout takes a dry fly, a ring forms on the surface and spreads out into a series of concentric circles which eventually fade away with the current. This is the result of the sucking action of the trout at the surface of the stream.

A nymphing trout, on the other hand, works a foot or so under the surface, turning now to the right, then to the left to eat the nearest of the many nymphs on their way up to hatch into flies. It is the twisting, the turning, and the up and down movement of the fish which disturbs the surface of the water. Sometimes these resemble little tent-like splashes. Frequently water movements like those occurring in the wake of a propeller are created. In the rapids, however, we cannot see the trout's "sign" of feeding on rising nymphs because the water is too ruffled or turbulent, but we note that now and then an escaped, hatched mayfly comes floating down. This, then, is our unmistakable clue of the rising nymphs in such waters. It is the signal to switch from the wet or dry fly to the nymph fly if we hope to catch trout there.

My first attempts to get trout with my imitations of the nymph flies weren't successful. It was several weeks before I learned through continual experimenting that my flies must be cast upstream during the rising of the nymphs. I found that a tapered line and leader was most necessary and that the rod tip had to be held right over the surface of the water, about 6 inches, after my imitation nymph had sunk beneath the surface, with line and most of the leader floating.

The fly had to be kept moist so it would sink on the first cast. More casts than that would dry the fly and would not let the fly sink immediately, as it must, to reach the feeding trout a foot or two under the surface. The hook must not be too heavy for this type of nymph fishing. It is true that day in and day out angling with the nymph fly under other conditions calls for heavy hooks, as we shall see later. But during these particular kind of rises, only a hook of regular wire would do.

I cast the nymph upstream in the center of each trout's feeding area—among the "boils" and swirls—and allowed it to drift along with the natural, unhampered flow of the current. In the trout ponds I used the same tactics. I accomplished this by stripping in the line which was held by the first two fingers pressed against the rod handle. The line was pulled through these first two fingers by the left hand. I used only short six to eight-inch pulls, stripping slowly when there was a slight current, or no current at all, and faster when the current was more pronounced. In this method one never has slack line between the leader and the rod tip.

This enabled me to set the hook in the mouth of almost every trout which seized the imitation because the strike was telegraphed immediately to the tip of the rod and along the line to the fingers clamped over the line at the rod handle. I then employed a smooth follow-through movement of the rod tip—held constantly about six inches over the water surface—with a deft push to the right or the left to set the hook. If I held the rod tip up in the air so the line bellied loosely between the tip and the water, there was no telegraphing of a strike to tell me to set the hook.

This stuff about striking at the flash of a trout means little to me during the rise of the nymphs. The trout are all "flashing" as they twist and turn during these periods. I always cast to and just above the nearest swirling sign. As soon as I feel a strike and set the barb, I hustle the trout downstream and net it below or opposite me. This does not spoil the water above for the next cast, and the trout I release is too tired to dash ahead and frighten the others. You actually can get almost on top of the trout when they are feeding in this manner if you do not send tell-tale waves ahead of you by fast wading. They lose their much vaunted caution during the time they are rushing at the nymphs and seem almost as fearless as bees around you in a garden. I have had trout take live nymphs between my legs, widespread, as I stood in the stream fishing.

WHY WE FISH THE NYMPH FLY

You can well imagine how my experience with the nymphing brook trout further aroused my curiosity about nymphs. Eventually I learned there are many other fascinating aspects about these underwater creatures. Likewise, I hope the beginning fisherman has his curiosity stimulated because it will speed the day when he becomes a successful all around fly fisherman.

On the following pages are shown nymphs I have gathered in trout streams in various parts of the United States and Canada, together with the flies which hatch from them. Also shown are my imitations of both the nymphs and the flies. There is a correct time and place to use each of the imitations—nymphs, dry flies and wet flies—in your fishing.

The best way to familiarize yourself with nymphs is to get into a stream and collect specimens in a fruit jar. Take them home and put them in the bathtub so you have better opportunity to study the nymphs as they swim in the water. But if your wife screams "Ee-ee-eek!" and runs home to mother, don't blame me. It's all in the life of a fisherman who really wants to get down to fundamentals. Later you can preserve the nymphs for future study by bottling them in a five per cent solution of formaldehyde. This you can get from your druggist for a few cents or make it up at home. Use one ounce of formaldehyde to one quart of water.

There are thousands of nymphs in all our waters. But don't let that baffle you. For the purpose of fly fishing, nymphs and flies can be grouped into four general classifications. These include the mayflies, caddis or "sedge" flies, stone flies, and dragon flies.

"Where do we begin?" you ask. Let's start with the mayfly. Disregarding the egg stage, it has eight other stages of development which you will soon learn to recognize. When you become familiar with these you will know the right imitation fly to use for each. So let's get into a stream and look for some

FIG. 34.—The Largest of Our Mayfly Nymphs, *Hexagenia*. (Mature body one and one-half inches). Showing growth at 60 days, one year, two years and the mature nymph, ready to hatch at three years of age.

97

FIG. 35.—Mayfly Hatching From the Nymph, *Hexagenia*.
After three years underwater, the nymph swims to the surface. The fly emerges from the shuck at the top of the thorax, higher than shown in the photograph. It is now a sub-imago, called a dun by the fishermen. The three stages, dun, spinner and spent fly are shown in Fig. 38.

mayfly nymphs because obviously the nymph is the start of all the eight stages which concern you, the fisherman. In a half mile of stream we will have a million or more of them at our disposal.

Pick up this stick which lies underwater and observe the harmless little creatures running along it as the water drips from the stick. Take off a few of them and put them in that jar you brought along. Raise that small rock out of the water and drop a few more nymphs off it, into the jar. Lift a larger rock, a rubble stone about the size of your head, and there you will find more nymphs. Scoop up a handful of those dead leaves off the bottom of the stream and search them for additional nymphs. Do all these things in a slow run, a medium fast run and in the rapids to collect the different types.

Now let us wade over to that patch of black silt, that soft mud which the fisherman call, "loon silt." It is rich in diatoms which the giant mayflies eat. Dig deeply underwater to bring up a handful of the silt. As you hold the silt in one hand, gradually wash it away with water from the other hand. Continue this washing process until you find a long pale bug thicker than a match stick and about an inch and a half long, with a light belly, a dark back and long gray gills along its body. This will be the nymph of the giant mayfly. Figures 34 and 35. It is our largest mayfly, often called the "drake" by the fishermen. The moment you put him into the jar you will see that he is truly

Fig. 36.–A Very Little Fly (Both flies 7 mm. long).

Small mayfly nymphs which hatch into tiny flies like the tiny mayflies shown above. The nymphs, are right to left, *Ephemerella, Caenis* and *Baetis.* The mayfly at the left is a dun and becomes the spinner at the right. Note the complete change of color.

Charles Cotton could have meant their iron-blue dun which we also have over here. Just as we photographed the dun, it shed its outer skin and became the "Jenny Spinner." The white body with the end segments and the thorax of crimson changed it completely. One who had not seen the metamorphosis, from the dark body of the dun to the spinner would not believe it could be the same fly.

a giant among the smaller mayfly nymphs you have already collected.

Now go to another part of the silt bed and gently remove a handful of only the top half inch of silt. There you will find small to medium size nymphs. They live on the top of the silt while the giants live far below them. Some of the smaller nymphs are hard to see for they are extremely diminutive and crawl very slowly. Figure 36.

Do not bother to look for nymphs on sand beds because sand in a stream is more barren than sand on a desert.

Change the water in your jar now and then so all the nymphs will be alive when you arrive home. It's a good idea to empty the contents of the jar into white saucers or soup plates. This gives you a close-up opportunity to observe their actions before you preserve them in formaldehyde solution.

I am sure your collection will be a fair representation of the different mayfly nymphs which hatch into flies all over our country. By now it should be apparent that with so many nymphs available there is a vast amount of food on the bottom of every stream to nourish the fish.

They eat every nymph they can seize. It's an all year around food supply, too, and very sustaining. Chemical tests prove nymphs are as rich in protein as beef, pork or mutton. Trout, of course, would starve if they had to wait for the flies which can come only from hatching nymphs because no nymphs can hatch when the streams are covered with ice. Plankton is also high in protein content.

When the main, large, hatches of flies are over in the spring and early summer, the eggs of those flies hatch into nymphs. These again furnish much trout food for late summer and all during the autumn and winter.

Trout eat nymphs as naturally as we eat meat and potatoes. During the first few weeks of spring, flies which hatch from the nymphs are more like a dessert—apple pie, cake or ice cream. There probably are 25 nymphs eaten to every fly which is eaten during early spring for surely the trout have more or less forgotten about last year's flies which have not yet begun to appear again in vast numbers.

Mayfly nymphs provide their greatest nourishment for fish at the time they rise to hatch into flies. They are the richest morsel at this time because they not only contain the mayfly which is about to hatch—plump of body, full of eggs or milt—but they have the bulk of the nymphal shuck as well. That is why the trout seize them so eagerly and will not feed on hatched flies while they can secure the rising nymphs.

Of the eight stages in the life cycle of the mayfly which concern the angler, only two affect the nymph fly fisherman. The first is the period during which the nymph lives underwater after it has hatched from the egg. Some of these mayfly nymphs live underwater only six weeks, others as long as three years before they can hatch into flies. The second nymph stage of interest to the nymph fly fisherman is that brief period required for rising from the stream bed to the surface to hatch into a fly. Both these nymph stages call for different fishing techniques on the part of the angler.

The next six stages in the mayfly cycle—the winged flies—represent adulthood, lasting only three to four hours in some species and up to three days in others. When the angler imitates these stages, he no longer uses a nymph fly, but fishes with dry, wet and wet-dry flies.

The third stage in the life of mayflies is the dun, or subimago, which hatches out of the nymph. It is the first true stage of all dry flies which the fish turn to after the rising nymphs are not as numerous underwater as their hatched flies are on the water. The duns float down on the surface with the current—often for 100 feet or more in a good current—or lie quietly on the surface of a spring hole or a lake before their upright wings are firm enough and they have the strength to take off the water.

The trout sip the duns off the surface, causing those rings to spread across the water. This is an unmistakable "sign" to the angler that he should change his tactics immediately to fish with a dry fly.

Although most of the newly hatched mayflies, duns, are off the water within a short time, particularly in hot weather, hundreds are forced to remain in the water. Before they can take off they get caught in their drifting by overhanging branches which form triangles, by logs or other obstructions which trap them in the current, as well as by other hazards which hold them so their wings and bodies get wet. No mayfly can take off the water with sodden wings.

After there are no more floating duns for trout to sip off the surface, not all trout are satiated. These then eat the drowned duns. Some of the waterlogged duns are devoured at the place of entrapment, while others are seized as they drift under the surface with the current. These egg-filled or milt-laden drowned flies are all rich food. This, then, is the fourth stage of the mayfly cycle as it pertains to fly fishing, and it represents the first true stage of the wet fly. For the fly fisherman, it is then the time to follow up the dry fly hatch by fishing with an imitation of the sunken duns.

The fifth stage is when the duns have flown to the trees, shrubs, grass, cabin windows, or any other place they choose to anchor and shed a complete, very thin, outer covering. See Figure 37. They are then able to mate and are known as "spinners", or imagos. Often the male looks not at all like the female of the same species.

In some species of mayflies (there are more than 500 species and often millions of just one species will hatch on your favorite stream the same day) the trout again have an opportunity to eat them as dry flies. These light upon the water and the current helps strip their eggs. Other mayflies hover over the surface and

101

FIG. 37.—Mayfly Becoming A Spinner.

It has just cast the thin envelope of the sub-imago, the dun, and now become a spinner, an imago. It cannot fly until its wings are fully arranged.

drop their eggs into the stream from a height of two to 12 feet.

All egg-laying mayflies are regarded as "spinners" or imagos, whether they dip to the surface for just a moment to aid in stripping their eggs, or drop their 200 to 3,000 eggs from varying heights. A very few species crawl down a stone, stick or other object which enables them to "paint" their eggs upon a solid underwater surface.

Sometimes the "spinners" are trapped by fast water, spray or other hazards and are then eaten by the fish. When this happens they are in the sixth stage—drowned "spinners"—and are fished as wet flies. This stage, however, is not as a rule very important from the angler's standpoint as only a very small percentage becomes sunk while egg laying. Once in a hail storm I saw them knocked to the water by the dozens.

The seventh stage of the mayfly, the spent or death stage, is of much importance to the fly fisherman. The females, whether they have dropped their eggs from the air, or those species which must have the water help strip their eggs, die and a great many of them fall upon the water. The males likewise die after mating, dropping anywhere.

The mating is accomplished in the air, often far above the water and over the land. This causes a large proportion of the spent or dying males to fall upon the ground. I have found dead, spent males on the hillsides and on the meadows quite far from the stream when there has been any sort of breeze at all which blew them about.

The females fall upon the water later than the males because they must seek out the sort of waters which they prefer for dropping their eggs after mating. The wading fisherman will often see them flying along in great numbers at twilight. He will observe them more particularly where the stream narrows and branches come over the water so that small twisting open lanes are formed which concentrate the "spinners," for they always fly upstream seeking the right sort of place to drop their egg clusters of pink, yellow, white, green or other colors.

They seem quite discriminating, for they fly on and on just over the water until they come to some riffle, rapids or reach where there seems to be enough of a flow to oxygenate the eggs after they are dropped. It is important that the egg not be smothered by silt or sand. Thus it seems to me that nature insists that the flies do not drop their eggs right where they mate. It may well be that if they flew downstream from the point where they hatched and mated they would leave long reaches devoid of eggs and of the nymphs which hatch from these eggs. It could be that if mayflies always flew downstream after mating there would in a few years be no nymphs at all in the upper reaches, and the concentration of eggs and nymphs downstream would be so great that all the predators would congregate in the heavily populated areas and eventually wipe them out. To me, this is an instance where nature surely knows best.

After falling upon the water in the dying stage, their wings outstretched, these empty mayfly carcasses are called spent flies by the fishermen. Some species mate and die just after sunrise, others all through the day and at sunset and twilight. The fish eat them greedily. Therefore, this stage is very much worthwhile to imitate by the fly fisherman. They are not nearly as rich food as when their bodies were filled with eggs or milt, but in the absence of a hatch the fish will often be seen feeding noisily upon them. While it may be the fish eat them as much for roughage as for food, I think the complete change of form and color causes a fish to regard them as a fresh hatch of a different species of flies. Look at the dun and then at the spent fly in Figure 38 and you will see that it could seem an entirely new species to a trout, which always looks up from below. You will note that the fly appears at least twice as large as the dun, which shows hardly any wing to the trout, while the same fly spent shows a great area of wing and much more body, for with the spent fly the body lies entirely upon the water. On the other hand, the body of the dun rests only half upon the water and the long tails are hardly seen up in the air. Since every portion of the spent fly, including the tails, can be seen by the trout, I can use

103

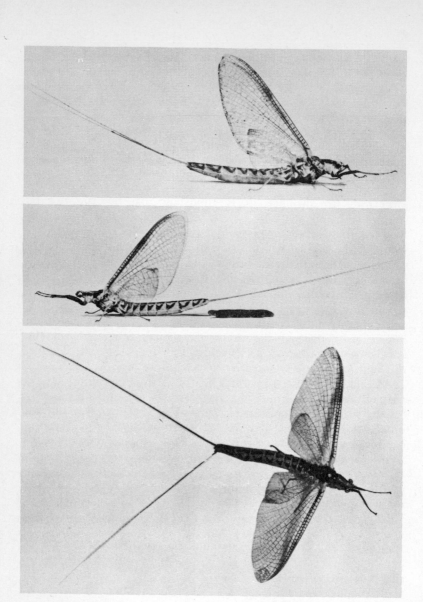

Fig. 38.—Dun, Spinner and Spent Mayfly *(Hexagenia sp.)*

This shows the mayfly in her two or three day aerial life. The dun,
the spinner and the spent fly, bodies one and one-half inch (head always
included). The spinner has just spent her two egg packets of some 3,000
eggs. Then, dying, and falling "spent" upon the water with wings outstretched, the trout sees an altogether different view than they have of
the dun or spinner.

a size 2 or 1 hook in my imitation of the spent fly. When imitating the giant mayfly dun I can tie an imitation as small as a size 6 hook and get away with it as far as the vision of a fish is concerned.

The eighth stage, the spent fly drowned, has not as good a chance to take fish as flies tied in the other stages. But the fisherman should always have two patterns, one light and one dark, so that when his observations tell him to tie on a sunken fly he will have these two imitations in his fly box, tied on hooks from size 10 to 4.

Drowned spent flies lose their effectiveness when the water and weather is right for a hatch of an entirely new species of mayflies. When this happens, the trout naturally turn from their diet of drowned spent flies to the new hatch of rising nymphs and then the duns of those nymphs. Also, there may be no new hatch coming on, but the flies of yesterday are mating and dropping their eggs, so that again the fish spurn the wishy-washy drowned spent fly of no substance. It simply does not make sense to expect the fish not to prefer the plump mayflies seeking to lay their eggs.

Nevertheless, one may often see no food on the surface for several hours after the spent flies have become waterlogged and come down sunk. That is the time to tie on a soppy-winged imitation of the spent fly and fish it wet. The fish may still be looking for food. Failing to find any upon the surface they may hover near the surface, in midwater. A spent fly, fished wet, has brought me many a trout under these circumstances.

I carry 8 dark-bodied white calf tail flies, two of each in sizes 10, 8, 6 and 4. The body is usually of black chenille with a rather thick "spray" of calf tail for wings. Doped heavily, it will float the way I want it to so that it imitates the spent floating mayfly, with body flat upon the water. Wetted with saliva and worked hard in the water until it sinks quickly, this same pattern can be fished to imitate the spent fly drowned, without the need of changing flies. Thus the one pattern serves for both the seventh and eighth stages.

I also carry white calf tail flies tied with white, ivory, or pale yellow bodies. These simulate the mayflies which have no dark markings on the upper body.

THE CADDIS NYMPH

Next to the mayfly the most important fly is the caddis, also known as the sedge. Although most of our angling literature and

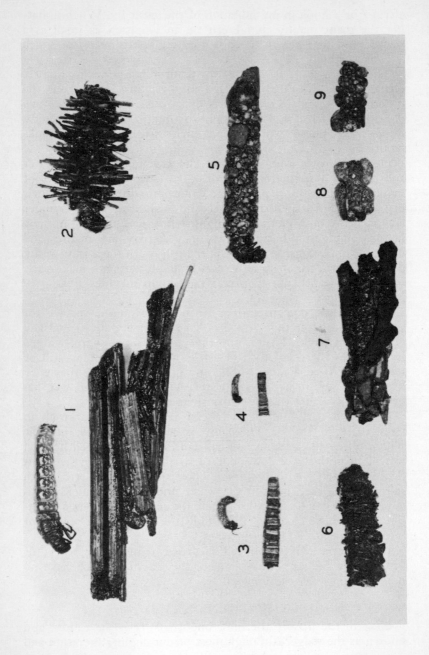

Fig. 39.—Caddis Flies and Their Houses (Order of the *Trichoptera*).

1. *Astenophylax species*. For scale the actual length is three-quarters of an inch. The *eruciform* type of nymph (larva) is shown above the house.

2. *Platycentropus sp.* Izaak Walton's Strawworm or Hedgehog. Paul Young's Strawman.

3. *Brachycentrus sp.* Bright green nymph, black head. House of at least 25 strips of glued bark. The larvae of the Grannom Fly.

4. Same as number 3. Half grown. It glues strips of bark to the house as it grows.

5. *Hesperophylax sp.* Izaak Walton's "Cockspur" may fit here. I have no specimen of the more curved *Platyphylax sp.*

6. *Limnephilus sp.*

7. *Phryganea sp.*

8. *Rhyacophila sp.*

9. *Hydropsyche sp.*

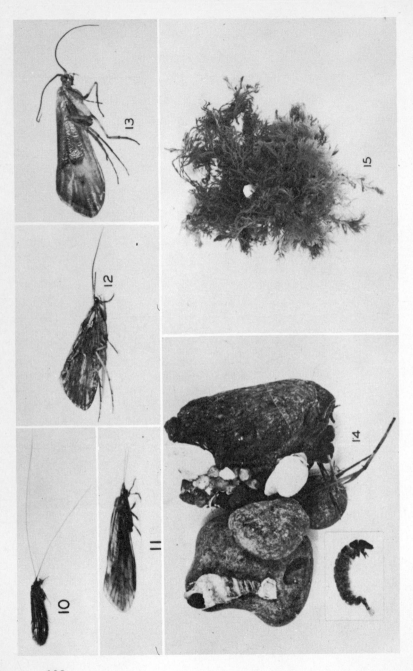

Fig. 39 (Continued).—Caddis Flies and Their Houses (Order of the Trichoptera).

10. *Hydropsyche sp.* The caddis fly.

11. *Platycentropus sp.* The caddis fly.

12. *Astenophylax sp.* Our largest caddis fly.

13. *Phryganea, Neuronia, Hesperophylax* and other species. Enlarged to show the legs which move like pistons when swimming down to deposit their hundreds of eggs.

14. *Thysanuriform* nymph (larva). The "Fantail" caddis nymph, shown bottom left in number 14. Lives free and differs from the *eruciform* nymph in that it glues sticks, stones, moss or leaves on solid underwater objects. There it builds tunnels and weaves a net, at each opening, to catch food. Sometimes it will leave its tunnel by spinning a strand so that it may return, an easy prey for the fish then. Note the large stones it has glued to the river bed. To the stones it has glued a snail and two small clams. Snail-like caddis houses, *Heliopsyche sp.*, have selected one stone to anchor their homes, one at the top to the right of the small fingernail clam. There are two more at the bottom of the same stone near the reeds. They are our smallest caddis flies.

15. Another shelter, glued together, of pieces of moss. The white piece of paper was the entrance to the tunnel of the *thysanuriform* nymph.

fishing talk deal with the duns and spinners of the mayfly, there are as many species of caddis flies in our country as there are mayflies. In fact, in my observations I have found the caddis nymphs, larvae, often are more numerous than mayflies. I feel sure an actual count would verify these observations in many streams across these United States, particularly in fast waters.

Caddis nymphs build houses which they attach to sticks and stones, or crawl along the bottom dragging their house with them. These houses are formed with bits of sand, gravel, sticks and other substances. If you pluck one of these houses off a rock and squeeze it gently a small worm will appear. As with other nymphs, the caddis is an important food supply for the fish and is greedily taken when it leaves its house to come to the surface to hatch into the caddis, or sedge, fly.

The caddis flies are the least understood of all waterbred flies by the fisherman, but best understood by the trout which eat them all winter long in their wood, gravel, bark, pebble or sand cases. The trout, however, do not eat vacated or inert houses. The fish must see some sign of life at the head of the case caused by some movements however slight, by the living nymph within the case. They eat the cases so that the nymphs (larvae) inside the cases will digest in their stomachs and the disintegrated cases will pass on through their intestines. In the spring, summer and fall they not only eat the cases but avidly devour the nymphs which emerge from them to swim to the surface to hatch into caddis flies.

Seldom do we imitate the cases of the caddis nymph, although there are some good imitations, such as the Strawman brought out by Paul H. Young. This Strawman, Figure 40, was aptly described by Izaak Walton in his famous book, *The Compleat Angler*, way back in the 17th century. Walton says: "There is also another caddis called by some a Strawworm and by some a Ruff Coat, whose house or case is made of pieces of bents, and rushes and straws and waterweeds and I know not what. Which are so knit together with condensed slime that they stick to her husk or case, not unlike the bristles of a hedgehog."

Our scientists of today describe it thus: Order of *Trichoptera*, Family *Limnephilidae*, Species *Platycentropus*.

How much easier it is to understand and appreciate good old Izaak's description, "Strawworm," or Paul H. Young's "Strawman."

110

Walton never imitated the caddis cases he observed. His adopted son, Charles Cotton, on the other hand, imitated the caddis flies wonderfully at that time, so well in fact, that today I still use some of his tieings with good success.

The female caddis fly drops her eggs in the water, or swims or crawls down underwater to "paint" them upon some submerged object. The moment the worm hatches from the egg, it begins to build a tiny house, enlarging it as it grows. Living in this house for many months, the worm finally seals itself up and a thin case comes over it, within the case, where the

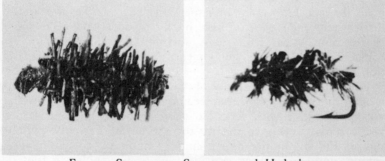

FIG. 40.—Strawworm, Strawman and Hedgehog.
Surely this must be the caddis house which Izaak Walton named the Strawworm. Paul H. Young's imitation Strawman does justice to it.

nymph now lies dormant. It is then called a pupa, like the butterfly in a cocoon. When the time comes to hatch, it bites its way out of the sealed case so only its head and forelegs appear out of the house, but it is still enveloped in a thin pupal shuck. Once the nymph protrudes out of the shuck, its forelegs begin swimming like mad, in a determined effort to rise to the surface to hatch out as a caddis fly. Fishermen often call them sedge flies when they have hatched. Sometimes you will see them, mostly at twilight, struggling to the surface only to go down under again. Sometimes they swim up again and again, turning and twisting in the thin pupal shuck. Many, however, pop right out of the shuck the moment they reach the surface.

The fish devour the rising nymphs very rapidly at this time as the nymphs by their activity show the trout that here is life, here is food which will get away from them in a second or in a moment. The fish do not see the rough body of the caddis which emerges at the surface. Neither do they see the

111

large wings, roof-like over the body of the hatched caddis flies, nor the hairy wings which are described in the chapter on the Wet-Dry fly. They merely see a thin case, packed with the wings, the body, the rear legs and antenna of the not yet hatched caddis. To get a fair idea of a caddis pupa, place your finger over the barb and bend of my imitation shown next to the caddis house, in plate 94. It is the second from the left in the second row, which shows the house, the pupa, the fantail caddis and the caddis dry fly.

When the beginning fisherman sees things like that, he will reason that surely there should be an imitation fly of this type in his fly box. He cannot buy them anywhere as far as I know, but he can tie his own or have his fly tieing friend make some up for him. What trout, bass or other fish does not fill his stomach with such good and plentiful food every time he has such an opportunity?

Assuming you have one of my favorite imitations, drop it over the swirlings of the feeding trout you observe on the stream. Work it with jerks, so short that the line and leader hardly moves, yet give the fly the short, fast, trembly twitchings of the fly in the pupal shuck coming up to hatch, now sinking, now rising, now drifting four or five inches, a foot or two among those rising trout which are smashing at or near the surface at the fast swimmers, the caddis.

Only a wide quill wrapped over a fat body will do for my imitation flies under such circumstances. There must be no tails, and the hook must not be of fine wire nor of heavy wire. Only a hook of regular wire allows the fisherman to manipulate the fly as it should be. Just thick, wide legs such as can be imitated by a few wide hackles from a pheasant tail, grouse neck or wood duck feather of the black and white tips satisfies me as a simulation of those few "oars", those exposed, fast moving, swimming forelegs of the rising fly. Although in the hatched caddis the body is short, much shorter than the wings, the body in the pupal hatching stage seems as long as its wings, packed as it is with the wings under that transparent pupal shuck. Therefore, the imitation fly for this stage need not be tied with differing body and wing lengths.

Day in and day out, a size 10 hook is staple for this fly. The fisherman may want to cast a fly as large as 6 to 4 when he sees the largest caddis flies hatch, and down to size 18 when he observes the smallest caddis flies hatch. As for me with my staple No. 10, I weep not if I am short of the other sizes.

Caddis flies are not short-lived like the mayflies which survive but a day or two, and about four days at the most for some of the largest mayflies. The caddis are hustling, bustling flies which swarm over the tree tops in great numbers, dancing with frenzy for hours. They live many days, and I have often seen them drink the maple syrup water I put out for them at camp. I believe they eat lichen—algae-moss—on the trees, for if you look closely at them you will see their mouth parts moving as if devouring food. Scientists claim they have kept caddis flies alive for weeks.

The caddis offers varying "styles" for the dry fly fisherman to imitate. Some females skid along the surface of the stream, using the water film to strip the eggs from their bodies, while others drop and rise, drop and rise in their egg laying. This means that while a mayfly imitation should be drifted naturally with the current, the caddis fly imitation can be skidded on the surface. The best evidence of the naturalness of this technique is shown by the way the trout hit the imitations fast and furiously in this type of fishing. Flies for this kind of casting call for light wire hooks and the very best game cock hackles obtainable and bodies which will not waterlog quickly. Thin leaders, at the risk of losing large fish, are most necessary for this skidding business as a heavy leader will sink the fly rapidly. For ticking the fly on the surface, the same tactics apply. A two-pound test for tippets will do excellently.

Other caddis flies dive to the surface from the air to drop their eggs in little bunches upon the surface, or to swim down and lay their eggs underwater, whereas mayflies crawl down. Out West, in British Columbia, caddis flies have a habit of lighting upon the water and fluttering here and there. The fishermen I met there called them "traveling sedges." These are not the species of caddis flies which swim down under to lay their eggs, the wet-dry flies to which I devote a whole chapter in this book.

"How do you distinguish between the mayfly and the caddis?" you ask. The mayfly has single wings like the sails of a boat, straight up in the air over the hull. The caddis fly has wings that resemble the roof of a house. Its wings come to a peak over the body, which is always much shorter than the wings.

While a fan wing Coachman is a good imitation of a hatching mayfly coming out of the nymph, a squirrel tail fly is a good imitation of a drowned caddis, as well as a drowned stone fly. A fly tied "buzz", an all hackled fly, whether it be a palmer or with hackles only from the eye to the middle of the hook shank, is unquestionably a very good imitation of the fast moving four wings of the caddis fly. He who wishes may call it a mayfly or a stone fly, but to me, the reasons for the trout hitting a hackled fly can be attributed mostly to the great number of caddis flies over the water from early spring until late fall.

The helter-skelter manner of flying, the "hurry up and take me before I have gone" appearance of some of the caddis flies means that the fly fisherman's fly box should never be without a few hackled patterns of every size, ranging from size 18 to 6 or even 4. The hackles can be gray, dark brown or tan.

To me, there is no better imitation of a flying caddis' wings than the mixture of brown (red game) hackle wound on with gray hackle. The greatest attraction of the trout to such a fly as the Adams is its close resemblance to the flying caddis wings, even if many do tie the Adams with spent wings to represent a mayfly.

Caddis flies are mostly drab in color—grays, tans and browns in various shades—but others rival the rainbow in their different hues, although they are in the minority during the daytime. He who will use the Adams pattern of the hackle and wishes to tie in slanting wings like the caddis if he prefers to fish with wings, can go any place in the country and have a commonplace, staple imitation of the caddis in just this one pattern.

Whether one uses the caddis as a floating fly—a dry fly—or fishes it wet—a drowned caddis—he must of course see that it is tied to suit its purpose. Almost any pattern of a squirrel tail, tied with a silver or gold body or just a plain

Fig. 41.—Stone Flies And Their Nymphs. (Order—*Plecoptera*).

1. Stone fly and stone fly nymph. *Pteronarcys sp.* Our largest specimen. The fly shows why a squirrel tail fly or a streamer fly takes trout and bass. Fly is two inches, head to end of wing.

2. Same as No. 1, but with its four wings expanded. Measuring the wing spread is called the "alar expanse" by the entomologist. Often the wing length, as in number 1, is given as well as the "alar expanse," the full wing spread. This is a good habit for the fly tier to follow on his home waters.

3. Stone fly and nymph *Perla sp.* Called "medium stone" by the Scotch, English and Irish fishermen. They use them in bait fishing and are called creepers.

4. Typical of the many smaller stone flies from tiny "Yellow Sally" of the fishermen to the size shown here.

5. Stone fly nymph, *Acroneuria sp.*

6. The "Curler" stone fly nymph of fishermen who use all stone fly nymphs for natural bait. *Perla sp.*

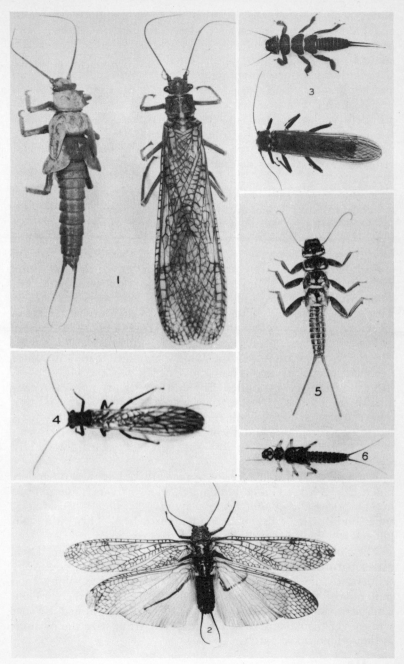

body, will be accepted by the trout if the hook is heavy enough in the iron to carry it down to and near the bottom of the deeper holes and the good eddies. A size 6 on a 4X stout wire is an excellent all-season fly for such fishing. A fly with a hooded merganser wing, tied low over the body, is another staple which should be in every fly box, in sizes 10, 8 and 6. Any gray downwinged fly with the hackle tied in a bunch lying under the eye—none above the eye—will complete the list of staple caddis patterns necessary. You may add many more, but with these three you can catch brooks, browns and rainbows in any waters where they live.

THE STONE FLY NYMPH

When fishing with nymph flies in any rapids, I consider my stone fly nymphs the most necessary of all. The trout eat all they can seize. Stone fly nymphs are plumper than any caddis or small mayfly nymphs, and inch for inch they outweigh them.

Fortunately for the angler, he needs but few patterns of stone fly nymphs in his fly box. They are not hard to imitate, and if the right hooks are used, are easy to fish with. The largest fish in the rapids or riffles—fast, short or long runs—hit them hard and quickly. Stone fly nymphs are found in fast water or where fast water spills into a good pool because there they get the oxygen they require which is more than any other nymphs in the stream. Their tiny claws get a good grip on the most slippery of stones. Some stone fly nymphs are cannibalistic, and carnivorous, too, eating every mayfly nymph they can seize. I often think the reason so many mayfly nymphs let go of their homes and allow the current to carry them away is to escape being eaten by the stone fly and dragon fly nymphs.

Stone fly nymphs have an upper crust, but a soft under-body. The small nymphs look much like many mayfly nymphs except that they do not have waving gills along the sides of their bodies, the gills being under their legs. Their life span underwater ranges from one to three years.

They do not swim up to the surface to hatch, however. Their claws permit them to climb to the top of boulders, to bridge timbers, to the banks of streams, or into the grass. They then pull out of their shucks, and leave them clinging there. They emerge as stone flies, slow in flight and distinguished by flat wings over their bodies when at rest. The trout seize the nymphs as they climb up to hatch.

116

The stone fly nymph fisherman strives to drop his imitations on the rocks, alongside of bridge timbers or in fast water. He fishes his imitation so its action resembles a foot-loose nymph unable to swim, which is tumbling along, or as a hatching nymph trying to climb to the top side of anything which juts out of the water and to which he can attach his claws to leave his shuck. Just as the beginner never makes a mistake by employing a varied action of his imitation mayfly nymphs, neither does he err in the manner he fishes his stone fly nymph when he works it in fast or other well oxygenated water, whether he fishes up, down, or across the stream.

A stone fly nymph tied on a size 8 hook, heavy in the iron, ball eye, 2X or 4X stout, should be in every fly fisherman's fly box. Stone fly nymphs run from a size 16 hook to a very large body for which a size 1 hook shank is not too long. But for consistent fishing of stone fly nymphs, a size 8 4X stout heavy or strong wire is best because there are so many thousands of nymphs of this size in our waters, and it handles nicely in its drifting.

As the beginner goes along in his fishing he will observe all the stone fly nymphs illustrated here and can then use his own judgment, for there are thousands of them in good waters. He will soon find out for himself that the waters will reveal to him every type on the sticks and stones in all good, fast water. He can then carry a few size 12 nymphs and a few size 6 and 4, but I am sure that the size 8 hook will become his favorite as it has mine, except in deep pools at the end of a rapids. It is then that size 6, 4 and 2 hooks should be used for deep sinking.

OTHER NYMPHS

I shall not here discuss the many water-bred flies such as the deer flies, horseflies, crane flies, no seeums, black flies, gnats or midges which are about the water in countless numbers. Like the caddis, the underwater creatures which hatch from the eggs of these flies are called larvae by the entomologists. They are, however, like worms and do not lend themselves to good looking imitations, nor are they the fish getters that the true nymphs are, or the caddis "nymphs" when they come up to hatch. See Figures 42 and 43.

There are many beetle nymphs, but many of them so closely resemble the mayfly nymphs that it is needless to imitate these slow burrowing crawlers separately. These are *Hemiptera*.

117

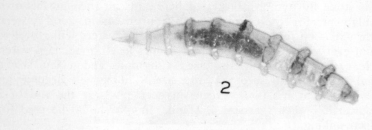

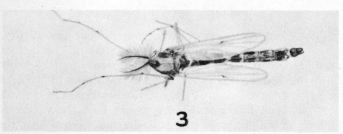

FIG. 42.—Odds And Ends—Numerous in Our Waters.
   1. and 2. The biting deer fly which only the best of fly dope will keep away. Its worm-like larva gives one an idea of the larvae of the crane fly, No. 4. and the midge, No. 3, The larva of the crane fly is very much larger while the larva of the midge is very much smaller and thinner.

FIG. 42, *Continued*. Odds and Ends.

5. *Gammarus*, a scud which we fishermen call "freshwater shrimp."
While it never hatches into a fly, it is a grand animal to imitate. The
fish eat thousands of them. I have heard them called "curly jukes" by
Easterners. When full grown, three-quarters to one inch.

6. This two inch giant water beetle which will pierce and kill
everything which lives in the water, from fry to nymphs. Note the sharp
beak, like a stiletto. Its nymph is just as bad a killer. Our June Bug
spinner probably owes its fish-getting qualities to the beetle-like shape.

FIG. 43.—Hellgrammites.

1. Left: The real hellgrammite, *Corydalis*, from which the great Dobson Fly hatches after the nymph has lived three years under water. The fishermen use these nymphs for bait. Some wrongly call the nymph of the Dragon Fly "hellgrammite". Mature nymph three inches long.

2. Center: The Fish Fly. *Chauloides.* The fish fly is about half the size of the Dobson Fly but resembles it greatly.

3. Right: The Fish Fly Nymph. *Chauloides* lives one year under water and is often mistaken for the bass bait nymph *Corydalis.*

The larvae of the dragon flies, *Odonata*, are nymphs and very large, yet I have not found it advantageous to use them except in lakes, ponds and pools. Usually I carry but one pattern on a size 6 hook. It is an easy nymph to, tie, to cast, and to work in the water as the majority need a size 4 hook to imitate them. These jet propelled nymphs were on earth long before man was here to dream of jet propulsion. Place one in a saucer and observe how he shoots the water from the opening of his posterior

Fig. 44.–Dragon and Damsel Flies. *(Odonata)*.

1. Our largest dragon fly with her egg packets.. Three inch body.

2. Dragon fly nymph. Tongue *(labium)* pulled down. This folding tongue, held like a mask over its face grasps a trout fry or anything else it can eat. They are a pest in a fish hatchery. One and three-quarter inch body.

3. One of the smallest dragon fly nymphs. I collected it at Paul's Lake in British Columbia, where the Kamloops trout had so much publicity among American anglers.

121

Fig. 44 (Continued)

4. The underside of one of the largest dragon fly nymphs. About one and one-half inches. I have seen the fly require 35 minutes to emerge and fly away.

5. The Damsel fly. This slow flyer is over two and one-half inches long. These slow flyers are of the same order, *Odonata*, as the dragon fly nymphs. Of many colors, but the one shown here has jet black wings with emerald green or brilliant blue bodies. Again we see why streamer flies will be taken for these many colored insects.

6. Damsel fly nymph, not enlarged. Its three wide paddles, tails, at the end of its body identify it quickly.

122

where he breathes and jets himself forward at the same time. See Figure 44.

Dragon fly nymphs sprawl upon the bottom, eating every nymph and tiny fish they can clamp down upon with their great folding "tongue". See Figure 44. Nothing can get away from them when in their grasp. In the waters where they abound —they are in every type except the rapids—I have found them so crowded in trout stomachs that it seemed as if a machine had packed them solidly so they resembled sardines in a can. These trout were taken from spring holes and trout ponds. Their relatives, the damsel fly nymphs, are numerous, too, and furnish much food for fish. See Figure 44.

I have also found many crayfish packed in the stomachs of trout. Also, I have found dozens of small snails and small clams in the stomachs of brown trout—54 in one stomach— but these, too, have given me no desire to imitate them at my fly tieing bench. They belong to fishing with the spinning and the plug rods as much or more than with the fly rod.

HOW TO FISH THE NYMPH FLY

Fishing the nymph is a comparatively recent art in the United States, although it has been practiced for almost a century by the English, Scotch and Irish. By 1932 fishing the nymph had become old stuff with me, but when I wrote an article about nymph fishing for *Outdoor Life* that year, I was surprised by the many letters I received. Since time immemorial they have used the living nymph for bait fishing—they call them "creepers."

It turned out that I had written about an entirely new subject as far as the American fisherman was concerned. There have since been numerous articles written about nymphs and nymph fishing in our American publications, but even today it is amazing how few fishermen really use this principle in their angling. By all odds we are still primarily a nation of wet fly and dry fly anglers.

Having learned about the nymphs, the beginning angler is naturally anxious to see what he can do with his fly rod and his imitations of the nymphs. But first he should devote another hour to gathering more live nymphs from the stream. He should release them in the water, one by one, so he can observe their action. This hour of observation will show him how to fish his imitations in the right manner. It will provide

FIG. 45.—The Mayfly Blasturus.

The gills along the body of the nymph show why peacock herl is such a good imitation for nymph bodies. Note the shorter middle tail on the three-quarter inch fly.

him with a nymph fishing pattern to be used in all his days of fishing, at the right time and the right place.

As he lifts a crawling or a running nymph from an underwater stick and drops it in the stream, the angler will note that it cannot swim upstream against any fast or medium fast current. It must drift along with any appreciable current, swimming gradually down until it gets a foothold on a plant, a stick, a stone or upon the bottom. There it seeks a home to its liking. This should suggest the importance of letting that particular imitation nymph act in the same natural manner, otherwise the trout is not fooled.

Right now is the time to find out why you should always have some Coachman or Royal Coachman flies in your fly box, despite the oft repeated statements that these flies resemble nothing on earth. Drop one of those live mayfly nymphs in the palm of your hand. It will not run along the hand and drop off, like the claw-footed stone fly nymph which is often found with the mayfly nymphs in fast water, and looks somewhat like them. If there is no water in the palm of your hand the mayfly nymph will lie there motionless. Now put a little water in your cupped palm and watch the sides of the body of that nymph, back of the wing cases. You will readily see fast moving gills along each side. Figure 45.

These are characteristic of thousands of mayfly nymphs. They take the air from the water for the nymph to breathe just as the gills of a fish enable it to breathe air from the water. If the windings of peacock herl used on the shank of a hook on both the Coachman and the Royal Coachman fly isn't the most perfect material we have to imitate those moving gills, I'll eat every nymph in the "crick" and starve the trout. And when we see the nymph and the fly emerge at the surface, who can ask for a more natural imitation than our Coachman or Royal Coachman, fan wing, lead wing or any wing of the color of our mayflies? Peacock herl, as well as muskrat fur and cut saddle hackle for other types of nymphs, will be discussed in the chapter on fly tieing.

Running nymphs are flat nymphs, and like all nymphs which live above the bottom, they thrive upon algae, the slime which the fisherman despises when he slips upon the rocks while wading. The angler may not like the algae, but for nymphs it is their hay, oats, vegetables and meat. It nourishes them so they grow from an almost invisible creature out of an egg to the full grown nymph, shedding its skin as many as 20 times during the months or years before the wing pads show that it is fully developed and ready to hatch into the mayfly.

When you drop live nymphs into the river be sure to pay close attention to the action. I cannot stress too strongly that it is the same, natural drifting of the nymph with the current when you drop it into the water that you, the angler, must strive to imitate. The way the nymph acts when you drop it in the water is exactly the way any nymph of that species must act when it loses its hold upon its home. Knowing that there are thousands of such nymphs in a river, and that often some of them drift down with the current, you can see that you can cast your imitation nymph fly—tied with peacock herl gills on a hook which matches the head to tail length—upstream, across, or up and across. If there are no dry flies on the water, or drowned flies, and the trout are down near the bottom, why shouldn't they take your imitation when it drifts past their noses like a live nymph?

But not all mayfly nymphs are drifters. Some are darting, dashing, swimming nymphs which trout also relish. These nymphs do not shun the daylight or live on underwater sticks and stones like the running, or the burrowing nymphs. These live in the open, among the plants, the gravel, over the silt and in our fastest rapids. Drop one in the water and you will see it can move swiftly. It will stop and start, swim or jump, usually but a short distance. It can be captured with a fine net or screen only. Figure 46.

An imitation of this humpbacked nymph tied on a size 6, 8 or 10 hook will allow any beginner to take trout, for some grow

FIG. 46.—The Bucking Bronco May Fly Nymph. Formerly *Baetis*, then *Chirotonetes* and now *Isonychia*. (Body one and one-eighth inches).
I call him the "Bucking Bronco" for he darts and dashes with such speed that seldom will you be able to catch one in the fast or slow water where he will live. Note the "basket" of his two front legs with which he gathers drifting food. His cousins, *Callibaetis* and *Siphlonurus* are half his size, but they too are speedy, one minute here and the next second a foot or two away.

to a full inch in length. The imitation should be tied on a hook heavy in the iron, such as a 2X Stout or 4X Stout, with the body tied as shown in the fly tieing chapter. The angler should let the current have its way with this imitation in fast rapids, but should work it in slow "jerks" in the pools or slow runs. He can fish it upstream, downstream, or across and upstream.

This imitation should be the beginner's—and the expert's—staple nymph, for it is impossible to make a mistake no matter how he fishes this imitation of the darting nymph after he has learned to control his fly and feel a strike. The easy method of doing this is explained in the chapter on casting, and illustrated with pictures of a nymph fisherman.

There are other nymphs which look much like this darter.

126

These are running nymphs which cannot swim well, but they have humpbacks (prominent wing cases), too, and the trout eat them every day in the year, winter and summer.

Study the live nymphs for size, color and appearance, and I am sure the stream will show you how you can keep your patterns down to just a few. But you must use different weight hooks on those patterns for bottom and midwater, and sub-surface fishing of the nymphs. Use heavy hooks for bottom and midwater fishing and regular wire for the subsurface, the hatching nymphs. During the rise of the nymphs, a quick glance at one or two empty shucks—the *exuvia*, as the entomologists term them—will often tell you what sort of patterns to use if you do not see a live nymph coming up.

We now wade over to a silt bed. Before you start digging for the giant nymphs, remember the slow, crawling nymphs you found on TOP of the silt bed. As you watch the slow, very slow action of these small nymphs—ranging from a size 18 hook to a size 10 in body length—you will know that over a silt bed your small imitation nymph can be fished slowly, dragging it along or close to the bottom in quiet waters, morning, noon or night. The trout should take it when they are in a feeding mood.

Now that we have finished with the smaller nymphs which range from hook sizes so small that we could not hold a trout in fast or cluttered waters—sizes 22, 20 and 18 hooks to those whose imitations we tie on size 16 to 6 hooks—we shall turn to the homes of the "giants" of the mayfly nymphs.

Digging deeply in a silt bed we find a few of the largest nymphs which lie buried in the black silt. These are diggers, burrowers, which shun the daylight and eat the silt continually. As we wash off this two-inch long nymph which lives three years underwater before it comes up to hatch into our largest mayfly, we drop it in the stream. The moment it strikes the water its powerful digging legs are folded along its body, for it does not use its legs when swimming. Its great gills and undulating body carry it downstream at the fastest, bottom-seeking level its gait and the current will allow it to go. In still water it swims like a minnow, but not so fast, going where it chooses.

Watch it closely and you will see that it is far from being the dumb creature one might think. As its undulating body and constantly waving gills give it the power to swim lower and lower toward the bottom, it is in a great hurry to burrow into any black bed it can find. Throw such a nymph over a white sand bed and note that it will swim like a minnow, but downstream with the current, not stopping until it sees a patch of black. The patch may be a few dead leaves no larger than your hand, or a good patch of silt, but there the nymph exerts itself tremendously.

It swims down fast now, almost a dive into the black silt, then its great digging legs work like a steam shovel, throwing the rich but very soft silt aside. It is out of sight so quickly you marvel at its digging speed. Now it is again among its own species of large size. If you examine the top silt very closely, you may find, in August, the smallest size which hatched out of the egg just 40 days previously—a mere baby "giant."

What leeway this nymph offers the fisherman and the fly tyer! He can imitate these nymphs ' with their light bodies, dark backs and waving gills in just about any size hook from 8 up to our largest size 1, yet fish true to nature.

I prefer size 4 and 6 hooks because sizes 1 and 2 are too large for nice handling in the daytime, although I am never without some in size 2 for very deep waters. With the 4's and 6's the beginner can drift his nymph fly in the rapids where the trout will take it for a wave-washed nymph. He can fish it deeply in the pools and give it a starting and stopping motion like the real nymph which pops out of the silt seeking a new home, and seeing the daylight, dives down again to dig in. I use leaders no finer than three pound test at the fly end on my tapered leaders for the giant mayfly. Anything under one and one-half pound test for fishing the smaller nymphs, hooks 16 to 10, is wholly unnecessary.

At night, with a flashlight, I have seen many a trout with his nose almost on shore, over a shallow silt bed, waiting for the large mayfly nymphs which often come out then to swim around in search of a richer silt bed or to shed its old skin like a crayfish. The beginner should learn to examine the black silt fringes underwater along all trout streams where the current is not too strong. He will see the small holes which these nymphs the night before burrowed as they left the water before dawn to avoid the light of day. If he digs there he will have good collecting because the holes are not washed out for 24 hours or more.

I have never seen a rising nymph, one coming up to hatch into the mayfly, swim upstream at that stage. The only way to fish this kind of nymph fly during its hatching time is to cast it upstream and allow it to drift down towards you in that foot or foot and a half field underwater, when you see the swirls and "boils" which so clearly tell you the trout are feeding there. At any other time than this, the giant nymph fly can be fished downstream, upstream, across stream, and up and across. It is up to you to judge the water as you decide what method to use at any given spot. Naturally, any nymph cast upstream is always your best bet because the trout might take it for the beginning of live nymphs coming up to hatch. This is truly an example of outwitting the trout.

It's my guess that not one fly fisherman in a thousand fishes the nymph fly often. This is because he has not taken the little time necessary to observe the facts which are right before his eyes. Yet nymph fishing—done with the same rod, tapered line and tapered leader used for all dry fly fishing—will add so much to his enjoyment, ability and catch. As for his wet fly level line and level leader, or leaders tapered to a three pound or one and one-half pound test, he can use these when the nymphs are not hatching. The waters will tell him which leader to use with his level line or a watersoaked tapered line.

I realize, of course, that the average fisherman in his quest for knowledge about nymphs and flies has no intention of taking the subject so seriously that he aspires to become a dyed-in-the-wool entomologist. He doesn't have to. But he should give enough attention to the "bug" life on his lakes and streams to apply this knowledge to his fly fishing.

Now that we have discussed at more or less length the different nymphs and how to imitate them when fishing, a capsule summary of the eight stages of the mayfly should prove helpful. The tabulation presented herewith names each stage, gives the fishing technique to imitate it, and tells what type of hooks I have found most satisfactory. The chapter on fly tying gives a more detailed explanation of the various wires for hooks.

Stage	How Fished	Kind of Hooks
1. The growing nymph.	Fished deep.	Heavy hooks, 2X or 4X stout wire, ball eye.
2. The rising, hatching nymph.	Fished 18 inches under the surface.	Regular hooks.
3. The hatched mayfly, the dun (the subimago).	Dry fly.	Light wire, 1X fine.
4. The drowned dun.	Wet fly.	Regular wire to 4X stout.
5. The "spinner." Mated and dropping eggs (the imago).	Dry fly.	1X fine wire.
6. The drowned "spinner." (Least important stage)	Wet fly.	Regular wire to 4X stout.
7. The spent fly.	Dry fly, body semi-submerged.	Regular hooks.
8. The spent fly, drowned.	Wet fly.	Regular to 4X stout.

CHAPTER X

The Dry Fly
Tempts Many Fish

THE STREAM PINCHED a little, just enough so the constricted current washed the bottom and kept the gravel and rubble stones clear of sand and silt all the year long. I knew there would be thousands of active nymphs in that reach and intended to have some good fishing there.

The afternoon sun threw long shadows of the birch, sugar maple and ironwood across the stream. As I started to rig up my fly rod, I saw a wading fisherman coming around the bend.

He appeared to be a middle aged man. While I felt a little sorry that I could not have that stretch of water to myself, his first few casts interested me. I could see he was throwing a wet fly with what seemed a lot of know-how, for his fly dropped smoothly and without effort on those spots where I, too, would judge a fish to lie. The drift of his fly brought it right where I expected a trout might take it. He struck and a trout was on.

But I saw something which made me wonder just how good a man he really was with his fly rod. There was a ring upon the water not over 40 feet from the spot and to his left. Then there was another ring which spread over the same quiet water. Observing him closely, I saw him lift his line and leader out of the water with a quick flirt of the rod tip. He snipped the fly off the leader, reached into a pocket of his wading jacket and brought forth a fly box.

While he was tying the fresh fly onto the leader, I waited with questions in my mind. Was he merely changing to another wet fly or did he observe that which I saw upon the water? I needn't have been concerned, though, for I saw him dip his fly into a small bottle to oil it.

Soon his line, leader and fly were in the air, driven by a wrist which had grace and power. While he was making his

131

false casts, getting the fly out to where he wished it to drop, another break showed on the surface nearer him and the rings widened as they spread over the water. He quietly changed his position just a trifle and let his fly drop a few feet above the center of the ring above him, as lightly as thistledown.

I wondered what pattern the fisherman had decided to use. As I watched it come floating down towards him with the current like a natural, living fly, a trout's nose appeared and the fly vanished. There was a smooth turn of the wrist, and line and leader pulled taut. The broad back of a nice trout showed for just a moment as the fish turned down to make his fight in the deep water of the pool.

The fisherman lifted his rod a little and calmly ·made the fish take the strain of the rod. The arched bamboo became too much for the trout, and under the angler's masterful handling the fish was netted and released. Here, indeed, was an artist! He had demonstrated he was a versatile fisherman because his eye had seen the trout feeding on the surface and he had quickly changed from the wet fly to the only imitation which would take that trout, a dry fly.

The fisherman, beaming with satisfaction, looked up and said, "Better get in the crick, looks like a mayfly hatch is coming on."

"Thanks," I replied, "I'll get in at Tamarack Eddy." I headed upstream, following a faint trail. Just as I approached Tamarack Eddy I saw several trout working on the surface. I was sure I was in for a good evening's dry fly fishing if the hatch continued.

Before stepping into the river I greased the tapered line with Silicote line dressing so it would float upon the surface, and soaped the 7½ foot tapered leader so it would sink quickly. With a sweep of my hat I caught a mayfly in the crown as the insect was flying off the water. Examining its wings and body, I decided the nearest imitation I had for size and color was a Light Cahill fly, size 10.

To assure good floating, I oiled the fly with Silicote oil and worked it out with a few false casts so that I could drop it about two feet above the fish feeding nearest me. As the fly dropped lightly upon the water, the drift was perfect for the fish I was after. The small rainbow which hit the fly was hardly worth mentioning, but the float, the strike and the play was an appetizer for the larger brown trout which I knew would soon come on to feed.

Fishing the dry fly—imitating a living, floating fly upon the water—is one of the most intriguing methods of our fly fishing. It is also the most misunderstood, misused method of fly fishing practiced upon our streams. It is so often used by fly fishermen who have no conception or knowledge of the insects upon which trout feed, and who will not study the behavior of the trout, that the beginner must be warned not to fall into such habits.

There is hardly any greater thrill than offering a trout a fly in such a manner that you can watch every foot of its smooth progress as it comes floating down upon the surface, and see a trout seize it before it becomes necessary for you to lift it off the water and cast it upstream again.

Although the nymph comes first in nature, then the dry fly, (the floating fly) and then the wet fly, (the drowned fly) I am very glad that my fishing education was bait first, wet fly next, then the dry fly and last the nymph fly. Prior to 1911, the year I first used the dry fly, I owed much to the trout for showing me their feeding habits. Had this not been so, I am afraid that I, too, would have succumbed to the poor habit of fishing the dry fly to the exclusion of all other methods as so many fly fishermen are now doing.

As the beginner goes along perfecting himself in dry fly fishing on lakes and streams, he will find there are two situations when he should offer the fish a floating fly. One is to place his fly so it will drift over the fish which can be seen plainly right there before him, feeding upon insects which are floating upon the surface. The second situation, and the most uncertain to hourly success, is fishing the dry fly where he thinks a trout might lie and be willing to take the imitation if it floats over him in a natural, life-like manner. It is here that the beginner must intently strive to be observant and gradually pick up enough knowledge of the fish, the water and the insects so he will not spend the best hours of his angling in "throwing his arm out" with poor results.

Many a fisherman goes along the stream hour after hour, casting his dry fly upon the surface, proud of its water-riding qualities, enamored of his casting skill, and enjoying the warm sunlight, the verdant woods and the wildlife. Though he comes home with an empty creel, he has honestly enjoyed every minute of it, even if there were several hundred trout to the mile in that stream.

To such fishermen I have no objection, but when I go fishing

133

I want to catch fish. Therefore, I avoid the tendency to fish the dry fly continually by also fishing with the nymph, wet fly and wet-dry fly, each according to the behavior of the insects and the fish. The tackle, the art of casting, and the beautiful sights of nature are then secondary to me for my enjoyment is enhanced a thousandfold when my diversified efforts are capped with success in angling.

Only then, in my opinion, is a fly fisherman on the road to mastering a grand art, fly fishing. Who would care to sit down to a table which has no refreshments, no matter how grand the setting? Catching fish refreshes your mind and body if, now and then, all your skill and knowledge allows you to out-think your worthy opponent and sink the hook home. You can release him unharmed to fight another day and derive much pleasure in so doing. Yet the fact that you have so copied nature that the wary fish has put the sign of approval upon your methods brings so much satisfaction that only you can appreciate it to the fullest.

No fish feeding upon surface insects can fool a beginner for a moment upon a still pool, a slow run or any smooth surface of the water. The trout's mouth, engulfing the floating insect, inevitably leaves its "sign" for you to read as plainly as you read this print or as easily as you can see where a pebble tossed into the water has created much the same "sign."

Trout must break the water film, the *meniscus*, when they sip a tiny or a large insect from the surface. This break in the film sends out rings, ever-spreading circles over the water. One quick glance shows where the ring is centered. Smooth casting with a fly tied to float well, dropped a few feet above the spot where you see the trout feeding (center of the ring) will come within the trout's range of vision and should be taken if the fly is handled rightly.

In broken waters, however, such as long rips (rapids) or short rapids, one is sure to miss seeing many a rise to a floating natural fly. Also, when it is raining heavily upon smooth water, or the smooth surface is ruffled by a moderate, fresh or strong breeze—13 to 30 miles per hour—it is likewise difficult to discern a rise. Only a sharp break or an occasional ring upon the water under these circumstances tells you that a floating fly might well be tried.

If you see many flies rising from such hard-to-read water, that is a good "sign" for you to try the dry fly then, but do not confuse the swirls or "boils" of trout feeding upon nymphs below the surface with the "sign" of trout feeding upon surface flies. It is utterly useless to cast with the dry fly if it be rising nymphs that the fish are seizing. By the same token, if you see trout making rings all over the stream, it would be absurd to continue fishing with a nymph, wet fly or wet-dry fly. Give those feeding fish what they are eating, a floating fly.

While it is a simple matter to drop a dry fly two or three feet above the rings made by a feeding trout in quiet waters and allow it to drift toward the fish as if it were truly a water-bred fly, it is quite another story to work a dry fly in fast to fairly fast water. This calls for pin point accuracy in your casting.

In the faster water the dry fly angler must use the "tick cast" if he hopes to catch trout there. This he does by allowing his fly merely to touch the surface several times in rapid succession, and then dropping the fly on the water for just an instant in the hope it will immediately fool the trout into thinking a living insect has alighted. This easily perfected cast is great fun. It will drive trout or bass frantic. Use a short line.

If the fly is allowed to remain in the water for more than an instant, the current will make short work of pulling line, leader and fly under the surface. It then ceases to be a dry fly, and woe betide the dry fly man who would rather perish than be caught fishing wet!

There simply must be no drag of the dry fly in these faster waters. It is a most unnatural sight for a trout to see a floating mayfly pulled along the surface by faulty action of the line and leader in the varied maneuverings of the current. Toss a live mayfly upon fairly fast water and see what happens. Although the water seems too broken for it to remain floating for long, the living fly often does. You can't hope to achieve that kind of a float with your dry fly in fast water, but you can achieve it partly by using the "tick cast."

If you have dropped your fly on slow water but your line is in fast water, a drag invariably sets in. As the current tugs on the line, the fly plows along the surface as if it had an outboard motor attached to it. Then down goes the trout.

But for the beginner, the drag may well be the best thing that can happen to him. After he has spent several troutless hours on a stream, with no regard to the drag of his dry flies, he'll suddenly realize there's more to dry fly angling than merely dropping an imitation fly here and there for a hungry trout to hit. He'll analyze his faults, the most obvious of which will be the drag.

135

He'll find that the drag compels him to learn current, to study every foot of water upon which his fly, leader and line will occupy the moment his cast is made. The drag will teach him to take a position in the river so that he mentally "sees" the action of his fly before he even starts to strip the line off his reel to make the cast. He will decide that his fly, to look natural to the trout, must be dropped two or three feet above the beginning of a quickly flowing run, and must be dropped so that it will float nicely—with absolutely no drag—over the entire 15 foot channel of the run.

No cast the beginner might make across the run would carry his fly afloat along the channel because the quiet water at the side would hold the line. The fast moving water would take the fly and leader for a moment, but the line held back by the quiet water would act as an anchor, with the result the fly would skate across the channel. There could be no perfect float of the fly from head to foot of the run, just a drag of the fly across the good water, and no trout would hit it. Figure 47.

After studying a run, the beginner will see that there is but one logical position to take if he wishes to fish that water with his dry fly. He moves 15 feet below the end of the run and keeps low in the water so the trout cannot see him or his rod when he begins his upstream casts. Now he makes several false casts for accuracy, and when he judges the oiled fly will drop lightly three feet above an eye-marked spot in the channel, his 30 feet of line and leader carries it right there. The fly drops, the leader sinks and the greased line floats in the same channel, all moving smoothly at the exact speed of the current. No drag occurs, and the beginner has learned how to handle such types of current right there.

There will be many current situations to meet, but the beginner will soon solve them in the only manner possible, trial and error. Each hour will bring less error if he will continually have in mind the all important thought, "pay more attention to current than to the pattern of the fly." He must constantly realize that the trout each day take dozens of live land and water-bred flies, but they take them only when they come floating down in a natural manner. When his imitation fly comes along with the current in a "natural" manner it looks like one of these insects and the trout will probably hit it.

Too many anglers become so obsessed with the dry fly that they forget about the behavior of the trout. When they go along the stream hour after hour, dropping a dry fly on

136

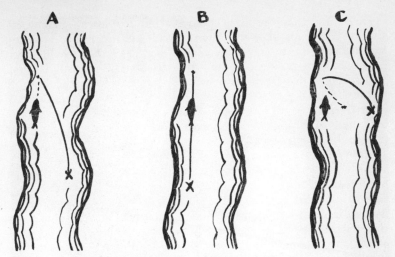

Fig. 47.—Offering A Fly To A Trout.

Fig. A. When the line, leader and fly are on the water from X to the position shown, the wet fly, dry fly or nymph drifts along the dotted line. It comes to the trout in a natural drift of the current. He does not see the line and the leader is not a hazard.

Fig. B. When the line, leader and fly drop at X, you are "lining" the trout. He runs from the sudden drop between his eyes.

Fig. C. When the line, leader and fly drop on the water from X, the pull of the fast water "drags" the fly past the trout in an unnatural drift. He refuses the fly.

the water, they actually are telling the trout, "You'll take this dry fly or nothing." How can any fisherman, observing the trout eating nymphs underwater, offer them a floating fly which they cannot see, or seeing it, ignore it completely and continue feeding upon the fat nymphs?

How can any fly fisherman look at deep water in the bright sun, or on dull days for that matter, and expect a little floating fly to bring a resting trout up to a fly which he cannot see? Not that way are trout taken regularly in the daytime. A deeply sunk nymph or a wet fly may bring the angler much joy on that water, a dry fly only frustration and a reflection upon his knowledge of water and the trout.

How bright the world seems when you see that floating flies are on the water and the trout begin to feed upon them. With great anticipation you note the size and color of the fly, tie on the nearest imitation you may have and take fish. The bait, wet fly and nymph fishermen are then as out of date as Aunt

137

FIG. 48.–A Reach On The Brule River.

During the day the angler takes up a position at Y working the near water to his right with short upstream casts, fine leader, and small dry flies, if the fish are rising to midges and mayflies. If the trout are taking nymphs which are coming up to hatch, he covers the nearest swirls with a nymph of the same type and size. There may be 25 trout working on the nymphs ahead of him, but the angler does not stir in his tracks until the nearest trout are taken and fought below the water at Y.

Ida's old bustle in the attic. Your one thought is, "Can I so drop my fly over the feeding trout that it will compete with the dozens of naturals, all of one species, which he is taking? Can I reach out with my fly and take the nearest trout so that he will not put down the others in the play and the netting?"

And, having caught the trout, can you go on and take the next nearest trout and the next? Such action, turned into trout, can come only to him who is climaxing the hours of trial and error, theory and practice.

It is by no means impossible to get more than one trout if you see a number of them feeding in a certain area. But you have to make sure you do not let any fish create so much commotion that he puts down the others.

Before you begin your upstream casting, you get well below the feeding trout. You first try to take the nearest trout during his first risings. Obviously, it would be very foolish to slam line and leader over the nearest fish, or others near him, to reach out for a bigger one 10, 15 or 20 feet ahead. Like sheep attacked by coyotes, they would scatter wildly, warning all the calmly feeding fish ahead of them. Figure 48.

You might take that bigger trout you reached out for, but that will be all. But if you catch that nearest fish first, then the next nearest, and so on, you can probably catch them all, even the big fellow way up front.

After each fish is caught, your well-oiled dry fly should be washed quickly in the stream and should be dried by several hard and fast false casts. This unconscious drying is done with your rod hand, not your mind. Your mind is busy studying the spot where the next closest fish is rising. You study the water for the right placement of the fly and decide it must go near to the edge of that broken water ahead, but not in it, so the fly will float down nicely without drag to the trout which is feeding three feet below in quiet water.

While you have sort of kept the fly in your vision all during the hard driving to dry it, you now watch it closely. You shift your wrist to "aim" at the spot you wish it to go. You intend to drop it on the water at the end of the next false cast. When you see that your aim is right, you have in mind that your final cast must be a smooth one, a cast for delicacy as well as accuracy.

Just as the fly is over the right spot, you release the five feet of spare line you have been holding between the thumb and forefinger of your left hand. This "shoot," as it is called, "kills" the hard driven line and the five feet of loose line speeds through the guides. This causes the fly to pause in the air and drop down as lightly as a natural fly upon the water.

Now the loose line on the water is stripped in very rapidly, underhand, so that no slack line and leader is between the rod tip and the fly. See Figure 49. The rod tip is held right over the top of the water, pointed at the fly. The line, leader and fly are now in a straight line before you and no kinks or curls will form on the surface before the fly floats over the trout you saw feeding.

If he hits, an easy, but quick six inch movement of the rod handle to the right or the left *over the water*, sets the hook firmly and the play is on. Be sure you set the hook with that side movement, not by lifting the rod tip in the air. A lift takes the fly away from his mouth, a side push of the fly sets it in the corner of his mouth or in his lip.

Four trout like this and the master looks around. Can you

Fig. 49 and 49a.—Rod Tip Over the Water. (See Text).

With the rod tip over the water, the line is now placed between the two fingers, as shown. Fast water is worked with short casts and no stripping is required when the rod can manipulate the fly easily.

blame him if he thinks, "Who ever said fishing with the nymph or wet fly can hold a candle to the dry fly?"

But now that you have had a few hours on the stream and have a good idea of how and where to place your dry fly so it will float over the area you wish to fish, comes the problem of what fly to use. That's easy enough. The fly you choose will be the one which most closely resembles the varying stages of the living flies the trout are taking off the surface of the water.

Since there are hundreds of species of mayflies, nymph hatches

140

FIG. 50.—A Male May Fly and its nymph *(Stenonema sp.)*.

Observe the small pair of claspers at the end of the body, under the tail. They appear only on a male for they are used to engage the female's body while mating. This is the only male mayfly shown in this book. The only way we amateur entomologists can be sure of identifying the male and female of the same species with sureness is to capture a mating pair. A swipe of the hat, or a net, will show the sometimes vast difference between the male and the female of the same species. Some call this the March Brown Fly. I know of no mayfly hatches in March and no two fishermen can agree which of our reddish-brown flies are like *Ecydyurus venosus*, the mayfly to which the British gave the name "March Brown."

are likely to come on at most any time. No matter what the species, each mayfly nymph produces a floating dun. Figure 50. Since these duns appear on our waters in such great numbers throughout the fishing season, you can readily see why this phase in the life cycle of the mayfly offers such great opportunity to the dry fly angler. His main problem is to determine the general characteristics of the duns on the water at the time he is fishing, and to fish for trout with the closest imitation he can produce.

Whenever you see duns floating after they have hatched out of the underwater nymphs, pluck one off the water and examine it closely. You have plenty of time to do this because large duns float many feet downstream before their wings become strong enough, or fill out with sufficient fluid, for them to fly off the water. It may be that you will note a pale yellow underbody, dark markings on top of the body, light-colored wings, and long,

141

dark legs. Its body probably will be about the length of a size 1 hook.

You look through your fly box and decide the closest imitation of this dun is a light-bodied fly, whose hackles are of light colored game cock feathers, with long tough hackles at the tail to aid in its floating. While the living dun has an inch long body, it arches itself so that it rests only half an inch on the water. You therefore select a pattern tied on a No. 8 light wire hook, about half an inch long. After tying this fly to your leader, you oil it, and using ordinary dry fly tactics, drop it over the nearest feeding trout and take him.

The next stage in the life of the mayfly giving opportunity to the dry fly angler is that of the "spinner." Duns change into "spinners" after they have flown off the water to rest a day or so in trees, bushes, grass, or anything like that along the water's edge. After mating, it is the female that becomes the "spinner." She flies over the water and touches the surface repeatedly as she "spins" her eggs, and then flies away quickly.

When you see "spinners" laying eggs, seize one in your hand or capture one with a sweep of your hat through the air. Observe that fly in the same careful manner that you examined the dun.

You probably will find the fly somewhat resembles the dun of the previous afternoon, but now the body is much brighter, the belly lighter in shade, and the dark markings on the back much sharper. If you reason that the "spinner" is of the same species as the dun you caught the day before, tie on a dry fly of similar body color but longer in the hook shank. You use the longer hook because unlike the dun, the "spinner" does not float upon the water with half its body curled off the surface, since she must extend her body full length on the water to utilize the current to help strip, or "spin," the hundreds of eggs from her two egg sacs.

Therefore, you tie on a size 4 hook, of light wire, with the body color as nearly like that of the living fly in your hat or hand. You cast it as you would any dry fly over the fish. The trout, you will find, seem to take the "spinner" quicker than the duns, since the "spinner" is off the water in short order after dropping her eggs. When a trout misses several flies in a few minutes time, he adopts a faster hitting tactic, more of a slash than a slurp.

If the "spinner" you have examined is not like the dun you caught the day before, you will conclude she is of a different species of mayflies and will pick out an imitation which resembles her as closely as possible. A size 10 hook probably will match her body length.

Within an hour or so you note there no longer are any "spinners" laying eggs on the water, but you can tell by the rings on the surface that the trout are still feeding off the top. Also, you hear them because they are now feeding more noisily, sucking and slurping like little Willie downing a chocolate soda. The rings, too, are more pronounced than before.

Again, you should corral one of the flies upon which the trout are feeding, for here you will discover a third opportunity for the dry fly man. You should carry a very small net in your creel for this purpose, like those for dipping minnows from a bucket or pail. The fly, you will discover, is most likely the "spinner" dropping to the water in the form of a "spent fly." Emptied of eggs, the "spinners" soon die. As they are carried downstream by the current, the trout suck them off the surface. The males die, too, after they are emptied of milt, but many of them fall dead upon the land instead of the water.

As you look carefully at the fly you have scooped out of the net and placed in the palm of your hand, you will see how the large wings are spread out flatly, revealing their full size. When those flat wings are similarly spread out over the surface of the water, they are readily seen by the trout. The dark markings on top of the fly show through plainly because the fly is now a mere shell. The 'spent" flies are by no means the nourishing dish of the mayfly in either the dun or the "spinner" stage because the vitamin-packed eggs, or milt, are gone. Nevertheless, "spent" flies are taken by trout which are still hungry. Who knows, maybe they are like figure-conscious people, looking for food that's not so fattening?

Whatever the trout's motive, to catch him now you tie on an imitation "spent" fly, one with a long shank and widespread wings with a matching body. A fine wire, No. 1 regular hook, is none too small for this large species. You oil this fly and cast it to the trout just as you would any other dry fly.

In your efforts to present imitations of the many thousands of duns, "spinners" and "spent" flies you see on the waters, it is by no means necessary to try carrying the more than a thousand patterns listed in the catalogs or tied by amateurs. You merely look at the living fly and select the nearest color shade you have in your fly box. This means you should carry some of each shade, light, medium and dark-colored bodies. Any white, yellow or ivory body is viewed as a light body by the fish below. Any tan, light gray or dark yellow is a medium body while dark brown, brown red, dark gray and black are dark.

As for hook sizes, you will soon observe the living mayflies range from a size 20 hook to as great as a 2/o hook shank. The latter is the size of our giant mayflies. That hook is so large that it really is big enough for fishing muskies. In our fly fishing we never use a longer hook than a size 1, and we seldom use one larger than size 4. Even a hook as large as size 4, regular shank, is hard to handle as delicately as we would like. Rather than use hooks of enormous size, we prefer the smaller size long shanks if it is length of hook we are after. A long shank hook is often missed by a trout, and it is harder to "set" in a trout's mouth.

If a stream is not deep and is of *very clear* water, nothing I know of can beat Paul H. Young's moosehair body fly, tied on size 16 or 18 hooks when tiny flies are on the water. The sharp hackles can be all black, black and Plymouth Rock, or brown and Plymouth Rock. When you use flies as small as these, add a foot and a half of one and one-half pound test tippet to your seven and one-half foot tapered leader. The nearest water MUST be carefully covered first before extending your cast.

Another favorite dry fly body with good floating and lasting qualities that I use frequently for larger sizes is made of the shaft (rachis) of poultry saddle hackle stripped of its hackles (barbs) and wound on like moose hair.

This nicely tapering body material was brought out by the English authority H. C. McClelland in his excellent book, *How To Tie Flies For Trout*, published in 1898. McClelland wrote, "A friend to whom my first acquaintance with this material was due, makes a very beautiful red spinner of the shaft of a saddle feather of dark red game cock."

The color range of "shafts" in the various breeds of poultry enables me to obtain the color of any dry fly body I desire to tie.

For all practical purposes, the dry flies you carry in your fly box should come in but four sizes, 16, 10, 8 and 4. For the beginner, 36 dry flies is enough for his fly box. He should carry three of each shade of color—light, medium and dark—for each hook size. That adds up to nine dry flies in size 16 hooks, 9 in size 10, 9 in size 8 and 9 in size 4 in regular shanks. All should be tied on 1X light wire for easy and long floating of the mayfly.

Work with these dry flies for a full season while observing the flies natural to your waters. Carry more of some than the

144

others if you find you need them in your area, but with the color selections and hook sizes I have recommended you can go on any waters in the world and take fish.

Writers of the past have so stressed the mayfly fishing that anglers are most apt to think only in terms of mayflies. But it is wrong to overlook the caddis flies in your dry fly fishing.

When I observe the nymphs (larvae) of the caddis flies in all our streams, I realize, and I am sure you will also, that there are just as many caddis flies hatched from our waters as there are mayflies, and in some streams many more. Like the mayflies, they must return to the water to deposit their eggs, and thereby they also become important in our dry fly angling.

Trout will often hit a live caddis fly (sedge) harder and faster than a mayfly, for the caddis flies act much more "nervously" upon the water. They fly quicker, move faster off the water film, and lie much lower on the surface when laying eggs, thus showing more of the entire fly than any dun or "spinner" of the mayfly. One caddis fly touches the water many more times than any mayfly in its egg dropping. I often use a sedge fly which "skates" over the water and take fish with it for this reason. This fly is tied "bushy," a palmer, size 10 hook.

In the midst of a big hatch of mayflies I often successfully confound the trout by offering them a quick moving caddis fly. The only explanation I can offer is they have become so intent feeding upon a hatch of mayflies that they turn to the imitation caddis fly for a quick change of diet. If the mayflies they are devouring are dark bodied, I offer them a light bodied caddis, and vice versa if the mayflies are light bodied. I feel that when little Willie spears a juicy pickle while his mouth is full of good beef, just so will a trout turn to a caddis fly when he is gorging himself upon mayflies.

No dry fly fisherman should be without at least three patterns of caddis flies in his tackle box. If you purchase them in a tackle shop, you may find they are also called sedges. They should run in hook sizes from 14, very small, to size 1, very large, in overall lengths, but the body is just about half of the length of the wings which are rooflike over their bodies.

I carry caddis flies in four hook sizes, 14, 10, 8 and 6. For each size I have three of each color, gray, brown and light-colored wings and bodies. Three of each size and color gives me a very good choice on any water. One gray, size 10, would do the business for all three if you do not tie your own flies.

There should be considerable method to the way a dry fly

145

fisherman comes to his favorite stream for the evening's fishing. First off he rigs up his tackle at the stream side and greases his line so thoroughly that it will float all through the evening. He rubs the soaked leader lightly with a piece of wet pumice soap to make it sink well.

He starts out with a No. 10 fly, possibly a Royal Coachman. But in oiling his fly he must be sure that none of it gets on his leader, or it won't sink. I mention the Royal Coachman because I know it is a fly that is readily mistaken by trout as one of the thousands of insects they are accustomed to devour. Any other well-tied dry fly will probably do as long as it has white wings to make it visible to you in the twilight. Figure 51.

The fisherman works his No. 10 Royal Coachman until twilight and takes a few trout here and there. If the nymphs come up to hatch into mayflies he will lose a grand opportunity to catch many trout by not tying on a nymph during the hatch. But since this evening fisherman will fish nothing but the dry fly, that is one of the penalties of being a one-style angler. He may not care for many fish, or may be one who releases every

Photograph by Norb Vette.

FIG. 51.—A Pool on the Pine.

Dry fly water in the late evening. A large mayfly floats about one foot per second here. The brown trout feed leisurely then on surface flies. On bright days a heavy nymph is best, while a streamer, a hair fly or a large wet fly is best in the evening if there are no fly hatches.

146

FIG. 52.—The Wolf River in Wisconsin.

A slow and fast reach finds the trout in the pool above the rapids in the evening where the dry fly does good work. During the day the trout may drop down to the rapids. The fisherman stands at Z and drops a large stone fly nymph in the quiet water above, allowing it to drift into fast water. After several casts he proceeds slowly downstream covering every foot of water with his stone fly nymph.

trout he catches while waiting for a "big game" specimen, a large cannibal trout. Possibly he'd rather catch only the really big ones, helping rid the river of a tremendous fish eater and secure a trophy at the same time.

When twilight comes on, the fisherman changes from a light tapered leader to one of at least four or five pound test at the fly end. Now he uses a size 8 or 6 dry fly unless there is a hatch of large mayflies occurring about a half hour after sundown and go on hatching for an hour or two. In the dim light he uses the same casts he uses during the daytime, but much shorter line. Carefully he works every feeding spot of the large trout.

If, in the faint light he discerns a dimple here, a large bubble there, he casts his dry fly about three feet above the spot and at an angle so it will not "line" the trout, not slam line and leader directly over his head and body.

147

Soon it becomes so dark that it is hard to make out the fly on the water. Now is the time to tie on a large spent wing, size 4 hook, of regular wire. The leader now must be stronger, at least six pound test at the terminal. The fly is cast wherever a feeding fish is spotted in the near darkness, or wherever a fish in total darkness is heard feeding.

If there is a good pool, lined with grasses or shrubs, the fisherman decides during daylight the best spot from which he can stand to cast in the darkness, and how much line to get out to place the fly near the shoreline on the quiet water of the pool. He knows large trout lie here waiting for the giant mayfly nymphs which come out of the silt to moult. The trout well

FIG. 53.—A clear cold, *hard* water springhole in the upper peninsula of Michigan. Limestone springs feed it with a water temperature of 44 degrees—an ideal home for brook trout.

148

know the nymphs shun the daylight to shed their outer skin, just as a crayfish sheds its skin. What a luscious fat morsel these giant nymphs are for the trout.

And, if by midnight the dry fly fisherman has landed a prize trout, who would deny that he has found contentment in his chosen method? As for me, I'm home in bed by that time, for I prefer to see the water and my floating fly when I fish.

SPRINGHOLE FISHING

In this crystal clear, hardwater springhole near my home town, I have stood at "T" and taken and released 50 brook trout without moving from that spot. They ran from 7 to 10 inches in length.

They would hit every knot on my leader as it moved along in the water. The knots resembled the water fleas (daphnia) which were so numerous in the five acre spring fed pond with its inlet and outlet of two small brooks.

It was a different story when I wanted to find real opponents. Then I would have to wade over to the spot marked "V". Alongside and in the downstuff large brook trout held the good cover. The small trout dared not come too close for fear of being eaten. Figure 53.

One 16, 17 or 18 inch brook trout was worth a dozen of the little fellows and they were by no means easy to tempt. Beautifully marked with their bright red and white fins, red meated from feeding upon the freshwater shrimp which abounded in the water, only a fisherman could appreciate the thrill of their fight to get back to their cover.

One had to take advantage of every cloud over the sun and every light breeze which ruffled the water. A 9 foot leader with a fly of orange body and gold ribbing did nice work when worked along the good cover. On days that were too bright, a shrimp fly or a mayfly nymph on a heavy hook would be allowed to sink to the bottom for a full minute. Pulled very slowly along, rod tip over the water, an underhand stripping in of the line telegraphed the instant strike of a good fish. It was a fisherman's heaven. Only a hundred feet away a doe and her fawn might be feeding upon the bright green filamentous algae in the pond, looking at you only when the buzz of the reel brought its unaccustomed sound to them. I'd talk quietly to them and they would resume feeding.

At twilight the wood ducks came winging in to their nests in the trees; the woodcocks would thrill me with their mating

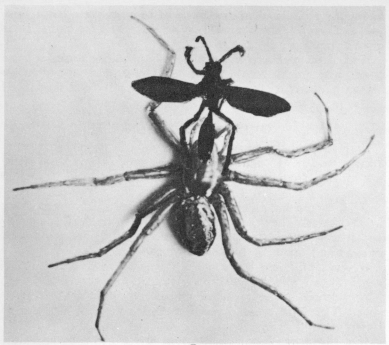

FIG. 54.—Our Largest Woods Spider With *Ichneumon* Fly. Spider's body five-eighths inch; flies wings one and three-quarter inch; alar expanse.

gyrations, directly over my head; the ruffed grouse flying in silently to the hemlocks for the night. Twice I saw a timber wolf, and several bear crossed at the inlet.

Returning after several years absence, I visited my secret spring hole. I came upon a hard packed trail. Along it and around the little jewel of the pond, cans, bottles and wrappings of every description littered the land.

Someone had foolishly cut away the cedars to get at the trout! The grand cover you see along the shoreline in the photograph was gone. My heart wept a little as I retraced my steps.

See Figure 54. If a fly tier brought forth a dry fly like the above combination, he would be accused of nature faking. It was right there at "V" in the spring hole that I saw a large woods spider come sailing along on the water film. As it came past my thigh, I noticed that its legs were not moving. Then I saw a miniature helicopter on top of the spider. Too heavy to lift, the ichneumon fly was buzzing its wings so fast that they

150

were hardly visible, yet the fly was propelling the spider at such a rate that I was forced to wade at a fast walk to keep up with it. When it came to a dry spot ahead of "V" it tugged and dragged the spider among some dry branches, inserted its ovipositor and flew away.

It had evidently caught the spider at the water's edge, paralyzed it with its stinger, rendered it helpless, then skidded it along the water film until it came to a good spot to deposit it. The egg, or eggs, it then forced into the spider's body would hatch in a few hours and the larva would have living food until it hatched into a fly. I have seen this happen several times since then, sometimes on a very quiet reach of river. I often wonder what a chemical analysis of the liquid in it's "hypodermic syringe" would show. I was strongly tempted to take the spider home but why should I destroy one of man's best friends, an ichneumon fly?

CHAPTER XI

The Wet Fly
Is Intriguing

"MAY A TROUT take my sunk offering in his mouth, then it's up to me to do the rest."

That, in brief, sums up my idea of fishing with a wet fly.

It's all that any angler can ask of his wet fly for he must depend upon his tackle and skill in handling it to let him set the hook and land any fish which may be hungry enough to mistake the fly for something good to eat.

Sometimes, I must admit, the fish is more skilled than I and ejects the fly before I can set the hook in his mouth. How many, many times this happens we have no way of knowing because the angler cannot always see his wet fly in its entire progress underwater. Neither can the angler always see the flash of the trout's body as it turns to seize the fly and eject it.

It is this unknown, that which we cannot observe underwater, which appeals so strongly to the fisherman who handles the wet fly well. This kind of fishing is much harder than dry fly fishing, for the taking of a floating fly is plainly seen.

A wet fly fisherman does not become expert in just one season. Even after years of experience he never fully feels that he can call himself proficient. With the wet fly he continually strives for expertness, even until the day he finally lays up the rod forever.

Not until we have learned just what the water will do with each particular fly we cast to the fish will we have gone a long way towards becoming a good wet fly man. And not until we ponder greatly about the flies we use can we link up the four great principles of fly fishing, *the water, the fish, the cast* and *the fly*.

It was around 1900 on my home waters in Northern Michigan that I first took up wet fly fishing. In those days few, if any, anglers fished that territory with flies.

To my mind there was going to be nothing to this wet fly "game," for I had many times seen the trout and bass take drowned flies while spurning my bait. At times they ignored the bait so persistently that I became frantic and developed a deep-seated grudge against the finicky fish.

A little practice enabled me to dunk my wet fly almost any place on the stream. Soon I was catching dozens of trout. There really was nothing to it; the trout were so plentiful.

Yet something was wrong! For every large trout I formerly "hooked into" with the old telescope steel rod and bait, I now would hook and land 10 or more small six, eight and ten inch trout with the bamboo rod.

All that first spring and summer it was the same story, over and over. It rankled me to think that with the wet fly I had become a quantity but not a quality angler.

I tried desperately to take steps to remedy the situation the next summer, and the next, but apparently I was too thick-headed to comprehend why the wet fly would not take large trout. There was no one with whom I could consult, so through experience I finally learned.

I had pitched my tent by a little spring near the Whitefish River. All afternoon I offered wet flies to the trout in that stream, catching and releasing many small ones. As the afternoon wore on, I decided to keep the next three trout for my supper.

I was tired, so did not bother to change the fly tied to my leader. There wasn't much left of the hackle or the body because the fly had been badly chewed by the trout I had caught downstream.

The late afternoon rays of the sun slanted so that when I waded across the stream to drop my straggly fly where the waters of a cold brook emptied into the Whitefish, I saw the bottom of the pool very clearly.

I counted at least 50 brook trout of all sizes schooled in mid-water. The small trout were in the downstream end of the pool and I noted that the fish were progressively larger towards the head of the pool where the brook flowed into the river.

We wore no waders in those days so that didn't prevent me from standing in the water almost up to my armpits. To get a good eyeful of the school of brook trout I hung onto a stump at the bank with my left hand, and held my fly rod aloft with the right.

I saw the trout descend, as if by command, to the very bottom of the pool. Suddenly a "whale" of a trout hove into sight. "The bully of the pool and how I'd like to take you," I thought as I observed his long, upturned, undershot jaw.

With some effort I remained as immovable as the stump to which I clung. Slowly the huge trout cruised over the descending school of smaller trout, then turned and headed towards me, coming so close that I felt I could almost reach out and touch him before he casually turned upstream.

I made a quick short cast. My fly dropped about two feet in front of him and sank quickly in his path. Without changing his course, the trout opened his jaws and the fly disappeared. I sent the hook home so hard that I lost hold of the stump and had to tread water before I again felt solid bottom under my feet.

This was by far the largest trout I had ever hooked with the wet fly.

When he became so tired that I could bring his head up and make him take air for a few moments, it was easy to extract the hook and let him go. I wanted to see if I could catch him again the next day.

Here then was the first real lesson in taking large trout that I had experienced in my fly fishing career. I was sure it unfolded a whole new outlook upon my fly fishing. That night, in my little tent by the spring, I lived over the entire performance many times, and planned my strategy for the next day.

Unable to sleep, I was on the stream at dawn. By 5:30 that July morning I once more had the big trout in my power. I had used the same tactics with my wet fly. The procedure again paid off the first week in September.

Even today I can visualize that trout and analyze every move I made and every move he made. He had revealed to me two fundamentals of wet fly strategy which I have since used with success for more than 50 years. These two principles are: Use a heavy hook with sparse dressing, and, in deep water, cast the fly upstream.

Why? Because a hook heavy in the iron, if cast upstream, will drift down and toward a trout's mouth as naturally as if it were a drowned fly of nature.

Once I had learned this technique, I ceased casting "here and there," the haphazard "drop and draw" stuff, and consistently began taking larger trout. Also, I became a "slow" fly fisherman. Not once did I drop my fly into the stream without first "sizing up the water." Even now, wearing Polaroid glasses, I

155

quietly walk the bank on a strange stream to observe a good reach before getting in the water.

Every cast was made with the hope that a big fish might lie there and take the fly as it came to him in a natural drift, in the same underwater course of any natural, drowned fly in that particular spot.

An angler should always remember that a fish has no hands. If he sees no enemy around, and something comes floating down with the current before his eyes, he seizes it with the only means in his power, his mouth. If it's food, he accepts it. If he judges it inedible, he shoots it out of his mouth as if it were jet propelled.

All his life he has secured his food in this manner. I do not believe it is anger, curiosity, jealousy or many of the other reasons which fishermen so often give as to why he takes our fly or lure. I firmly believe it is just plain "appetite" on the fish's part. This being so, it makes sense for us in our wet fly fishing to tempt each trout in its home to seize our submerged offering as food.

In a measure, trout are handicapped against a good wet fly man. That's because nature sends thousands of land flies such as house flies, bees, moths, butterflies, to say nothing of ants and grasshoppers, in the trouts' direction each season.

Also coming to him are the thousands of drowned waterbred mayflies, stone flies, caddis, dragon, damsel, horse and deer flies, plus mosquitoes, gnats, midges and others which hatch right there in the water.

Why, then, shouldn't a trout fall for our wet fly when we permit it to drift naturally toward him underwater, just like the real insects of nature?

There can be no excuse for hurried casting over good-looking water. Just one trout caught in such water is evidence enough that the water temperature is right, the oxygen content is surely good, the water is pure enough and has ample food. Otherwise the captured trout would not have lived there.

It cannot be emphasized too strongly that when a trout sees a fly coming towards him in a natural manner, he has no fear and takes the fly calmly. Our whole aim, therefore, must be to see that our imitation wet fly is of the right weight and the hook so dressed that it will come to him in a "natural" manner, like a drowned helpless fly in each particular type of water we fish.

It is folly to drop our wet fly on the surface, and seeing

it sink, allow it to drift but a short way, then pick it out of the water and cast immediately to another and more remote spot. That would be an unnatural drift of the fly. The angler who uses such a method is only casting, not fishing.

A wet fly should be allowed to search the water as if it were on a stick and we could push it along in front of a trout's nose so he could suck it off the stick.

We are, however, handicapped with a rod, a long line and a fly attached to a soft leader with which every whim of the current has its way. While we can force no part of our equipment, from our rod hand to our fly, we can learn to look at every run and riffle, every eddy and pool with a sure knowledge that if we but select the right weight fly, we can rely upon the current to drift our offering to a trout's mouth.

A fisherman has a much better understanding of what the current does to his wet fly if he realizes each stream has three layers of water, and that each layer flows at a different rate of speed.

When, in 1939, I first called this three layer factor to the attention of anglers in my Hunting and Fishing column, I was challenged mightily. Old time wet fly men knew, of course, that the flow of river water differs at varying depths because the current action with their wet fly told them so. Yet the idea of three separate layers struck many as being somewhat fantastic, although the principle of three layer lakes seemed plausible enough to most of them.

In a stream, the first layer is of rather fast water. The second layer is always the fastest water in a stream. The third layer, the bottom layer, is always the slowest water.

A confirmed dry fly fisherman could well insist that I am omitting a fourth "layer." This is the meniscus, the water film which contact with air forms over all water. To the dry fly man, this film is of great importance because it contributes much to the success of the dry fly fisherman. This is so because it is this layer that enables insects to float long enough to deposit their eggs, and is the basis for our dry fly technique. The angler's greased line floats for a long time on this film.

If you doubt the natural floating power of the paper-thin film, prove it by gently laying a heavy hook on the surface of a glass of water in your home. A hook as large as size four will float there all night if it is undisturbed. With a light breeze blowing over a river, you can even see the surface film move upstream!

157

The fastest moving second layer is good wet fly water. Here are carried many of the drowned insects that fall upon the water. Flies with which you intend to search this layer for feeding fish must be fairly heavy in the hook and hackled sparsely enough so they will sink fast one to three feet below the surface. It is amazing how many fish you can catch in this midwater when they come up to this level to feed.

The third layer is both wet fly and nymph water. This level is usually the daytime resting place of the fish. To work these deeper waters properly, heavy hooks are essential, and the sparser the hackle, the better. This layer often yields the biggest fish, but anglers who do not realize that the current at this depth is much slower and trickier than at the top of the stream, miss many opportunities to drift their flies toward the fish at the natural rate of the current.

Bill O'Gara, one of my associates in game work and lake and stream improvement, and I timed the layers with a Price current meter. We found that an average trout stream, five feet deep, shows a wide variance of speed from top to bottom. Our readings disclosed a current speed of .35 fps. (foot per second) at the bottom, 1.06 fps. at the surface, and 1.20 fps. at one and two feet below the surface, or *more than 200 per cent faster in midwater than at the bottom.*

We also found that the surface water at the bank moved along at .32 fps., but that the surface water five feet from the bank traveled at 1.40 fps., a *speed increase of more than 300 per cent!* See insert in Figure 55.

These are tremendous discrepancies. They account for the difficulty so many anglers experience with their wet fly fishing, as well as in overcoming the drag near a bank with their dry fly.

A beginner can soon learn current speed by sitting down at a stream which has *clear* water and observing how natural "drift stuff" behaves in any appreciable current. He will soon see how the "particles in suspension", such as dead leaves, bits of grass, drowned flies and other underwater drifting material is carried along. He will note that the "top stuff" moves along at a rapid rate, and how much it slows down when it comes near the bottom.

In the bottom foot of the stream he will see how the particles swirl and eddy upstream, downstream and all around before moving on in the water. If the beginner will tie a light fly to his leader and dangle it along in the faster upper current, he will realize why I stress the use of the right weight hooks.

FIG. 55.—Trout or Bass Under Branches.

The water at the bank runs .32 fps. (about one-third of a foot per second) as shown in the insert in the photograph. Where the author stands, the current has a speed of 1.40 fps. (about a foot and a half per second). The bank is obstructed by trees and shrubs. The author is unable to wade close to the bank and fish the fly, dry fly, wet fly or nymph so that the line, leader and fly will drop in the slow water which friction causes along every bank.

By standing out in the stream, using an underhand cast to drop the fly under the branches, the fly will have a natural drift from point 1 to the arrow. The fly, line and leader must then be picked off the water with a roll cast. Beyond the arrow a heavy drag of the line would set in, caused by the faster water between the author and the end of the line. A large fish would refuse to hit the fly, during the drag. The insert also shows the difference in the current away from the bank, 1.06 fps. at surface to .35 fps. in the bottom water. We'll assume that the author, working from the ledge he is standing upon, has thoroughly covered the upper water under the branches before moving downstream. He is fishing upstream and across stream but wading downstream. As the great majority of our trout streams are wooded, the underhand cast is a must for every beginning angler to learn. See photographs of "Mike" in the casting chapter.

159

That light fly simply will not go down. But a heavier hook, in a size 10 to 4 on 4X stout wire, tied with quick-sinking, water-absorbing materials, will descend toward the bottom. If given the freedom it must have down there, the heavy wet fly will

FIG. 55a.—When we allow ourselves to be put in this position we miss more than half our fish, probably two thirds of those which do not hook themselves. We would have to fall backwards to set the hook and take up the slack. This method is practical only when using a very short line in broken waters, or easing a fly down stream along the banks. Compare the instant control and the ease of striking when a fisherman uses the method shown in Figure 55.

be carried toward the fish in the same natural way that other "drift stuff" moves along with the slower underwater current.

Knowing that every stream has three layers of water, (four layers if you add the *mensicus*, the film) the angler should look at every few feet of stream and figure out the speed and drift of his fly. No expert can beat you in your own home streams once you have learned the "pace" of the waters you fish constantly. I'd rather know a thousand feet of river thoroughly than fish five miles of unknown water, even if the five mile stretch is reputed to be well populated with trout.

A good wet fly man, whether he fishes upstream or down, works with his fly in a manner best suited to each stretch of water he may encounter. To do this he must acquire an understanding of runs and riffles, rips (long rapids), quiet reaches, eddies and pools. He will succeed best if he will first regard the fly and water as one, for the river "talks" so plainly to us in every foot of its meandering.

FISHING SLOW AND FAST WATERS WITH THE WET FLY

Suppose you are on Wisconsin's Brule River and have come upon a little run for your initial study of the combination of fly and water. The run may be 30 feet long or it may be but 15 feet. Whatever the length, it will give you an idea how to fish that kind of water properly.

The depth is three feet and the water runs over a gravel bed. The *clear* water shows you plainly that a trout can see you if you approach too closely, so you decide it is best to fish this run by getting behind him and casting your fly upstream.

You do not want to frighten a fish below the run and have him dash into the run and scare the good fish above him which you hope to catch. The larger fish may well reason, "If that little trout coming into my spot in the run isn't afraid of big me, there must be something more dangerous than I. Guess I'll vamoose, too." Consequently, you should approach the run by quietly fishing all the water below, and if you hook a trout, you should fight him downstream away from the fish in the run.

If, in spite of your precautions, the trout in the run should have been frightened, it will be wise to stand quietly about 15 feet below the run, giving the trout about five minutes to get back into his feeding position. Fish the water down stream while waiting.

161

From your fly box you select a wet fly, one that will sink quickly, possibly a Professor tied on a size 10 regular hook. You tie it on a six foot nylon leader tapered from six pounds to three, a leader easily handled for short casts.

You drop the fly into the water behind you to let it soak, or you wet it in your mouth with saliva for quick sinking. You want it to enter the water the moment it is cast. Standing 15 feet below the run means getting out 20 feet of line and leader to drop the fly gently so it will have a five foot drift before it leaves the lower end of the run and comes back to the quiet water near your feet.

Twenty feet of line can be handled nicely with the rod tip alone. If a trout hits the fly, a quick lift of the rod sets the hook and the trout is hurried towards you and made to fight below the run. In this manner he will not scare away any trout which lie ahead of him, upstream.

Having caught this trout, you try for another about five feet further upstream. You stand at the same spot and strip five feet more of line from the reel to cast on the unfished water. The thoroughly wetted fly drifts down and along the run. If it is taken by a trout, he is handled and netted below the run in the same manner as the first.

Let us assume that in the first five feet of the 15 foot run you catch no trout at all. The run is about 10 feet wide, so it is possible your fly did not drift in the path of a waiting fish. You should thereupon make another cast with the same length of line, but this time let the fly drop three or four feet to the right so it will search five feet of different water in its drift down to the end of the run. If this fails to bring on a fish, make a third cast three or four feet to the left of the first one.

Three such casts at the most will cover this 10 foot width of the pool. It is now time to reel off another five feet of line to make three more casts into the next upstream part of the run. You stand right where you are in making these extended casts.

There now remains only the upper five feet of the run to be fished. Once again you strip out five more feet of line, and without changing position you cover the 10 foot width with three more casts. You are quite likely to take a fish on one of these tries. It is advisable to give that fish as much pressure as you can. With the rod arched, fight him down below or in the run. You do not want him to scare away the fish which

162

may be in the quiet pool above the run. That is where you intend to fish next.

You approach the pool by wading quietly and slowly through the run you have just fished, even though the faster water of the run helps prevent sending tell-tale ripples ahead of you. Before you get to the upper end of the run you stop and carefully size up the pool which lies immediately ahead. You make mental notes, something like this:

"A pool of *clear* water, 10 feet from the head of the run where I am now standing. The water deepens. I can barely see the bottom. The pool seems to be of good depth, about six to eight feet, within 20 feet of where I stand. There might be a trout here at the foot of the pool, just 15 or 20 feet in front of me. No need to change my Professor fly. I'll make at least three casts here before I change my tactics."

Possibly you take a trout there with your 15 or 20 foot upstream cast. If you do, hustle the trout down towards you and make him fight opposite or below you. Otherwise he will most surely frighten trout in the deeper water above.

If you take one or two trout from the lip of the pool, do not let your love of that size 10 Professor bias you. The time has come for a change. Since the Professor has already produced trout for you, it is safe to conclude that the pattern must be a good one today. So you stick with it, except that you now tie a larger size Professor to your leader, a No. 6 or a No. 4, of stout wire. The dressing on this larger fly should be sparser than the size 10 hook you have been using, because the larger the hook the less body and hackle it should have to do a good job of sinking and searching the deeper waters of the pool.

In this situation you do not want your Professor to ride near the surface, nor even in midwater if you can help it.

In the event you do not have a No. 6 Professor on a heavy hook, but do have a No. 6 tied on the lighter weight regular wire, your cause is by no means hopeless. Use your leader snippers or a pair of scissors to trim off and thin out much of the hackle on the fly. Also, snip off half the tail and some of the wing. "My beautiful Professor ruined", you moan, but when properly wetted, how deeply that trimmed fly will sink. You resolve, of course, to bring along heavier hooks and sparser hackled flies on your next trip, but no one runs home when he is on the stream. You make the best use of that which you have.

To be thoroughly convinced of the proper sinking action

of your fly, try it out before casting upstream into the pool. Wet the fly in your mouth, cast it close to your side where you can easily see its action. You should cast it again, and note that it will sink no lower than on the first cast. That is the riding depth of this particular wet fly.

If it's a No. 6 tied on light wire, it obviously will not sink very deeply. But if the fly is trimmed, it will sink more rapidly and perhaps as deep as it needs to go for proper fishing of the pool above. If the fly is a sparsely hackled No. 6 tied on a heavy hook, the sinking action will be immediate and the proper depth will be attained to drift along in the slower bottom layer.

Having satisfied yourself that you have a Professor with the right action, you are now ready to cast into that pool ahead. You stand in the same position, at the head of the run. Your cast must be a longer one, so you drop 35 feet of line and leader on the water above. The fly you have cast upstream will sink faster and farther than the same kind of fly cast downstream because there is no underwater drag by line and leader. It is important that you realize this. It explains why you are more likely to get a strike in this pool fishing upstream than you would if you were casting downstream.

Assuming the pool is of *clear* water, a hungry fish may see your fly and come for it. If the pool is of dark water—*brown, tan* or muddy—your chances will be less because the bottom lying fish in that kind of murky water would never see your fly unless you spaced your casts very closely.

The 35 feet of line and leader sinks as much as you dare allow it before beginning the draw of the fly towards you. There must be some tension on the line or you would not be aware when a fish strikes your fly. With rod tip over the water, line between the first two fingers on the rod hand, you use short, six-inch strips to retrieve the line. To me, this is the best way to feel a strike. See Figure 49, Chapter 10.

If you have your rod tip and some 20 feet of line up in the air, you are vastly handicapped because the fly will be ejected from the trout's mouth before you can set the hook.

If a trout strikes, you move your rod to the right or left with a little push of the wrist, with the rod tip held about 12 inches over the water. You continue the short, six-inch strips under the rod hand until the fish is pulling strongly against the now arched bamboo. The rod is then held up in the air while playing the fish.

Soon the trout is tired. You force him to the surface and make him take air every time you possibly can. When his back

FIG. 56.—Poor Strategy.

The line on the water is moving at a rate 300 per cent faster than the fly and the leader at the bank. The drag sets in almost immediately and the drift of the fly will be unnatural. Your reflexes are too slow to set the hook if a trout struck—with all that line dangling in the air you will lose a large percentage of the strikes. Such water calls for fishing along the bank up stream or, as in Figure 63, easing your fly downstream and bringing it back in the manner shown.

and sides begin to show upon the surface, he is a tired, "air drowned" fish. Your fingers are clamped against the line on the cork handle while the reel is turned and all the slack line at your feet is reeled in until there is just enough line out for you to lead his tired body towards you and over your *deeply* sunk net. You now lift the net to release or creel your prize.

Just as you did in the run, you work that pool thoroughly by extending your casts five feet upstream on each new try in unfished water. The pool may yield several more good trout.

Above the pool you come to a rather long stretch of rapids. Since the rapids are more productive and much easier to work with downstream fishing, you might as well pass them up for the time being. There is a long, quiet reach above the rapids which looks more promising for upstream fishing.

Water of this kind definitely is a problem for every phase of angling, whether it be wet fly, dry fly, nymph, or wet-dry fly. Some reaches of this kind don't offer good prospects if the weather becomes too warm, especially during the months of July and August.

165

FIG. 57.—Netting A Fish Correctly.

We'll assume Mike has fought and tired his trout. Sinking his net before he brings the trout smoothly over it, is good strategy. Jabbing the net at a trout causes him to make a desperate effort, and we look sadly at a broken leader.

Brook trout get out, and stay out, of long reaches if the water warms up over 70 degrees. Rainbows will not stay there either, for they do not like water over 70 degrees if it is quiet. They will, of course, remain in water up to 78 degrees, even as high as 80, if there is plenty of air, say seven to 12 parts per million of oxygen. Riffles, rapids and eddies create such a condition, but not the long, quiet reaches warmed too much by the mid-summer sun. Brown trout might lie in the quiet reaches if the water is as high as 78 degrees, but even they do not like it. They come on to feed in such water only at night, during the hot months.

But this is late June up north, so the long reach you are about to fish is only 65 degrees. All trout feed nicely when the water is not warmer than that. Besides, this reach happens to have some underground springs. You can feel the coldness on your legs when you approach the areas where the springs bubble forth. Look closely along the bank and observe the water-loving plants, such as the sedges and water cress, growing in those little cuts on the bank. That is another good sign that spring water is trickling there and into the river. Learn to "feel" the temperature of all water when it touches just below your waist-line. Check your guess with your thermometer. Soon you'll hit it within two or three degrees.

Knowing that there are springs here, there can be no question but that you must learn to fish water such as this. It will be good now, and it will be just as good, or better, during the hot months to follow, thanks to the cooling influence of the spring water.

Here, too, will be a good supply of food for the trout. The bottom of the reach is covered with creeping caddis houses with a fat worm in every house. Snails and clams are here in great numbers, and in this *medium hard* water stream there will also be crayfish, shrimp, dragon fly nymphs and mayfly nymphs. While the trout eat the snails, clams and caddis houses, there is too much bulk in the form of shells and sandy grit to satiate the appetites of the fish. The crayfish would be an extremely tempting dish for trout, but they're not anxious to be devoured. They burrow into the banks to be safely out of reach. You can find this out for yourself by reaching under the edge of the bank. You'll most probably scoop up a whole handful of the growing crayfish within a short distance.

So it's the nymphs, shrimp and flies which nourish the trout most in the spring-cooled reach. And that is the food you imitate

167

when you fish here. The nymph fly is your best offering, but this is also good water for using the wet fly. This is so because many land flies drop into the stream here and drown. Any gentle breeze is bound to shake many an ant, spider or caterpillar off the swaying branches overhead. Most assuredly the trout are feeding on this tasty and satisfying fare.

I cannot stress too strongly that no wet fly angler should ever neglect a long reach of this quality on a day when there is a breeze. It is the prize stretch of any stream, so good that we feel compelled to desert the pools, runs and riffles to come here and "make hay."

There is no need to hesitate over what fly to use here, day in and day out. Only one pattern is needed, a Coachman tied on size 8 hook. The wire, however, should be heavy, a 2X or 4X stout. The hackles should be sparse and not too long, and the two or three whisks of tail should be short. The Coachman should have lead-colored wings, not white, and there must not be too much wing. The lead-colored wings will not be as conspicuous as the white. Thus the wary trout will not detect the fraud as quickly when the fly comes near him. If he hits it hard, it will then be too late for him to eject it.

This is no place for a heavy 6 foot leader, for you want the trout to see only the fly. A 7½ foot nylon or gut leader, tapered to no larger than a two pound test, is your best bet. Use a level line, or an ungreased tapered line to do the business at hand.

As in the run and at the pool, you will continue casting upstream. This kind of quiet water calls for careful wading lest warning ripples put down the trout. A downstream wet fly fisherman would take few trout out of this reach.

Long casts, 30 to 40 feet, and a quick entry of the fly in the water with the help of a sinking line, is the method to employ. The fly will then go right where it should, nearer the bottom than the top, slightly below midwater. In all our fishing, it is the trout's view of our fly which we must consider, not our view. Then our fly box is not cluttered with useless flies because each pattern serves its individual purpose.

To ease into the reach as quietly as possible, lift one foot at a time, sort of sliding along so that no waves or ripples go out from your upstream wading. Even so, there will be some ripples, and you must get into position in the middle of the stream so you may, without moving your feet, work both banks of the 60 foot river with your fly.

It is advisable that you wait patiently for at least five minutes before beginning to cast. If you are a "weaver," you might as well go home. Not until you master the art of casting without moving your body can you expect to get results on quiet waters, or on a beautiful spring hole bordered by hemlocks and cedars. A weaving body constantly sends forth ripples, and even the dumbest trout will refuse to strike.

If you haven't yet learned the knack of casting with either hand, now is the time to do so. It is only a matter of casting left-handed 15 minutes out of each hour if you are right-handed. You will become proficient in just a few days on the water.

You drop your wetted fly—soaked with saliva—as delicately as possible upstream and near the bank, 30 or 40 feet to your right. The rod tip is held just over the surface at the end of the cast and the underhand strip must be used to work the fly slowly, ever so slowly, towards you. The slack line, of course, must be stripped in quickly the moment the fly has dropped on the water. The fly is then worked at the same speed as the current.

A trout looking at your Coachman sees a mayfly nymph with wings half out of its shuck, coming slowly through the water towards him. The slightest nip of a trout will be telegraphed through the line you are stripping. A smooth push of the wrist sets the hook firmly and the exciting play of a surprised trout is ample reward for this strategy.

If you are successful in hooking a trout on your first cast you will know that every act was as it should be. You will next turn to fishing the left bank of the stream with your left hand and will not move your feet and body until you have worked the water around you like the spokes of a wagon wheel, the spokes spaced 10 feet apart.

When you have covered the 60 foot width of the stream in this fashion you will have made seven 40 foot casts and worked over 200 feet of water with your fly. Not until then should you move your feet, oh, so slowly, to take up another position in the center of the stream some 30 feet above you in water which you have already covered. There you will wait another few minutes before executing the same tactics as before. Here is where slowness and patience really pay great dividends.

When I see an angler wade right into a beautiful reach such as this, from the upstream end, and continues on down, kicking up silt and sending great masses of cloudy water ahead of him with widening surface ripples telegraphing his approach so visibly to the trout, I groan and feel sorry for him.

But when I hear him say, "This quiet water never was any good," I'd like to grab him and shove his nose down there among those wonderful underwater springs and hold him there until his violent struggling tells me he has decided to quit slurring that glorious reach. A good fisherman appreciates, but never depreciates, good water.

Now that you have fished the wet fly upstream in a run, a pool, and a long, quiet reach, it must be thoroughly apparent what the fundamental plan of action has been for all three types of water. It must now be firmly fixed in your mind that in each instance you have been searching the bottom waters for fish, using the only logical method for doing this, casting upstream with a wet fly so heavy in the hook and so sparsely hackled that it sinks rapidly and is carried below midwater toward the fish with a natural action by the current. I can assure you that far more heavy trout will come to your net with this kind of daytime wet fly fishing than will come to the dry fly.

I dislike to disagree with so eminent a wet fly fisherman as Charles Cotton when he says: "That fly, I am sure would kill fish, if the day were right; but they only chew at it, I see, and will not take it. Come, Sir, let us return back to the fishing house; this still water I see will not do our business today."

When fish start coming to my fly, "chew at it," I feel that they are hungry and willing to feed. It is "dinner time" to them. If I fail to connect with them, there is something wrong with that fly or I am presenting it to them in the wrong manner.

I am either not getting the right drift, not offering them the right fly or nymph or, as Cotton says in Izaak Walton's *Compleat Angler*, "He saw you." I keep low in the water, change to a deeper sinking fly, let it have a natural float and throw at least 35 feet of line and leader.

A "chewer" is usually a "follower" and a follower comes up from the depths and has too long a time to examine it, to suit me.

FISHING A WET FLY IN THE RAPIDS

Working the wet fly in rapids and riffles calls for downstream angling. These, too, are productive waters.

Because of the varying current action in a rapids, it is reasonable to conclude there must be dozens of good spots where a trout can lie. The water may be churning all around the fish, yet between a few small rocks and boulders he lies at ease in the quiet water the obstructions create on the bottom. He exerts himself only to dash into the swift water to seize a drowned fly, a struggling minnow or any other bit of food which comes sweeping by him.

In a rapids the water is too fast for you to fish upstream. Your line is always slack and the fish ejects the fly without you being aware of it. Unless he hooks himself, which is seldom under such circumstances, upstream fishing of very fast water is absurd.

If the water of the rapids is shallow you need not worry much about your fly, but in fast water over three feet deep, the fly, if light in the hook, will be carried along nearer the surface than the bottom. A fish either cannot see it or will not fight a fast current for what seems to be a small fly going by.

The rapids you are going to fish happens to be four feet or more in depth. A tapered line will not do here, for it will float and drag your fly too near the top of the water unless you allow it to become water-logged before using. A level line is better.

The fishing procedure here is simple. All you need do is see that your fly searches out every trout's resting spot in the turbulent, churning water. But in doing this, you will have thrilling sport, for you call upon your eyes to show you the likely spots, your rod hand to guide the line and leader, and

Fig. 58.—A Stretch Of Brule Rapids.
White water is always interesting water to fish.

171

the current to drift the fly where you wish it to go, with your legs firmly guarding you against a spill in the fast water.

These rapids are similar to those shown in Figure 58, a scene on the Brule River, Since the Brule raises brook trout, browns and rainbows through natural reproduction in its many gravel beds, you can expect to catch any or all of these species here. For "schooling" purposes, let us assume that your rapids are long enough to provide an hour of intensive fly fishing before you turn your attention to the pool and the eddy at the end of this stretch of water.

The weather has been hot for several days. In the bright sun we are experiencing, you can reason the fish will be lying in the rapids, and, you hope, feeding. Trout like the rapids during hot weather because the churning waters create much more air in the water than long, deep pools or slow reaches. This keeps the fish both active and constantly hungry, just as a cooling breeze causes us to stir more vigorously and whets our appetite.

There are but two ways to fish a rapids easily and comfortably. One is with an "up and across stream" cast and the other is with a downstream cast. Either way, you are wading downstream, not up. A good wet fly man will never use the one cast to the exclusion of the other since for almost every "up and across stream" cast he should follow through with a downstream cast if he hopes to cover all the water with a good drift of his fly.

You want a fly which will show plenty of wing and hackle action, will ride low in the water and will help the current take the fly down, in its swirling action, to the quieter spots ahead and behind all rubble stones and boulders which lie in the rapids.

We know that the greatest number of water-bred flies in a rapids are caddis flies, for we have picked up the rocks, gravel and water-logged driftwood and noted there are thousands of caddis houses.

When you offer the trout in the rapids an imitation of the caddis fly you are merely giving them something which they are accustomed to seeing and feeding upon, right in that stretch, every month from April until October. Here, then, is no good spot for a size 16, 14, 12 or 10 fly. Hooks that small will hardly present a tempting mouthful of food, nor can they do much more than ride near the top of the water out of sight of the fish.

A size 8 hook is the very least you should consider, but you can go to sizes as large as 4, 2 or 1. Why don't you compromise

Fig. 59.—Fishing A Rapids On The Brule.

Around the boulders, try first for the speckled trout behind the boulders (S). Then try for the rainbows (R) and lastly the Brown Trout (B). When, by repeated casts, you are sure you have given the trout plenty of chances to look your fly over, proceed to X and cover the waters at 1, 2, 3, 4. See text.

by choosing a caddis fly tied on a size 6? The main reason for this size is that you feel it is easier to cast than a larger one. True, it will not sink as quickly nor as deeply as a size 4, 2 or 1, but you are after accuracy as well as sinking quality to search out each likely looking spot.

Your No. 6 hook will be on 2X or 4X stout wire, heavy enough in the iron to help it sink quickly. The fly should have a rough body resembling many of the bodies of the thousands of caddis flies. These bodies range from browns to grays and to light colors in yellows, greens and whites. A wet Hare's Ear fly is always good in a rapids if it is tied on a size 6 hook of 4X stout wire.

I know you are tempted to use a leader tapered to 1 pound test, but perish the thought if you expect to hold a large trout in such fast water. My advice is to use the smallest size leader, you dare, say a 4 pound test. I know that the finer the leader the more it will allow the fly to swirl with the current and be carried deeply, yet in this kind of water it would be folly to have too fine a leader. The 4X stout wire compensates for this.

Look at the three large boulders in the picture of a Brule River rapids in Figure 59. A brown trout will lie upstream by each boulder at B, a rainbow will lie at either side at R and a speckled trout will choose the water at S directly behind the boulder. Thus, there are always four permanent homes for fish around each large boulder.

The reason for this is that when water hits an obstruction there is an eddying current created just ahead of the boulder, a slowing down of the current, and this makes a home for a trout. This "cushion" will not be large but it will always be large enough to allow a trout to lie there in comparative comfort. Here he has first choice of all the drifting food which is washed down to him from above.

And what a varied choice of food he has. There are grasshoppers, caterpillars and luckless land flies which have dropped on the fast current. Augment this with the nymphs of every species which are carried down by the current, and then add the hundreds of drowned or floating mayflies, caddis, stone, gnat and midge flies along with all the bottom food such as crayfish, small clams and snails.

Truly this is a hotel and grocery store for the fish which by right of might occupies this best spot at a boulder. Lying in that fairly quiet "cushion" of water, he has but to open his mouth and "inhale" the food which comes to him so easily.

174

Fish will not hold a place in fast water hour after hour. They will seek out these resting places in fast water which allow them to eat without effort, although they dash out now and then for a large piece of food just outside the drift which did not bring it directly to their mouth.

The rainbows lying on either side of a boulder find this a quiet place, for the current is split by the obstruction and the full force is lost for a foot or two on either side. No fish ahead of the boulder can glean the entire washings of a fast current, so many a morsel comes to fish which lie on either side of a boulder. A rainbow is faster than either the speckled or the brown trout and will go a little farther and more often into fast water to seize anything which appeals to his appetite.

The brook trout is a heavy eater, but is never as ravenous as the brown or the rainbow, nor has he the ability or inclination, pound for pound, to withstand the attacks of the brown or the rainbow. A pound brown or a pound rainbow will bunt a pound brook trout out of a good home and occupy it himself. Thus our speckled trout lives in the water behind the boulder when there are rainbows and browns in the same stream. But he is not so badly off, for here is the quietest water near any boulder. The first thrust of the current is thrown so far away from the boulder that a large V is created at the downstream end and the brook trout has three times the space of quiet water in which to lie, compared with the other three homes. While he takes the leavings, there is still much food for him to eat in that wide part of the V.

Never neglect a boulder or anything which is anchored to the bottom and juts above the surface of the stream. Trout know that there is not only food being washed to them by the current but that there is much "surprise" food for them there.

Little *Baetis*, one of the small mayflies, may light there, fold her wings around her body and ramble around underwater until she finds a good place to deposit her eggs.

Next a large or small stone fly nymph may crawl up from the bottom and slowly climb the rock to anchor its body above the surface and emerge from its shuck. A damsel or dragon fly nymph may be next, while a mated caddis fly may light on the obstruction and walk down at a fast pace to paste her eggs there.

A trout which lives behind the boulder does not have the first choice of drifting food, but the "surprise" food compensates for this. A small hook hone should always be in your pocket so

175

you can resharpen the point when your fly strikes a rock in your endeavor to allow it to light on and slide down the boulder.

Fishing a boulder soon becomes child's play compared with picking trout from the main body of a rapids. Let us now fish a boulder so that we may have a set pattern for all boulders.

First we drop our fly behind the boulder, or directly on it and allow the fly to drop off into the quiet water behind where a brook trout might lie. If he accepts the fly, a strain on the leader, as much as it will bear, turns him down to fight in the fast water below. Here we make our play, and after he is exhausted we bring him to the net. In this manner there has been no disturbance in the waters above the boulder.

Next we turn to the better spot on either side of the boulder. Our aim is to take the bigger fish first. Sizing up the water on both sides, we note that the larger area of quieter water is on the right side. We fish there in the same fashion we fished the V behind the boulder, dropping our fly on it or in the water just behind the upstream "cushion" where the stream meets the boulder head on.

We are not yet ready to tackle the brown trout in the "cushion" ahead of the boulder. We reason that if we can make the rainbow at the side of the boulder hit our fly, we can cause him to make his fight downstream. The brown trout, whose view is shut off, will not be aware that any fight is going on.

Next we turn our attention to the left side of the boulder and try for the rainbow which may be lying there. The same strategy is used here as on the other side.

Finally we offer our fly to the brown at the head of the boulder.

As shown in their lettered homes in the picture of the boulders, Figure 59, it is a case of S, R, R and B. With the speckled trout it's S, the rainbow trout R and the brown trout B.

Those of us who like to consider ourselves good wet fly men recognize these places instantly and work them carefully with our flies and nymphs. No beginner is likely to have the experience of catching fish here, and he is lost until his trials and errors drive these facts home to him when he catches fish there. Soon he says to himself, "There is nothing to fishing a rapids."

But rapids are not all boulders and he finds that he knows little when he turns to the rest of the churning waters in that stretch. Let him understand right here that those who think themselves experts in fishing rapids which show no boulders have nothing on him.

176

A small rock underwater will furnish cover for just one fish. That fish will lie behind a small obstruction on the floor of a rapids. There is not enough of a "cushion" ahead of a small rock, nor on either side, so a trout lies directly behind it where there is always a quiet spot. This much we old timers have learned in all our fishing, but since we are not fish swimming beneath the churning water we cannot easily see where those quiet spots are created. The fast broken water acts as a blanket and covers those spots from our eyes.

The beginning fly fisherman can learn much from us in HOW to fish all rapids, but he can never learn from us WHERE to fish such water. This is because we cannot see the trout lying under broken water any more than he can. The only method we can use is to cause our fly, in our casting and the drifting of the fly, to search out every foot of the bottom, the floor of the rapids.

I was such a dumbhead in school that I merely got by in algebra. But I never forgot that X means an unknown quantity. In fishing a rapids, almost every spot is X to me, Xcept the white water, for trout do not make their homes in the white stuff. They only dash in there for food. Look again at Figure 59 for the only sound information I can give you about trout in a rapids. Where you see the smooth spots near or around the white spots, there a trout may lie.

I have marked several of these spots 1, 2, 3 and 4, and it is these that I search with my fly in every rapids. This is the unknown quantity that we must solve. I leave it to you to look at the rapids in the picture and fill in the rest of the smooth spots where you think a trout might lie.

Standing on or close to the shore, I work the nearest water first. Fifteen feet of rod, line, leader and fly is used to cover every likely looking spot in that distance. I cast the fly out to its full 15 feet, dropping it up and a little across the stream.

Then I allow the fly to drift with the speed of the current in the same natural manner a drowned fly would take. At the end of the swing of the fly I do not pick it out of the water. I draw it upstream, with only a lift of the rod tip, for about three feet and allow it to return slowly downstream.

Not being able to see underwater, how am I to know but that a trout may have followed the fly to the end of the swing and missed it in that fast water? He may still be lingering there before turning back to his permanent home, so I give him another chance or two at it by drifting the fly to him again in the same water and in the manner described.

Believing that one little fly, drifting at a speed of five to seven feet per second, cannot search fast water thoroughly on just one cast, I then lift the fly out of the water, and, using the same 15 feet of distance I work exactly the same water I did on the first cast, and in the same way. In fast water, trout often miss a fly, so I give them three chances every time before I extend my line.

Stripping off another 10 feet of line, I now work the waters at No. 2 for 25 feet slightly up and across the stream in the same fashion as when I used 15 feet of line. After searching out another 35 feet and another 40 feet of the rapids at No. 3 and No. 4 without moving from my original position, I leave that spot and move downstream about 50 feet. It is foolish to cast more than 40 feet in such waters for I would miss many a strike.

Where I can wade out a little way in a rapids, I do so, but where the current is too strong I wait until I can get over to the other bank and work the waters there that I cannot reach from my side of the stream. The trout cannot see me in broken waters, so I have no fear of putting them down in my wading or casting.

The whole idea in working a rapids is to cover every bit of water while you are right there. On wide rivers with wide rapids, however, where the water cannot be waded easily, we have no choice but to get out every bit of line we possibly can. This may be as much as 90 feet after you have carefully covered all the water nearest you.

On the Soo Rapids at Sault Ste. Marie, Mich., between Canada and the United States, such heavy and deep rapids calls for long casts and nothing smaller than 10 pound leaders. When the gates are open and the water from Lake Superior rushes through to St. Mary's River, at a speed of over seven feet per second, huge rainbows strike with extraordinary force. Under these conditions I have discovered to my sorrow that not even a 10 pound leader is strong enough to withstand the assault of a charging fish.

I first ran the Soo Rapids with Joe Rousseau more than 50 years ago. Such powerfully swift water never loses its appeal to any fisherman even though he "throws his arm out" for many an hour without getting a strike. When a trout does hit, the terrific jolt it gives your rod-arm is never forgotten, for it feels like the kick of a mule.

178

My friend, Scotty Stephenson, who lived along the river, took several *Field & Stream* prize-winning steelheads and rainbows there when he was living. It was a thrilling experience to go with him of an evening as he poled his large canoe out into the treacherous rapids just below the international bridge and dropped anchor between huge boulders, some of them as large as a small house.

Here we would cast until almost dark. When rainbows hit, they would run out as much as 300 feet of line and backing, and what a battle it was to bring these five to 12 pounders to net. Scotty frequently hooked much larger rainbows, some as heavy as 15 to 20 pounds, but they either smashed the leader at once or held position so firmly down among the boulders that there was nothing else to do but break the leader and dream about that fish ever after.

I have also enjoyed fishing the lower waters of the Soo Rapids from the motor boat of Dr. B. I. Marks. He works these waters almost every late afternoon during the summer, and has many a prize catch to his credit. He loses almost as many anchors when the fast water jams them between the large underwater boulders as he does mammoth rainbows too heavy to be caught. His method is to drop anchor, fish the near water by casting his favorite Jock Scott fly, and then move to new water by paying out more anchor rope.

From these lower waters, one gets a commanding view of the mile long Soo Rapids, the mighty Soo locks, the international bridge over which a train occasionally passes, and the two thriving cities on the American and Canadian shores. When twilight comes over that scene, even the strike of a big rainbow can never erase it from your mind.

Fishing the Soo Rapids reminds me of other thrills on Pacific Coast waters; the Rogue, the Klamath, the Umpqua and the Eel when the steelheads come up from the ocean. The angler who has not experienced waters such as these has indeed missed something. Figure 60.

In some of our just average streams, we find fairly long stretches of fast water which are not classified as rapids. We should never make the mistake of fishing such reaches upstream. The short, fast downstream drift would find the fly returned to us so quickly that we would have no control and could not set the hook because we would not have the feel of the strike. Wading upstream in such fast water is exhausting and needless.

Long fast reaches should be fished exactly as if they were

rapids. We wade down, but cast up and across the stream and downstream, but we must keep low to avoid being seen by the fish, for such water is not broken as in rapids. We must fish slowly, covering all the water in 15 to 40 foot casts before moving down again.

Surely three or four casts in any stretch of water will show the angler, through the action of his fly, line and leader when to change from upstream to downstream fishing. Using his common sense, he conforms immediately to what the water tells him.

FIG. 60.—The Rogue River.

Momma and Poppa fishing the Rogue River, Oregon, in the year 1928. Little Willie? He's probably climbing the mountain chasing a grizzly bear with his hatchet. We feel sorry for the poor bear!

180

THE WET FLY AND AN EDDYING POOL

It is with a great deal of delight and some trepidation that I fish a good pool with an eddy. Here is a challenge to every wet fly, nymph and dry fly angler.

When there is a sparse to medium hatch of flies over the pool, great thrills can be had with the dry fly.

The pool is heaven to the nymph fly fisherman when the nymphs are just beginning to come up out of the silt and the trout are feeding heavily upon them.

Fig. 61.—An Eddy in the Brule River.

Trout, like all fish, always lie with their heads up stream. The enlarged photograph. Figure 62 shows how they face down river but not "down stream," in an eddy.

Today, however, there is no rise of the nymphs and no hatch of water-bred flies, so you will stick to your wet fly.

A tremendous amount of food is washed into an eddying pool. In Figure 62, the arrows show the varying current. Even a beginning fisherman will observe that the rapids above must carry every sort of food into and, through its eddying, around the entire pool before the pool spills its waters downstream. Every moment of the day and night the water performs as a faithful food carrier.

With aerated water flowing into the pool, with deep water in the center and shallower on the side, with such protective

FIG. 62.—An Eddy in the Brule River.

If the beginner will study this eddy carefully, he will have a pattern for all eddies. Each eddy has the same tell-tale signs, the floating matter on the surface. Throw a handful of dry grass or leaves on the surface if you are in doubt. Its progress will teach you the current.

182

cover as the large, constant patch of foam in the center, truly this IS a home for trout! Trout of every size and species, too!

To contend with a pool having an eddy, you must observe the habits of the fish, the vagaries of the current, the time of the day and the habits of the insects. You must also concentrate heavily on the best possible casting of your fly. A true fisherman never leaves such a pool and eddy with the guilty feeling he has not done justice to it. Most important of all is the necessity of knowing every inch of the water.

Your eyes will tell you the transparency of the water, thus indicating how far you need to space your casts to get the maximum results.

If the water is *dark brown*, you know that you must cause your fly to work every two feet of water in the spacing of your casts, for fish can see only about a foot on each side in dark water. If hungry, the fish will feed nearer the surface in *dark brown* water than in lighter colored water. This, as you know from your knowledge of transparency, is because nature cannot grow much fish food at the bottom of a pool in dark water because the penetrating growth rays of the sun are lacking. That accounts for the fish in a dark pool watching for the insects near the surface which the rapids throw into it.

The entire bottom of the pool will be covered with fish food, however, if the water is *clear*, or *very clear*, thanks to the effects of the sun's rays. Here large trout will forage on the bottom for food all during the day. They will also eat the smaller trout which are foolhardy enough to get within seizing distance. Thus, the large trout will not readily respond to surface flies or those which ride merely a few feet beneath the top.

While we are now primarily concerned with a discussion of the wet fly, there are such variable factors involved in an intelligent fishing of an eddying pool that I feel it best to mention other kinds of flies as well, especially the nymph. The cannibalistic trout in the deep, *clear* water pools are a case in point. In the daytime these can best be taken with a large, bottom dragging nymph fly.

A giant mayfly nymph on a size 2 hook of 2X or 4X stout wire is my best offering for such trout. The fly, however, must sink and be allowed to rest on the bottom for at least two or three minutes before it is slowly, in very short starts and stops, worked toward you DOWNSTREAM along the bottom.

The time of day has some bearing on your success in a pool. The fish usually lie deep if the sun is bright. This, however, means nothing if nymphs are coming up to hatch in the shallower water which lies around the pool. The trout will then be up and feeding there about a foot below the surface. Then only a nymph fly tied on regular wire, fished in the downstream current of the eddy, will produce for you, because the nymphs do not swim upstream to hatch. Observe the size and appearance of the natural nymph and tie on the nearest imitation you have to the size and color.

It is fortunate that trout, in their nymph taking during a hatch, are not at all choosy. One of two patterns will usually suffice. A medium, or dark-colored nymph of the right size will do. The chances are it will be only a dark mayfly nymph tied on a size 10 regular hook that will be needed.

If it is early morning on a *clear* water pool, and the fish are not taking a dry fly or rising nymphs, a wet Lead-wing Coachman on a heavy hook, size 6 with 2X or 4X stout wire, will go down to the trout and be taken. A Hare's Ear or a fly with a body of muskrat belly fur on the same size and weight hook is just as good if the sun is not bright. Should the sun be bright, use a fly of the same size but with a yellow, light green, or any other light body tied on a heavy size 6 hook. The fish will be lying deeper during a bright sun, and a light-colored fly under such circumstances does not seem to be noticed for the fraud it is until it is near them. Then, if you set the hook quickly, it will be too late for them to eject the fly from their mouths.

Rainy days find the trout feeding high in an eddying pool at the start of the rain. Should the rain last a few hours they go down and stay down, foraging on the bottom. It may be that they fear high water and know the bottom of the pool means safety for them. I then offer them my giant mayfly nymph since this is a time when many such natural nymphs are washed from the silt into the pool by the accelerated current. I use a size 4 or size 2 hook, tied on heavy wire to make sure it gets down toward the bottom.

When the rain has stopped and the trout and I both know the river will rise no higher, I find them foraging for land food in the flooded grasses and small shrubs. Such food is a real treat. It seldom comes to the trout except during a freshet which has subsided. Beetles, grubs and angleworms are probably their *piece de resistance* then, but I offer them a dark-bodied squirrel tail fly with a lot of wing or a white calf tail fly with dark brown or black body, fished wet.

184

Along about 3 or 4 o'clock in the afternoon large trout move around the pool, probably prompted by stirrings of hunger, but they keep down. Then it is only guess work on my part. I have had the most success with a heavy hook worked fairly fast and smoothly. Long, long casts across the pool with a white calf tail, black body and gray hackles on a size 4 hook are quite effective. If no results are forthcoming, I change to a large mayfly nymph. One or the other usually delivers.

Do not ask me why or when one fails and the other succeeds. I do not know. The white calf tail, I strongly suspect, is taken for our largest caddis nymphs which break out of the stick or stone cases on the bottom of the pool and swim up to the surface very fast to hatch into pale-winged caddis flies. I would say, though, that the mayfly nymph, which so closely resembles the actual nymph stage of the mayfly, is often taken much better by the trout earlier in the day under these conditions than the white calf tail.

Evening comes on, and the sun's rays do not penetrate the waters of the pool. I must now be very careful in my casting because the fish are up higher. I keep low, throw a much longer line—50 feet—and work the white calf tail. Unless I get a strike, I soon change to a gray squirrel, but now the hook is lighter, of regular wire. I alternate these two flies every 15 minutes or so if I get no response. Should I take fish, I stay with that one fly until they quit hitting it, then change back to the other.

Look at Figure 62. Surely you will see that beautiful patch of "snow" floating in the center of the pool. That is my pet spot, petted now and then with a pat of my wet fly. The patch, of course, isn't snow. It's made up of foam, an accumulation of the bubbles which are constantly created and carried into the pool by the rapids above.

This foam is herded and held continually in the center by the current created by the rapids spilling into the pool. The water of the rapids is too shallow, and the water of the pool is too deep for it to rush right through, consequently the fast water seeks a way out and down river. In this process a whirlpool is created, a maelstrom, let us say. The white foam shows the exact center of the whirlpool. Look upstream and note that the water rushes from the rapids at the right and runs downstream, but the heavy under body of water turns it, whirls it toward the bank on the left, (looking upstream) causing an eddy which runs around the outside edge of the pool. The patch of foam is stationary, always being added to and always being carried away at the edges only. It is perfect cover for fish.

Somehow, a dry fly dropped lightly upon the foam can be seen through the center and often a black snout will engulf it. But we are now fishing the pool waters with a wet fly. Knowing that many a morsel is trapped and held in the bubbles of the foam, we interrupt our pool fishing every 15 minutes or so to drop the wet fly as nearly as possible in the center of the patch. We give the fly a little time to sink, then drag it across and through the foam. It matters not what fly we have on our leader.

In this way I have caught many fish, so many that I have learned never to neglect a patch of foam on any place in the stream. The patch may not be larger than my hand, or it may be as large as the one in the photograph. Foam means eddying water, whether it be a whirlpool or just a tiny eddy caused by water fighting an obstruction, no matter what the obstruction may be, a log, stick, stone or a pool. The foam invariably means there is good oxygenated water there, an excellent home for trout. Failure to take fish there with wet fly, dry fly or nymph is often through sheer ignorance of the water on the part of the angler.

As all pool-eddy combinations are fundamentally the same, you should intently study the pool in the photograph, and forever after know the way of the water with your fly. Close concentration for 15 minutes or so should complete your study, thereby greatly enhancing your fish taking potential for all days to come.

On the stream, the best way is to wade into the water and feel the current, but a quicker method is to study the surface water of the pool. Assume you have taken up a position directly below the foam at the point marked F, Figure 62. It should be evident to you that the pool-eddy combination you are observing there, is merely a stream within a stream. The flow of that stream within the stream, a side stream in effect, can be judged by the bubbles, insects, grass, sticks or other floating material on the surface. Toss a handful of dry grass on the water and watch its direction if you are in doubt.

A pool-eddy combination such as this is always created by fast water running into a deep place in the river bed. There is, however, a rising in the river bed at the *downstream* end of the pool. This rise constricts the current, causing the water to spill

186

out at the *lower end* of the pool to become a long or short stretch which we shall fish later.

But if a lot of "short stuff" becomes anchored at one bank and narrows the stream to such an extent that the water is forced to back up on that side of the bank, a sort of temporary eddy-pool is created.

Nature often forms such a pool when a drive of logs piles up on one bank and a few remain there to catch and hold short stuff such as small logs, small trees and other drifting material which is finally anchored and held by sand and gravel washed up by the current. Sometimes these are temporary pools, terminating when the obstructions are washed away with a big freshet or the ice and high water of the next spring break-up.

In that eddy-pool you will see that the current has made a circle around the foam, literally a river running around the bubbles. But you notice that the bubbles and all floating matter begin to flow downstream at F and continue to do so all the way to the constricted place which forms the lip of the pool, downstream.

Here then, if you fish the dry fly, you would have to cast it ahead of you on what appears to be water flowing downstream but really is flowing towards you. Actually, the water flowing upstream towards you is going downstream in reverse because of the eddying of the stream. If you fish with your wet fly, the plan of action here is to drop it upstream so it drives towards you with the downstream flow of the current. If you strip in the fly slowly it will have good action.

A river within a river, and all of it happening in this pool! What a change is needed in your fly fishing methods if you wish to get the most out of your fly in such water!

First of all, it would be foolish to obey that impulse to start fishing at the rapids. If you should hook a fish there, you would have to force him into the waters of the pool. There might be a dozen fish in that pool and you would be putting them all down, ruining water from which you might take six fish instead of but one.

Having decided to leave the rapids until the last, you must now reason that the very best fish should lie where the water coming from the rapids into the pool is forced to turn and begin seemingly to run "uphill." When you take a position later under the clump of trees upstream, at the point marked X, to the left of the rapids pouring into the pool, you will notice that peculiar "uphill" action of the water because as you stand

187

there looking downstream, bubbles, grass and everything else floating upon the surface is coming directly towards you. As you look along the side of the river bank to your right, you see the same peculiar action of the water—everything comes floating towards you. If you were to wade into the river to follow this phenomenon you would see that all the water is running "uphill" until you get well below the patch of foam.

A lazy angler, or one who doesn't know his stuff, would walk right into this water and proceed to work it all downstream as he came within casting distance of each spot. But you intend to fish this kind of water intelligently.

You take your position in the deep water below the foam and drop your fly below the foam at the point marked F. Your heavy, sparsely hackled fly sinks slowly and you begin to draw the line across and down the stream towards you.

A trout hits your fly hard. You set the hook solidly with your rod and force the fish to your right, endeavoring to avoid ruining the good water to your left. After netting the fish you let the water rest while you study it closely and at the same time give the nearest fish which you feel should lie there a chance to get over any fright he may have had.

In this fashion you work your fly with the current half way around the patch of foam until you have covered all the bottom water. You then get out of the pool, take up a position at X in the water near the trees and work the water with your flies. In the water before you is the same upstream current you met up with below the patch of foam.

Not until all this water has been covered to your satisfaction do you quit fishing the eddying part of the pool to turn your attention to that long white strip of rapids, which is also a part of this big pool you are fishing. This water runs 300% faster than the pool water. Here you go on downstream, working the white water and the slower water just at the edge of the rapids where a good trout might be resting if you have not disturbed him when you worked the eddying waters.

With great satisfaction in having caught some fish in the pool-eddy, you are now at the lip of the pool. It's time for lunch. You select a likely spot where you can study the water while you munch your sandwiches and rest. Your observations tell you the water below the pool is a reach, and will best be fished upstream, just as you fished the reach before you worked the rapids and the pool-eddy, Figure 62.

Fig. 63.—Where the Water is Too Deep to Wade.

Where one meets up with ox-bows or reaches which have undercut banks, it is hard to take the large trout that rest there in the day time. The current is very slow along the bank, it runs three times faster two feet from the bank. A size 6 mayfly nymph, heavy in the iron, will often bring results when fished as in Figure 63 (a), 63 (b), and 63 (c).

With rod tip up in the air and 20 feet of line and leader dangling, as shown in Figure 63 (a) a gradual easing down of the rod tip allows the nymph to drift down and along every foot of the water at the bank Figure 63 (b). When the nymph has drifted to the limit of its distance, the rod tip over the water and short strips of the line will bring it back upstream. The nymph comes swimming slowly along, six inch starts and stops. This tempts good trout to hit, for it is behaving like a giant mayfly nymph looking for a better home in the silt under the bank. Slow, quiet, careful walking on the bank will not frighten the trout. A heavy tread will put them down.

189

THE STREAMER FLY

The wet fly angler will often grin at the dry fly fisherman who so frequently catches smaller fish. But he will look enviously at the worm or minnow fisherman who often takes larger fish. The trout fisherman who uses spoons and other lures with his plug or spinning rod on larger rivers will catch big trout, too.

Mulling over this bait and spoon vs. the wet fly proposition, the confirmed fly fisherman will resolve to adjust the situation to the best of his ability. He decides to use streamer and bucktail flies now and then.

Many contend the streamer flies imitate minnows, and that therefore the use of such flies is not in accord with the true principles of fly fishing. I disagree. As I see it, the streamer flies imitate countless large flies to be found in all our streams, as well as the drowned damsel flies too.

This is readily apparent by comparing the stone fly illustrated by Figure 41, Chapter 9, in its nymphal and fly stages with the streamer flies on page 191. These imitation flies with their mottled, barred feathers of the Plymouth Rock rooster, will behave underwater the same as the living stone flies if they are properly presented to the trout by the angler. The feathers of such streamer flies as Allen's Last Chance, Kidder and the Highlander patterns of the Cains River all give the effect of the large flowing, wetted wings of the real stone fly.

The gray squirrel tail fly also imitates the stone fly. The colored shadings of this hair, light to dark, resemble the venation of the stone fly wings as much, or more so, than the streamers tied with Plymouth Rock feathers.

Weber ties Cains River streamers—now called Weberkraft—in size 2, 4, 6, 8 and 10 hooks. These are by no means too large, because our biggest stone flies have a wing spread of a little more than three inches. When the stone fly is swimming down to deposit her eggs underwater, her folded wings and body are fully two and one-quarter inches long. Since Weber ties his regular hook size 2 Cains River streamer fly only one and one-half inches long, it is three-fourths of an inch LESS than nature's largest stone fly. This doesn't mean that his hook size is too small, either. Other stone flies range from one and one-quarter inches to less than a half inch in wing or body length. Figure 65.

The fly tier, then, has a legitimate right to tie his streamer flies on hooks as large as size 1 or as small as size 10. These will imitate the size of millions of our stone flies which live

Fig. 64.—Streamers and Squirrel Tail Flies.

The two Weberkraft squirrel tail flies, top left, are good imitations of stone flies. I trim about half the squirrel hair off, thin it out, but leave the stubs so they will not fray. The wings then drift loosely in the water about the same width as the live stone fly. Weber's bucktail, top right, represents a minnow when the various shadings, light belly and dark back, are correctly blended.

The three Weberkraft streamers are good imitations of stone and caddis flies, even if Weber sells them as "minnow-like" flies. Some patterns do look like swimming minnows but, on our streams, you just cannot beat that Plymouth Rock feather streamer for a swimming or a drowned and drifting stone fly. Shown, bottom row, at left.

FIG. 65.—Stone Fly Water.

Nothing can beat a stone fly nymph on such waters, for the naturals abound here. The current moves at the rate of five miles an hour, or about seven feet a second. Fifteen to 20 feet of line and leader will search out every trout's home, if you cover every foot of the water. Trout miss many a natural nymph here. Your nymph, handicapped by the line and leader, will be more often missed. Give the trout several chances by carefully working your fly never less than three times in each spot before moving down.

in every rapids or other well aerated waters on all our trout streams.

But there are other flies which also live in our waters and which can be imitated by streamers and bucktails. These, too, show a good wing length when swimming underwater. When drowned they have a much greater wing spread, too.

The caddis fly, is a good example. Our largest brown-tan species shows a two-inch wing spread when drowned and a one inch body and wing length while swimming. Here then is ample reason for tying a streamer with a fox squirrel wing fully an inch or longer. Similarly, anything tied as small as a size 10 hook with fox squirrel or gray squirrel will be recognized as an imitation of many natural caddis by the trout.

With regard to bucktails, there are many which are splendid imitations of minnows. They simulate the light belly, the center

192

dark lateral line of the body and the darker, upper or dorsal portion, of the small fish.

The fly tyer who wishes to imitate minnows should capture live ones in his home stream and decide which are the most common. Naturally he imitates those which are in greatest abundance. In Wisconsin I once collected 17 different species of stream minnows. These were an excellent guide for the imitations I tied by showing the variation in color and size.

At the fly tyer's command are various colors for bucktail patterns. I am sure he will find minnows in his home waters which range from the dullest chub to the golden shiner to the "rainbow" minnow. He need not know their scientific names.

If the fly tyer keeps in touch with the men who sell minnows to the trade in his area and places one of each in a 70 per cent solution of alcohol, he will acquire a collection of his own, and soon will become familiar with all the local stream minnows. If a scientist comes along he can have them identified if he wishes to know their scientific names.

Bucktails, however, are not taken by the fish only as minnows. Depending upon the colors used, when they strike the water they resemble some moths, some stone flies, and drowned damsel flies as well as a few species of caddis flies.

Some bucktails are tied entirely too short for evening fishing as far as nature is concerned. Our night moths often are as "big as a house," or, at least, their bodies are as large as one's little finger and their wing spread is enormous. In comparison, this makes our largest natural stone fly look like a Pygmy.

A large bucktail for night fishing, tied with two trailing hooks and dropped lightly upon the water where a big fish is feeding, has accounted for many a trout for me. It will for you, too, I am confident.

The one great fault I found at first in fishing with large streamers of feathers, squirrel tail and bucktail in the daytime was that they did not catch the largest trout in the stream. I knew there were bigger fish to be had because I saw them in pools and runs.

The reason, I discovered, was that my flies were too heavily loaded with fur and feathers, and the hooks were too light in weight. When I sat down at the fly tieing bench and reduced the squirrel tail wings more than half in hair content, my heavy hooks took the flies down to the trout and I had better success.

I thereupon made it a rule to quit loading my streamers with too many feathers, and tied my bucktails very sparsely but with

Fig. 66.–Fishing the Wet Fly and the Nymph.

Having covered the water along the bank, as in Figure 55, the author, wading downstream does not neglect the midstream waters immediately below him. Snipping the dry fly off the leader he changes to a heavy nymph, a large stone on a number 6 hook. It must be heavy in the iron to go down beneath the two upper fast layers of the stream and drift along the bottom.

With right hand casts he covers the water to the right and downstream. Where the angles demand it, he uses a left hand cast to reach water at his left which the right hand cast would cause the line to pull too sharply against the nymph, the wet fly or the streamer fly.

Using the underhand strip, rod tip over the water, a slight push of the wrist, to right or left, sets the hook firmly at the first feel of a strike. No strike? He doesn't hasten, works slowly, relaxed, hoping that every cast will bring a trout or a bass.

bodies heavy enough to sink quickly. My formula became: Sparse but large flies on 2X to 4X stout hooks for deep daytime fishing, bulky and large flies on regular wire for near and on surface night fishing.

I shall always stick to this streamer-bucktail-squirrel tail fly rule.

In the daytime I work the heavy flies in the water with starts and stops. Then I allow the fly to sink to the bottom, pull it slowly along the bottom and then bring it to the top now and then with a steady swimming motion. In nature,

194

thousands of insects behave in that manner, due to current action in the three layers of stream water. Figure 66.

When we throw a streamer fly at a trout and note that the fly rides on the top and does not go down to him and past him, it is foolish to persist in using that fly. We must make it appear suddenly with a swimming motion past the spot where the trout is concealed. With just his nose showing ahead of a log or behind it, in a small eddy created by a boulder, run or fault in the river bed, the trout is apt to seize it quickly and is soundly hooked.

On bright hot days when there are no insect hatches, we sometimes see trout lying over the cooler gravel beds, for gravel throws back no heat like silt or sand beds do. If you see them swinging their heads from side to side you may be sure the fish are feeding upon nymphs and caddis houses, not merely resting. There is no better medicine then than a heavy streamer dropped well above them. When it sinks to the bottom—nymph or squirrel tail—bring it along very slowly until it almost meets his nose or at either side of him. Quite likely he will swallow it calmly.

Whenever you catch trout under such circumstances, cut open the stomach of every one you kill. It will prove most conclusively to you that he was feeding there and that it was the action of the streamer which took him. In his stomach you will find a few caddis houses, probably three to 20 snails and a few nymphs. With this varied food you may be sure that this trout wasn't being too choosy. He was taking anything fairly true to nature. It is only during a rise of nymphs or a hatch of flies that a trout is at all a consistent feeder upon just one species. See Chapter 13 for a list of what I found in just three trouts' stomachs.

CHAPTER XII

The Wet-Dry Fly Offers a New Fishing Method

ON A BRIGHT JUNE DAY in 1937 I bent down to fill a flask for a water test of Wisconsin's Brule River, just below the well known Winneboujou Bridge. With my face close to the surface, I was amazed to see a caddis fly dive into the water before me. It was an ordinary gray caddis, one of the millions which hatch from the Brule waters each year.

As it pierced the water film, an almost unbelievable change came over that drab fly. It suddenly seemed to be encased in a bright gleaming bubble, so bright that it looked like a shining ball of quicksilver. Fast moving legs propelled the bubble, angling it down toward the bottom of the *clear* water. See Figure 68.

There the bubble crawled nervously over a rubble stone and stopped. What was that fly doing there? I watched the bright silvery insect for a moment or two, then reached down to seize it, but the fly let go its hold upon the rock and drifted away.

I put the flask in my pocket and watched the air and the surface of the stream. One caddis fly after another descended from the air and dove under the surface of the water. I tried to capture one with a sweep of my hat but was not successful. Later I caught several and scrutinized the rough bodies and wings, which, I reasoned, held air and formed that underwater bubble.

For quite some time I was puzzled over what I had just witnessed. It was entirely foreign to any previous experience in my many years of angling. When those caddis flies neared the surface of the water I fully expected them to float momentarily to lay their eggs, and then to fly quickly off the stream. Had I been fishing I most certainly would have prepared for some fun with a dry fly.

197

Yet those flies didn't stop at the surface. They dove right through the film and swam to the bottom. When they rested upon rubble stones, I could only conclude that here were flies that were laying their eggs at the bottom of the stream, not at the top.

I wondered what I would have done had I seen this strange performance while fishing. Surely this wasn't a situation calling for a floating dry fly. A wet fly wouldn't do, either, because here was no drowned insect drifting inertly with the current. Nevertheless, it definitely was a living fly, although it went underwater, a behavior I had heretofore associated only with the wet fly.

A wet-dry fly! That was the inevitable thought that flashed through my mind. Wet because it went underwater, yet "dry as a bone" with that quicksilver case over its wings and body. That bubble! Did it hold promise of a new technique in my fly fishing?

For weeks I discussed my experience with fishing friends,

Fig. 67.—The Wet-Dry Fly.

Here, where I judge the current to run about three feet per second, I first saw a caddis fly dive under water in the Brule River. I was astounded at the change which came over the fast swimming fly. Good nymph, wet fly and dry fly water.

but none said he had observed or read about caddis flies behaving in the peculiar manner I described. I went through all my own books on angling and referred to many more in the public libraries, still I could find no writings wherein fishing authorities discussed anything but the three types of fly fishing we anglers have practiced for the last 2,000 years or more, the nymphs, the dry fly and the wet fly.

Then I turned to the scientific works of the entomologists. As I suspected, a few had noted the underwater egg laying habit of some of the water-bred insects. I found nothing recorded about that underwater bubble, however. Oddly enough,

Fig. 68.—A Caddis Fly. One inch long.
When encased in the silver bubble, her six legs work with amazing speed under water.

neither the scientists nor any writer about fishing had thought to apply this insect behavior to the art of fly fishing.

Some English writers, though, came remarkably close to discovering that certain imitation flies simulate quite closely the actions of a living fly descending to the bottom of a stream to lay eggs. They knew these flies had some special trait that enabled them to catch many fish, but they didn't know why, and frankly said so. Had they seen the bubble created by underwater egg-laying insects, they would have known that their mystery flies had a certain flash that imitated it.

The Alexandra fly, with its silver body and brilliant peacock sword, is one example. It caught so many trout that many English anglers have barred it on their private waters. Those great English authorities, Halford and Skues, condemned it as not an "exact" imitation of any known insect, therefore not sporting. Actually it was no "exact" imitation, but in its underwater action it gave a shining effect of a living insect swimming toward the bottom of the stream.

Doctor Halford had also rejected one of my favorite flies, the Gold Ribbed Hare's Ear, with which I had done so well in 1911 when I first fished the dry fly.

G. E. M. Skues wrote that Halford gave it up because he could not explain its success to his satisfaction. Skues devotes several hundred words to this fly, and admits it was a complete puzzle to him. I am sure that neither he nor Halford had ever seen the action of the underwater swimming caddis.

You can easily find out for yourself how the fur of a Hare's Ear imitates actual insect behavior if you capture a live caddis fly and place it in a quart jar filled with water. If you up-end the jar so quickly that the water completely submerges the live fly, you will immediately see the fly swimming upward to reach the top of the water.

As it does so, the dull-looking fly will become enveloped in a shiny case. Its fast moving legs, working like pistons, wholly outside the bright bubble, propel the fly swiftly like a swimming minnow. If you keep tipping the water back and forth you will observe that the fly in its confused effort to regain the top of the water can swim backward as well as forward. You will plainly see the body of the fly inside the bright envelope, and you will note that its wings do not move. It is the rough body and wings which create and hold the bubble by trapping air.

Now drop a Hare's Ear fly into the jar and observe how its imitation body holds a bubble around the rough fur as it descends to the bottom, and how the gold tinsel of the fly's body contributes to the flash of that bubble. Up-end the jar quickly and again note how that bubble clings to the fur body for awhile.

After you have seen how both the living caddis fly and the Hare's Ear have that shiny bubble effect, you will know that your imitation fly does conform to nature, and how wrong Halford was when he spurned it because he did not understand its function. It is true that the Hare's Ear will not hold the airy envelope nearly as long as the living caddis fly, but it serves the purpose until waterlogged. I prefer the belly fur of the muskrat to the fur from a hare's ear for it is much more mobile in the water.

When I first brought out the traits of the underwater egg layers in *Field & Stream* magazine in August, 1939, I received many letters. Some doubted my findings, but not one entomologist questioned them. I wasn't surprised that there would be skeptics. After all, 2,000 years is a long time for something like this to be overlooked.

There are still those who are not convinced, but if they will study insect behavior intently, sooner or later they will have the enlightening experience of my good friend, Alan Miller, the camera and fishing expert who has taken most of the pictures in this book. Although Alan has long tied excellent flies for his nymph, wet fly and dry fly fishing, he made no effort to tie wet-dry flies until he saw for himself.

It happened the sunny day he and I went to a spring hole in Northern Wisconsin to gather some specimens of freshwater shrimp. After digging in the silt for awhile with my long-handled shovel, I straightened up and glanced at the sky as every fisherman is wont to do when he is around water. I saw 50 or more caddis flies sailing along like an air flotilla. "Here they come!" I shouted.

Small wonder that Alan thought I had suddenly gone balmy. I waded over to him and stuck my shovel in the silt.

Then we saw what looked like tiny raindrops on the water as those flies dove from the air into the water. One dropped so close to us that Alan for the first time observed the underwater flash created by a caddis fly swimming swiftly toward the bottom.

But that wasn't all! Alan pointed to the shovel handle. A caddis fly was working its way down the handle with the fast, nervous walk peculiar to this insect. "Well, what do you know!" exclaimed Alan when he noticed that the moment the dull gray fly walked under the film of the water the large silvery bubble I had so often described to him instantly appeared. Right then Alan told me what materials he was going to use to imitate that bubble.

If you tie your own flies impale a live caddis upon a hook while on a lake or stream. Dunk it in the water. Then try, just try, to imitate that confounded silver bubble with the fly showing so plainly *inside* the bubble. Please do not neglect those fast moving legs, entirely outside of the bubble. (Then we fishermen will bow down to you.)

I must admit that before my eyes were opened to the new possibilities of the wet-dry fly I had been more partial to simulating the various life cycles of the mayfly during my fishing than imitating the caddis flies. I now have become much more caddis-minded, realizing more than before that in many of our waters it actually exceeds the mayfly as a source of food for the fish.

After my closer observations of the caddis flies, it didn't take me long to reject the notion of those English anglers that

201

certain imitation flies should be spurned because they knew not in what way they simulated nature. In the same manner I soon developed a grievance against entomologists, even those of recent times, for telling us that the caddis fly is "nocturnal or crepuscular."

While I agree that most of the caddis flies hatch at night, as a fisherman and a naturalist of sorts I disagree most violently that the caddis is only a fly of the night or twilight. I know they also are *daylight* flies. This is now especially significant to me because this fact has direct bearing on my fishing with the wet-dry fly.

Even during the very brightest days, the caddis flies mate and some dive through the surface of the water on ponds, lakes and streams to deposit their eggs. I have seen them do this from very early daylight to dark, and as far as the fisherman is concerned, this is the most important time for them to behave in this manner.

The caddis fly isn't the only species of water-bred insects with the underwater egg laying tendency, although I have observed many more of them than the others. Quite a few species of female mayflies deposit eggs in this way, and certain species of the stone flies, as well as our bright green and bright blue bodied damsel flies with the black wings. The damsels deposit their eggs in underwater plant stems.

I have no definite idea what the percentage is for each species, but since there must be at least a half million flies of all species inhabiting a reach, such as that above and below the Winneboujou Bridge in the Brule River, I feel that among them the number of underwater egg layers is sufficiently great for the fishermen to regard them as a fairly substantial item in the seasonal diet of the fish.

The female mayfly descending to deposit her eggs doesn't have as much flash as the caddis, but most certainly is worth imitating. Mayflies are smooth of body and wing, which causes separate bubbles during their descent. The caddis, you will recall, is hairy of body and wing, and these trap and retain more air, with its entire body enclosed in a single, and therefore much larger bubble.

The mayflies must have the quieter waters for the underwater egg laying. They fold their wings around their body and crawl down upon a stick or boulder which juts above the surface. I have seen caddis flies crawl down, too, but in so doing a caddis never rearranges its roof-like wings. I have never seen a mayfly dive and swim down in the manner of a caddis.

The caddis flies are not always successful in their first attempts to pierce the surface of the water. I have stood in water where the current was moderately fast, two feet per second, and have seen where they sometimes fail to make it. As quick as a wink they are up in the air again at a higher level. With increased speed they hit the water film harder and this time they succeed.

Instantly they are swimming in a long, downward angling course to the bottom. With its fast moving legs, the wet-dry fly often seems to be swimming against the current, but in this endeavor it can make no progress. The fly finally yields to the force of the current and gradually swims to the bottom. But it is this struggle with the current that gives the wet-dry fly the animation that appeals more to the trout than a dead, drowned and shrunken morsel that passes its nose in the form of a wet fly.

The fly fishing methods which man has employed during the last 2,000 years or more are based essentially on the feeding habits of the fish. When we fish with the nymph, dry fly and the wet fly, our imitations simulate the food which the fish are continually accustomed to eat. So it is with the wet-dry fly. It, too, represents food that nature supplies, and you can be sure they have been relishing it for as many centuries as the other food.

I am certain the trout feed greedily upon insects with the underwater egg-laying habit. Why shouldn't they? Here is a fly with as many as 1,000 eggs in its body, as nourishing and appealing as ham and eggs. And in the same way that we smack our lips over the tantalizing aroma from the frying pan, the trout has his appetite whetted the moment he sees the flashy bubble that signals the descent of the egg-laying fly. What a live, plump morsel this "ham and eggs" is, compared with the drowned hull of a wet fly that drifts listlessly with the current, like wilted lettuce, or the spent mayfly, emptied of its eggs, that floats not too appetizingly on the surface of the water.

It is my belief that during the underwater egg-laying time of the caddis fly, the dry fly angler does not have nearly the thrills of the wet fly fisherman with his sunk wet-dry fly. I have watched trout take the living underwater flies with avidity, striking much harder than at an ordinary drifting mayfly. The trout are so thoroughly acquainted with the current of their stream that they know the exact speed at which their usual food comes toward them, but when they see the flash of the faster moving wet dry fly adding its speed to that of the current, they move quickly to grab it. Therein lies the secret of the far faster and harder strike.

Knowing that living flies descend to the bottom and sides of streams, and are therefore a source of food to the fish, our problem is to develop a fishing technique that presents this food to them in the same flashy way the living wet-dry fly does.

The right kind of fly is of prime importance. Some dry fly patterns are good. I oil mine the same as if I intended it to float for dry fly fishing. The oil helps the fly to retain a brightness so necessary to simulate the flash of the descending fly, but the light hook will not drift below the upper layer in the stream.

I prefer flies tied with the stiffest of hackle, game cock if obtainable. The fly loses its effectiveness if its hackle tends to mat. Matted hackle makes the fly look too much like a drowned fly, and it hides that all important silvery case, the underwater flash so attractive to the fish. The tail whisks should be of mallard, wood duck or golden pheasant tippets to help it sink, and the body should have gold or silver ribbing. No caddis fly, of course, ever has tails, but it does have extremely long horns, or antennae. In the water these lie back along the body, so I feel justified somewhat in believing that the trout will forgive me for the tails on my wet-dry fly, and eat my imitation.

In fishing the wet-dry fly I simply present the fly to the trout with normal, natural action. I use a level line or an ungreased tapered line, so that line, leader and fly sink rapidly. If I am fishing with a tapered line that doesn't go under readily, and have no spare reel drum containing a heavier line for better sinking, I add two feet to my 7½ foot leader and tie on a size 6 wet-dry fly, with 4X strong hook. This long leader is more awkward to handle nicely, but it allows the heavy fly to search the underwater fairly well.

By casting upstream or up and across, I drift my wet-dry fly much closer to the bottom than the surface, somewhat like a wet fly or nymph. I drop the fly 10 feet above the spot where I think the trout is feeding, enabling the heavy line to drag it down and tumble the fly to the fish in the same way that the rolling, tumbling natural insect would come to him.

While the wet fly angler must see to it that his fly does not travel faster than the current, it's different with the wet-dry fly, since the descending egg-layer in its swimming often travels faster than the current. The trout knows from nature that this is so, hence, if my imitation fly with its flash gives the impression of a living insect, the trout is likely to seize it for the juicy morsel he expects it to be. I find that if my wet-dry fly is heavy enough in the iron, I can slap the faster waters with my tick cast and strip the fly in faster than the current, and the trout will still hit it.

In my earlier fishing days I often called to a companion when I saw a trout offer at my fly, only to have me take it away. I would have my friend stand quietly in the water, telling him I would bring a trout directly in front of him with my little gold-ribbed, orange body dry fly. By dropping the well-soaked dry fly near the bank. I would sink it with a quick pull underwater, and would lead a trout to the center of the stream. There I would slow the speed of my retrieve a little. The trout would catch up with the fly and would take it at any spot I wished to let him have it.

I thought then it was my mastery of the art of fishing combined with fly tying skill that enabled me to do this. I know now I was merely conforming to the trout's behavior in pursuing a living caddis fly that has gone underwater.

A favorite spot for mayflies to lay their eggs underwater is immediately in front of or behind an obstruction in the stream that causes a dividing of the waters. This obstruction may be a boulder, log, or any other obstacle forcing the current to split and form a V.

Mayflies have a fondness for this location because wherever a V forms, there is a quiet, or dead spot of water from one to several feet behind the obstacle and a shorter distance ahead. The obstacle itself must be used by the mayflies to aid them in going underwater. It is here that trout are apt to be on the lookout for unsuspecting wet-dry flies, and it is here that the angler can put on an imitation wet-dry fly and expect to get fish.

If I see a boulder exposed above the surface I endeavor to land my fly on top of the stone, using the short line cast. A gentle pull on the line causes the fly to descend closely, very closely, along the side of the rock into the water. By keeping the fly near the rock I get it to sink rapidly into that quiet spot which water always creates immediately in front of and behind an obstruction.

The wet-dry fly can be fished on lakes and in spring holes as well as on trout streams.

Nymph fishermen have long held to the theory that nymph flies must be worked slowly in the quiet waters of lakes and spring holes. Long ago I recognized that as a fallacy because when I studied the mayfly nymphs I found they weren't the slow moving creatures that many suspected. I learned that some could swim almost as fast as minnows in quiet waters, and that others darted and dashed like bucking broncos. These darters can never be captured with your hands.

Now I know that the caddis fly can also be worked quite fast in waters which have no perceptible current, and still expect discriminating trout to hit my offerings. In so doing I am but simulating the living flies that go underwater just as frequently in spring holes, ponds, lakes, slow pools and quiet reaches, as in the faster waters of a stream.

I have not yet succeeded in finding fly tying material that will exactly imitate the bubble of a wet-dry fly. I just cannot seem to create perfectly that quicksilver effect, that airy, shiny envelope of air around its body and wings which I see so plainly in the living, swimming insect as it works its way to the bottom. Sometimes I get so frustrated thinking about it that I feel like smashing a thermometer in the hope of fastening a drop of its mercury to the body of one of the flies I am tieing. But how do you wrap an elusive ball of quicksilver around a batch of fur and feather?

Certain wet flies can be altered so they resemble the living wet-dry flies for a cast or two. Also, such shiny-bodied standard patterns as the Orange, Greenwell's Glory, Alexandra, Wickham's Fancy, Slim Jim, and, of course, the Gold Ribbed Hare's Ear will catch fish if properly presented. All gold or silver tinsel bodied flies show a constant flash to the fish, and those in the tackle shops will prove fish getters when fished upstream. Most any fly tied with a gold or silver ribbed muskrat belly is worth trying. The March Brown is a good example, and is taken for a caddis, I believe.

One of my favorite wet-dry flies is one that I tie for dry fly purposes. It effectively imitates the mayfly *Baetis* which climbs down underwater to deposit eggs. I call it the Orange Body Bivisible, although one of my friends caught so many trout with it that he flattered me by naming it the Sid Gordon in a *Sports Afield* magazine article. As for the fish-getting qualities I offer no protest. As for the name my friend gave it, I cannot say as much.

Now I'm going to turn the tables on my fly christening friend by naming one of my wet-dry fly patterns after him. It is the pattern which is the nearest imitation I have achieved to the living underwater caddis.

More than once I have had the urge to dunk my friend underwater in the same manner that I dunk the fly that henceforth will bear his name, because he's the editor and fisherman who talked me into writing this book and who hounded me for 15 years until I finally finished it. His home is in Superior, Wisconsin, and he's with *The Duluth Tribune*, but if there's a hatch on, you'll find him on the Brule River, somewhere around the bridge where I first noticed the silvery bubble of the wet-dry fly. His name is Seegar Swanson, and from now on that's also the name of my new wet-dry fly pattern.

The Seegar Swanson wet-dry fly very plausibly gives the effect of the shining bubble of the underwater caddis. It is tied with a fat silver body, which shows through the wings at every turn of the fly in the water. This pattern may not look like much in the illustration shown here, but tie one on a leader and dunk it in the stream or the bath tub. If the "gleam" doesn't surprise you, I shall indeed be disappointed. Figure 94.

The same goes for the other wet-dry flies I have created and illustrate here. These patterns are good for only a dozen or two trout. By then the sharp teeth of the fish will have cut the wings and it becomes necessary to sit down and tie some more.

While I cannot achieve the silvery case of the diving caddis fly, I get the flash effect with three openings of the body showing the bright silver tinsel. The trout hit this faster and harder than they do my ordinary wet flies.

Some day, someone will beat my patterns all hollow. I hope to be the first to pin a medal on whoever finally achieves that outer coating of quicksilver that I so far have been unable to simulate.

THE STAGES OF THE CADDIS

1. The Egg.
2. The larvae (nymph).
3. The house builder, *Eruciform*, "Tight" living.
4. The tunnel builder, *Thysanuriform*, "Loose" living.
5. The pupal house which all must build to pupate, like the butterfly, before coming up to hatch.
6. Biting their way out of the house, then swimming up from the bottom with only their head and legs free, body still encased in the pupal shuck.
7. The caddis fly hatched, dry fly.

8. The caddis with the silver bubble.
9. The caddis drowned.

THE IMITATIONS THE FLY TYER USES
1. The brownish green and green "fantail" nymph, *Thysanuriform*.
2. The house with the worm inside. Paul Young's Strawman.
3. The coming up to hatch nymph, still in the pupal shuck, quill body.
4. The dry fly caddis.
5. The wet dry caddis, underwater egg layer.
6. The spent caddis drowned, wet fly.

(For the dressings of these flies turn to the fly tying chapters.)

WATER AND FLY FISHING

I fear, respect and admire water. When I see the harm it can do in dangerous flood stages, carrying people, homes and the strongest dams and bridges before it, I realize how terribly helpless one small human being like myself can become in it. Fearing its power, I respect it.

As a fisherman, I think only of the pleasure to be had from it. The lakes when seen from the air, seem like jewels in their beautiful forest setting, and there is no song so sweet, no murmur so soothing to me as the song of a fishable river.

In long association with a good friend, we minimize his faults. Just so does a river make you forget the hardships—only pleasant memories seem able to be recalled.

Worm fishing, minnow fishing or bait casting on a river will not bring you these unforgettable moments. Only fly fishing will cause you really to study ALL the water. Possibly because we search the waters so carefully with the fly, do we become so intimate with the river. Or it may be that casting the fly consists of gentle motions, easy graceful movements, quiet, slow moving steps combined with placing that delicate fly so lightly upon the water that it lands as softly as a wind blown leaf.

In a stream one forgets the grief of last week, the daily hardships, the cruelties of life and finds such peace that it is a thing of wonderment.

Only the quiet fly fisher sees the mother duck with her fluffy offspring, the doe and her fawn wading at the bend, the partridge and the squirrel. All wild things are seen by him as his eyes search the waters for movement of fish and current.

The shot gun and the rifle are discarded by the hunter as he grows old. Somehow the desire to kill is taken from him by nature herself, but the fly rod is discarded only when we get so feeble that we can no longer go upon the waters.

208

I know of no finer, cleaner sport than that of fly fishing. It not only makes a fisherman of a young man, but it teaches him more about the woods and waters than any sport of which I know.

It doesn't make a sissy of him, for he must be able to "take" it, good weather or bad, excellent luck or the opposite. Every young man needs two things, fighting ability and persistence. Fly fishing gives him both.

Along with it comes an appreciation of the finer things of life, a little of art, a little of courtesy to others, a love and understanding of the ways of nature, all things which he may not be able to put into spoken words, but which last much longer than wealth or power.

Fly fishing will give your boy all of this. Doesn't it warrant the investment of a rod, a reel, a line and other small necessary things which need not mount into any great sum?

There is no true companionship with your son to be had in any other sport such as may be had when you are together on a river. The simple little meal which he cooks of fish and bacon, fried potatoes, the days of good fishing, the day you saw the deer or even the partridge. All these and many, many things which you forget are taken out and rolled around in his memories of you, long after you have left him.

CHAPTER XIII

Brooks, Browns, and Rainbows Are a Challenge

TROUT FISHING as I knew it in my boyhood days back in the 1890s is gone and can never return. This may sound like the usual talk of every old timer since the days of the caveman, but I assure you that it is true.

There is hardly any need for me to amplify the causes of our changed trout fishing. Why wail about the timber which was cut, the fires which burned off the countryside, or the beaver dams which warmed up the waters and are still killing off our trout? Why bemoan the millions of autos which bring hordes of anglers to the streams of today where only hundreds came with horse and buggy in days gone by?

With today's shorter work week, prolonged vacations, long holiday weekends and fast transportation by land or air, even a child can see why our streams are under tremendous fishing pressure. How can we expect trout to abound in their previous great numbers when they are relentlessly sought with angleworms, minnows, salmon eggs, spinning and casting lures, and flies of every description?

And then there is the problem of erosion, aggravated by our spring breakups and heavy floods. What terrific destruction the unimpeded waters cause to the spawning beds and trout holes! Figure 70. Our best hope here is the installation of adequate stream improvement devices to restore the gravel beds and cover, along with streamside planting to shade our waters.

Why then, the beginning angler might well ask, should he consider taking up trout fishing at all? He might even tell me that in this book I have given him the impression that one merely has to learn the technique of casting, then, with the right equipment he can go out and fill his creel.

With all the fishing pressure we have today, it is not feasible to guarantee the trout fisherman a full creel, but that isn't saying that the quest for trout has lost its fascination. If anything, it now requires more knowledge of the waters and the behavior of the fish than ever before, and therein lies its impelling incentive.

Trout fishing, in my opinion, is not for the indiscriminate angler. It is for those who do not expect to dunk just anything in the water and have a fish impale itself upon his hook. Today we may fish for two hours without as much as a strike, and sometimes we work a stream all day and catch but one fish. Yet we go back, time after time, if for no other reason than to live over the conquests of the past, and hoping against hope that history will repeat.

Today the thinking sportsman puts most of the trout he catches back into the stream. With an eye to preserving this great pastime for many years to come, he fishes mainly for the thrill of outwitting and outplaying the extremely wary trout.

It may well be that in our understanding of the trout we may even be tempted, now and then, to regard them as friends instead of foes. Why not? We enjoy our friends who give us good competition at bridge, archery or golf, do we not?

Fig. 70.—Eroded stream banks are responsible for the covering of gravel bottoms which the trout must have to deposit their eggs. Stream improvement corrects this. See Chapter 22.

The Brook Trout
Salvelinus fontinalis

To one who has fished the brook trout for more than 60 years it is difficult to give an unbiased comparison of brook, brown and rainbow trout. They all belong to the same family, Salmonidae, the salmon and trout family.

It was the brook trout which taught me to appreciate their wilderness surroundings, for they lived among the deer, ducks and the partridge. The finest trees which grow upon this earth, the white pine, shaded their homes in the clear cold waters of the north, and the clean gravel of the streams brought forth thousands of their natural offspring each season.

They taught us not only to respect them for their fighting spirit but to love them for their grace and beauty as well. Few of us in the '90s thought there ever would be a dwindling of their numbers.

Their eagerness to take the angleworm of the lad, the minnow of the grown fisherman and the flies of the few who fished with the wet fly brought thrills to every angler. No fish is as firm-fleshed nor as handsome as the brook trout, and no fish is better eating because he will thrive only in waters below 70 degrees.

Medium to *hard* water lakes and streams seem to have more parasites than those of *very soft* and *soft water*. It may well be that the acid waters help maintain the trout and thus offset the handicap of less food per acre. This is merely a guess upon my part. Only a qualitative and quantitative analysis of our waters will solve this.

The brook trout is the most timid trout of all, but give him a few moments to recover from his fright and he will take a fly quickly. You can take more brook trout out of a single hole or one stretch of water than you can rainbows or browns. While a rainbow has the same short memory of the brook, a frightened brown stays down for a longer time.

For ease of catching, I rank the brook trout first, the rainbow second and the brown third. For this and other reasons brook trout are not nearly as plentiful in our streams as they once were.

The brook trout is not as heavily armored as the brown or rainbow. In fact, his scales are hardly noticeable. Although I have heard more than one angler declare he has no scales, they are there. I believe his tiny scales cause him to be more susceptible to parasites and injuries than the heavier scaled brown and rainbow, another factor which may well account for his decline.

213

The brook trout is much more of a home-body and a daytime feeder than either the brown or the rainbow. This is also hazardous to his welfare since many more fishermen are on the waters during his feeding hours than those of the night feeding brown and the day and night feeding rainbow.

While he doesn't often leap, he is a great tugger and a longer fighter, inch for inch, than any other trout of his family, *the Salmonidae*. He feeds extensively on nymphs, caddis houses and all other kinds of underwater food. Like all trout, he turns cannibalistic as he ages.

The brook trout does not eat as many insects as the brown because many of our greatest hatches of insects are at night. He does not feed heavily after 8 or 9 o'clock in the evening.

For "bright day, bright fly" and "dull day, dull fly" fishing, give me the brook trout. In my opinion, he has better vision than the rainbow and far keener eyesight than the brown. The brook trout does very little cruising, but he will follow my bright fly pattern all across the stream if I move it fast enough to keep it ahead of him. In fast water he follows a lure, but if he doesn't take it, soon turns to his home behind a rock or other cover.

When there is a rise of nymphs, the brook trout will assume one position in the water and cover his little field, taking nymph after nymph. I have often taken and released 50 brook trout by standing in just one spot in a good springhole, not stirring from my position, but merely extending the line at each cast.

It is absurd to say the brook trout is not a dry fly trout. If there is a good hatch of flies he will take your dry fly with a happy little turn of his body and a twist of his tail. I'm positive he has a smile on his face as he goes for the fly, for I have seen it hundreds of times.

Of all the trout, the brook is quickest to change colors. Place him over a gravel bed and he assumes a pale hue in a very short time. Let him move to a silt bed, and the black earth is soon reflected in his dark belly, darker sides and upper body. It is then that the extreme brightness of his beautiful red and white fins is accentuated. How, beautifully he harmonizes with the brilliantly colored wood duck in the hollow tree above his home!

Have you ever caught brook trout whose flesh is a rich red and wondered why? I believe that some ultra nutritious quality in the food they eat causes this. My observations have indicated that the red-meated brook trout feeds heavily on those

214

plump shrimps and large mayfly nymphs that thrive in the silt beds. As for the lighter colored brook trout, they feed on the smaller food in and on the gravel, which in my opinion gives their meat a pinkish tint.

There is now a growing tendency to plant fewer hatchery brook trout, and to place emphasis on the browns and rainbows. Good fishery management can bring back thousands of brook trout for the angler of today if more of them are planted in the clear cold waters, rainbows are reserved for the fast as well as the warmer waters, and the browns are planted in the warmer but quieter waters. Most assuredly the temperature should be taken only during the hottest months in order to judge the suitable water.

THE BROWN TROUT
Salmo trutta fario

There can be no general rules to follow when we fish for the brown trout, because he refuses to be classified. The nearest we can come to a fair understanding of how to fish for him is to study each pond, lake or stream and plan our strategy for that particular water.

Having had only a quarter of a century of experience with the brown trout, but over 60 years with the brook and rainbow, I must confess the brown is a much more difficult fish for me to fool than either of the others.

While the British have fished for this trout for centuries, the brown trout did not get general distribution in the United States until the early 1930's. That explains why I did not have the pleasure of meeting up with him any sooner in my home waters.

How often we read about or hear some authority insist that the brown trout is primarily an insect eater, a surface feeder, a grand trout for the dry fly angler. It is true he is a surface feeder, but after you examine dozens of brown trout stomachs you soon learn he has other eating traits, and that you must take into consideration the entire content of his stomach to know the full truth of the eating habits of this fish.

After 4 o'clock in the afternoon, when you take a brown on a little Cahill dry fly, you find on opening his stomach that there are many winged mayflies there. The later you take him, if there is a good hatch of insects on the water, the more winged flies you will find. This definitely proves he is a surface feeder.

Suppose, however, that it is 10 o'clock in the morning and no insects are hatching. You tie a Leadwing Coachman to your

215

Fig. 71.—Alan Miller took this brown trout from a *hard* water stream, the Wolf River in Wisconsin. The plentiful supply of fish food in this limestone river shows in the small head and nicely proportioned body.

Alan informs me that the trout were so plentiful there that they grow on trees. He offers this photograph to prove his statement. As pictures and fishermen always tell the truth, I shall get out my lariat, ten gallon hat, cowboy boots and saddle my paint horse and rope a few.

216

leader and let the fly drift down in a natural manner before the nose of a brown which you feel might be there. He hits, and after a nice play, you net him. When you examine his stomach you will find a number of snails and finger-nail clams, as well as several caddis houses. A friend of mine, Lyman Williamson, once found 72 tiny snails and clams in just one brown trout's stomach.

Surely, then, you are justified in saying that the brown trout is a bottom feeder *and* a surface feeder as well.

But there are other traits which the brown trout will show. Nor can these be dismissed with a wave of the hand if you are to get the most out of your fishing.

Let us say it is now 11 o'clock in the morning. You are fishing diligently with your wet fly when you notice a mayfly appear on the water. Observing swirls and little boil-like rises on the surface, you know the trout are feeding upon something under the surface. There is no question in your mind that this is a sure sign that nymphs are coming up to hatch into dry flies. You note that trout are feeding heavily underwater on these rising nymphs. Judging from the newly hatched floating fly, you figure the nymphs to be about the size of a No. 10 hook. You cut your wet fly off the leader and tie on a size 10 mayfly nymph.

Working the water nearest you very carefully, you drop your nymph fly just above each break of the surface and take a trout or two. If the hatch lasts a half hour you may get your limit right there—if sufficient brown trout are feeding. The hatch over, you take time out to investigate the stomachs of the fish.

In the stomach of the first brown you caught here you will find only a few nymphs. You will find dozens of them in the stomach of the last trout you took. The conclusion is obvious— give a trout a half hour to feed upon rising nymphs and you'll find his stomach literally crammed with them.

Surely, then, we are not at all out of order when we say flatly that a brown trout is a surface feeder, a bottom feeder and also a midwater feeder.

And last, but not least, who is there who hasn't taken a large brown—16 inches or over—and found another trout in its stomach? I once removed four six-inch rainbows from one brown's stomach, and you will certainly do the same someday. What better proof need there be that the brown trout is also a cannibal trout along with his other "top to bottom" feeding habits?

So now, I hope I have clearly shown why Mr. Brown cannot be limited to any one classification if you wish to be an all around brown trout fisherman. This means, then, that we must turn to the water for our pattern of fly fishing for this trout. That is because only the water will enable you to judge the feeding habits of the brown at any given time.

After 25 years of brown trout fishing I cannot help but feel that he is a near sighted fish. His eyes resemble the large eyes of a walleyed pike which will not go a long way for a fly, plug or minnow because he cannot see at a distance. Neither will the brown.

We may think the brown is a lazier fish than either the brook or the rainbow, but I believe that this is only partly true. He is a cannier fish than either of the others and does not foolishly dash out from his home to hit some small gnat, midge or tiny dry fly which offers little food.

When the small gnats, midges and mayflies are in large number, then he takes up a position and feeds where the most food comes to him in one small channel. With his nose right near the surface he feeds steadily upon the one species that is in abundance. He is hard to take then, for our best imitations are so often ignored.

As evening comes on, the brown can often be caught close up against the bank, often with a wet fly cast upstream or up and across. Also, during the late afternoon and evening, browns seem to venture out of the deeper waters and feed in the shallows where they are quite eager to accept your fly, whether wet or dry. It is surprising how often you can drop a fly in water so shallow that many fishermen pass it up and find a good sized brown taking it.

It is, of course, impossible for a brown to fool a fisherman when he sees him feeding upon the surface or feeding fast just under the surface. We can be positive he is taking flies off the top of the water or eating nymphs just under.

Here we can classify him, but the hours of visible feeding are scant compared with his long hours of invisible feeding. This is because an entire day or half a day will pass without a rise of nymphs or a hatch of flies to cause him to come up for his feeding.

Although a brown trout can make his home in a stream whose waters are warmed considerably by beaver dams holding back the water of cold feeder streams, this adds to our problem. No fish feeds heavily in very cold waters, neither do they in water that is too warm. For this reason the brown trout in a fairly warm water stream does not begin his heavy feeding until the sun's rays no longer strike the water, except on a slant. Every hour after 4 o'clock in the afternoon finds the sun losing more and more of its direct heat on the water. At twilight the brown is quite hungry. Every hour after twilight he feeds heavier and continues until his stomach is crammed. Sometimes he feeds until 2 o'clock in the morning, for the cool nights chill the waters and his appetite increases accordingly. It is usually after 8 o'clock in the evening until 1 or 2 o'clock in the morning that we catch the big trout that gets mounted for the plaque in the den or dining room.

Since most anglers care little about fly fishing after the first hour of darkness, they are concerned mostly with the daytime brown. It is here that they must study every bit of water and use all their knowledge of current, correct drift of the fly, accurate casting and stealth in their approach to the home of every brown trout. Knowing this, I have turned many an otherwise blank day into a day of success.

The Rainbow Trout (Steelhead, Kamloops)
Salmo gairdnerii irideus

The rainbow is without a doubt the quickest thinker and the fastest actor of all trout. His speed in responding to the feel of a hook is something at which one marvels.

The rainbow is noted for his fighting qualities and his penchant for leaping out of the water once he is hooked. When he leaps I call him a "skyline" fish.

In mixed water which harbors brooks, browns and rainbows, the angler is always at a disadvantage when the rainbow hits. He never seems to be quite "on his toes" in fishing this kind of stream, for he isn't immediately sure whether he has a brook, brown or rainbow on the line. In working water which he knows harbors nothing but rainbow trout, he intuitively sets the hook quickly, but plays the fish from the reel the instant he strikes. This is because his reflexes are set for this fast fish, and he does not bring his rod up and attempt to snub him as he does with brook or brown trout.

Often the big rainbow tears the hook from his mouth or breaks the leader and is gone before the fisherman thinks to give him added line immediately following that instantaneous setting of the hook in the rainbow's mouth. Rushing tactics will never do, for you simply dare not "horse him in" as you can with a brook or brown trout.

In a stream where natural spawning conditions are so good that rainbows come along well in the one, two and three year old class, what a thrill the small rainbows give us.

The moment they feel the barb of your fly, they are out of the water and back into it so fast that you never get over the excitement those little eight to 12 inchers can give you. Every second they are on there is a great admiration within you for their wonderful fighting qualities.

When their parents, from a pound and a half to six pounds or more, hit your fly, they give you no time to plan. These speedy swimmers, tuggers and great jumpers are fought more by instinct than by plan. They bring forth every bit of strategy you have learned in all your fishing, for there is nothing automatic about them.

You try to react to their every move, playing them from the reel on that first mad rush, then lowering the rod tip here, raising it there, wondering when and if you'll ever begin to get control. The busy bee is a giant sloth compared with you at that time.

When you are forced to give him line off the reel, or lose him, until your first opportunity comes where you can turn him safely to fight in your direction, you feel that there might be a chance to land him. The battle turns in his favor, then yours, then his. When you finally have succeeded in tiring him so that he can be led to the net or beached, there comes a feeling of exultation that only a fisherman can appreciate.

Call him what you will—rainbow, steelhead or Kamloops—he is one and the same fish, regardless where you find him. He is a grand fish, for he will take most any fly you offer if it comes to him in the right manner.

Only in the catching of him can the beginner learn how to play and land him. In the stillest water, he will learn to set the hook firmly. Here a tightened line does the business.

In fast water, 9 times out of 10 the rainbow will hook himself. The reel is regulated a little tighter than for brook and brown trout because the rainbow must be allowed to take line off the reel after the strike. Then the rod is swung up so that the thumb on the butt is pointing straight at the sky, or in an arc over the water, which will give the fish the same tension as if the rod were held at or over the shoulder.

The angler makes a serious error if he points the rod tip

at the rushing rainbow without allowing the line to slide easily through the first two fingers of the rod hand, between the cork handle and the fingers. After that first, fast, desperate run, the fisherman must cramp his fingers against the outgoing line and control him with an arched rod and short strips of the line with the left hand, behind the rod hand. He gives the rainbow more line only when the pressure becomes too great. This can be learned only in the fishing.

In fast, heavy water I have had rainbows take out 300 feet of line so quickly that their first hard run amazed me. When fishing waters like that there should be at least 300 feet of braided 12 pound test nylon spliced to the fly line. Many a big rainbow or steelhead will take out 150 feet before one dares do any snubbing. Even then the leader is sometimes broken when there is nothing left on the reel but the knotted end of the running line, or backing line as some term it.

In our Lake Superior waters we have large brook trout known as "cruisers". They range along the lakeshore until August and September and then go up the streams to spawn. Brown trout have this habit, too. But the brook and brown trout are not nearly as great in numbers as the "sea run" rainbows.

These rainbows are generally called steelheads. They spawn in the streams from February to May, although some go up river all through the summer and fall, sight-seers, I presume. In our inland streams as soon as the large rainbows have spawned in the upstream gravel beds, they work downstream to the nearest big water they can find. It may be a small lake, a mill-pond or a wide water in a stream. Here we call them rainbows, not steelheads.

After the rainbow eggs are hatched, instinct seems to tell the fry to remain in their home stream until they are large enough to withstand the hazards of the big water. Almost invariably, at the end of their third year, they leave the home stream and return each year for spawning, just as do their relatives of the coastal streams from British Columbia to California. They are then called steelheads. In our Lake Superior and Lake Michigan waters, steelheads cruise up the rivers for awhile in the fall but spend the winters in the big lakes.

Our creeks—small streams 10 to 30 feet in width—are no criterion for judging the big rainbow or steelhead. He either smashes our leaders, breaks our rod tips or gets away somehow unless we use rods that are very heavy, lines which would hold a muskie and are rigged with large hooks, spinners, worms or salmon eggs.

The most exciting rainbow fishing I have experienced has been in the Soo Rapids at Sault Ste. Marie, Mich., and over on the Canadian side, too.

When the International Bridge between the United States and Canada has several of its 16 gates open, the Soo Rapids are faster than any on the Rogue River in Oregon. The water here is colder in July and August than any waters I found in the Rogue, Klamath, Umpqua, Russian or Eel rivers of the West Coast. These hardy rainbows in the Soo Rapids are just as fast as their parent stock which came to us in 1890 from those Western streams that empty into the Pacific Ocean.

Here, as in the large Western streams of British Columbia, Washington, Oregon and California, a long line must be cast. Sixty feet at the least, and 90 feet is better, is needed for the rainbows which lie near the bottom or in midwater. At the Soo the bottom is strewn with rubble stones and great boulders two to five or more feet in height. The fly must be tied to ride deeply. One can look at the always crystal clear water, calmed and shaded by his canoe, and see trout lying at the bottom as serenely as if they were in a quiet inland stream. There is little sign of the fast, rushing rapids down there, for the boulders take the thrust of the water and tame it at the bottom.

Rainbow, steelhead or Kamloops, he's a noble fish for any angler.

Now that the beginning angler has read about the characteristics of the Brook, Brown and Rainbow trout, let him take courage in his fishing by examining the stomachs of the trout he catches. If he will scan the stomach contents of the three species I took on the same day in Wisconsin's Thunder River, he will see what a varied appetite they have. It will also show that not one of the flies I used, and which over 15 trout hit that day, was in the stomachs of any of the three trout I killed for examination:

BROOK TROUT STOMACH CONTENT

3 medium size stone flies, *Perla*.
18 gnats, two paired, mating.
3 ants.
3 caddis cases, *Brachycentrus*.
4 loose caddis nymphs, *Thysanuriform*.
8 large midge flies.
3 mayfly nymphs, *Heptagenia*.
Caught on an Orange body dry fly fished wet. Size 10 hook.

222

BROWN TROUT STOMACH CONTENT

8 caddis houses, *Brachycentrus*.
2 flying ants.
12 mayflies, mostly wing expanse of 30 mm. Some larger, some smaller.
5 small, thin, round caddis houses, *Granonema*.
10 gnats.
5 mayfly nymphs, *Heptagenia*.
1 large stone fly nymph, *Pteronarcys*.
5 gnat larva, *Diptera*.
Caught on Orange body dry fly. Fished dry. Size 14 hook.

RAINBOW TROUT STOMACH CONTENT

62 black gnats, *Diptera*, size of a 20 hook.
5 medium size mayflies.
3 small snails, *Physa*.
5 caddis nymphs, *Thysanuriform*.
4 caddis houses, *Rhyacophila*.

Caught on Giant Mayfly nymph size 6 hook.

The brown trout in Figure 71 had three chubs and two trout, three to five inches in its stomach. It was caught on a Veltic Spinner.

CHAPTER XIV

The Bass Is a Worthy Foe--
Panfish Are Fun

EVERY ONCE IN AWHILE I feel as if I have butted my head against a stone wall after getting myself involved in a futile argument over which has the greater qualities, the bass or the trout.

How can anyone compare bass with trout? You might as well collate a blonde with a red head or a brunette. Why, I can remember when—Here! Here! We are discussing fishing!

No angler, whether he is addicted to the fly rod, plug rod or spinning rod, fishes for the large- or smallmouth bass without a glow of anticipation. He knows he is about to meet a valiant adversary, one for which no defense is needed. The bass will offer his own defense when he hits or refuses your lure.

When the angler sets forth in quest of bass, he calls upon all his knowledge of water, whether in lake or stream, and he pays extra heed to current when he is angling for bass in a stream.

The black bass is a favorite of thousands of fishermen from Canada to Florida, from the East Coast to the West. Here we have a fish that can inhabit water too warm for trout, yet makes every foot of that warmer water a compelling incentive for the angler who wants real action.

I have cut open the stomachs of too many bass not to recognize that they are primarily fish eaters, although they also eat nymphs rising to hatch and insects within easy reach. Whether we fish bass from a canoe, a boat, or while wading, their zest for food causes them to hit almost any plug, spinning lure or fly and spinner, if presented in the proper manner.

But when I am on a stream in a boat or canoe I care not for a fast excursion ride. What good does it do to cast the lure or

225

fly ahead of me only to have the boat or canoe pass the lure or fly before it has a chance to work the water?

Our northern smallmouth bass has special appeal to the fly rod enthusiast. It responds to the fly far more readily than the largemouth bass. In the fairly cold streams of *clear* water, the smallmouth can be counted upon to put up a terrific fight on a light leader of six pound test and a level or tapered line with a fly from size 6 to 4.

When fly casting for bass in a stream, I prefer to wade. I know from experience I cannot work my fly or lure as fast for a bass as I do for a muskie. Only by wading do I feel I can take full advantage of the natural action of the current with my fly. Because I need accuracy in casting to derive the full benefit of this current action, I do not care to burden my fly with the heavy weight of a spinner.

I realize, of course, that a spinner provides flash to draw the attention of the bass, but back in the early '40s I solved that problem by creating a fly with flash. I achieve that flash by ribbing my fly with wide, embossed silver tinsel. Its yellow body with an overlay of black bear hair and white polar bear hair adds to its effectiveness in attracting smallmouths. I give a detailed description of this fly in the chapter on fly tieing.

I named my bass fly the General Immell in honor of General Ralph M. Immell, who served so ably as Director of the Wisconsin Conservation Department during the years 1932 to 1937. In my opinion, the fly is appropriately named, because like the General, it gets results, It was he who reorganized the fisheries, forestry, game and forest protection division of the Conservation Department in 1932, and who instituted lake and stream improvement and inaugurated many policies that have enabled the Department to earn the wide prestige it now enjoys.

I have caught many smallmouth bass with the General Immell fly on such renowned streams as the St. Croix and the Namekagon in Wisconsin and the Escanaba River in the Upper Peninsula of Michigan. It will consistently take smallmouths in the Ozarks, and in any other stream which harbors this wonderful fish. Figure 72.

I prefer a size 4 hook, regular, but not one with a long shank. A heavier hook and a larger fly will not allow me to get the accuracy I must have to cast it under branches hanging over the stream. A smaller fly is not good either because in a stream with good current it will not go down under as well as a size 4. This is because current a foot or two under the slower

226

Fig. 72.—A Small Mouth Bass Stream.

Wisconsin's famous St. Croix River near Solon Springs. A hard water stream that empties into the Mississippi. Here, the author wades and fishes with the casting rod, but uses the fly rod in the more narrow reaches.

water film is faster than it is near the bottom, with the result the smaller fly would ride too near the water film.

It has been my observation that 9 out of 10 fishermen do not pay enough attention to current when fishing a bass stream. They get fewer strikes and catch less bass when they do not allow the natural action of their fly to conform to the feeding habits of the smallmouth bass.

In a river the bass know the natural drift, the speed of the objects coming to them, within a moment or two after they pick the spot where they station themselves. Although they leave this place to chase minnows, they do very little chasing for water-bred flies. Only when the flies come near them, dropping their eggs or preparing to fly off the water, do the bass make

227

any effort to take them. Also, when nymphs are coming up from the bottom to hatch into flies, the bass eat quantities of them, but not quite as leisurely as when they reach for flies coming toward them with the natural drift of the current.

I cannot emphasize too strongly that the beginner must make it a point to observe the action his fly gets from the current if he hopes to become expert in tempting smallmouths to strike. After just one half hour of such observation he will be convinced that it is up and across stream casting that enables the current to carry his fly toward a bass in the same natural drift that most food comes to him.

When fly fishing for bass I wade upstream, just as I do most of the time when fishing for trout. In this manner I can easily cast my General Immel fly up and across.

Some streams, however, are so wide and their current is so swift that upstream wading becomes too difficult. In such situations I wade downstream but continue to cast across and upstream.

Suppose we are on Wisconsin's St. Croix River, in an area where it is about 100 feet wide. Here the current is so strong that it is more comfortable to wade downstream. We note alders growing on the bank and decide that there is good cover for bass. We therefore wade out to the middle of the stream, about 50 feet, face upstream and now are in position to cast the General Immell up and across.

The alders on the bank are now 50 feet from me and about 10 feet above my position. But I have no intention of reaching out for those alders yet. I see a little disturbance in the current about 25 feet from shore, caused by some obstruction or lift of the stream bed, and conclude a bass must be there. He might be looking for crayfish which always frequent an underwater shelf.

One quick glance tells me that my fly, tied to a six foot, 6 pound test nylon leader, will require a drift of five feet before it can pass through the water film and be carried to the bass down and along the water by the faster current below the film.

Since I must allow room for my line and leader to straighten out on the water, I cast about 10 feet above the obstruction. Only then can the fly be carried down and along the current. By the time the current action has allowed the General Immell to assume the natural drift of an insect, I have the rod tip over the water, the slack line gathered in, and am ready to set the hook at the first touch of the fish.

228

If there is no drag caused by the line and leader, the fly goes almost into the mouth of the bass. How naturally he opens his mouth to test whether the fly is edible. A smooth turn of the wrist sets the hook and the thrilling play of a fighting smallmouth is experienced.

There is another likely looking spot nearer shore, but I figure it is too close to the alders where I feel sure the biggest bass of this stretch of water should be making his home. I do not want a smaller fish to run in there during the fight and play to disturb the potential big fellow, so I pass him up.

I wade about 10 feet closer to the alders, for I now want to be assured of greater accuracy by using 40 feet of line and leader instead of 50. Making the usual allowance for the current there, I drop my fly on the water about 10 feet above the alders so it will have the natural drift of all food coming down to that big bass.

Having caught the big bass, let's now wade back to the middle of the stream, wade down about 25 feet and fish some new water upstream and across. And when this new water is fished, let's go further downstream for more new water. Success is bound to be repeated if we continue to delude the bass into mistaking our flies for natural food drifting down with the current.

When a smallmouth hits, is netted and released, I do not pride myself upon my casting with the good rod and line, nor the painstaking job I did in tieing my General Immell fly. I do take immense satisfaction, though, in the fact that I judged that current correctly and handled it the way the river and the habits of the bass have taught me.

Whenever I find myself gloating over my fishing ability, something inside of me says, "You poor dumb cluck! The current was always there, the bass were there long before you came upon this earth. Why did it take so many years for you to figure out the obvious?"

Somewhat deflated, I go along with the "expert" casting. I think of how I used to fish rivers like the St. Croix or those of the Ozarks in a canoe or a boat. I would cast "clean across the crick" or 50 feet ahead of me. What a nice long line I could throw! The miles I used to cover! But I'd get only one bass where now I get at least five.

I vividly recall how the current would carry the boat so fast that I'd be on top of the fish before the fly had any chance for a natural drift. The bass, of course, would be frightened

Fig. 73.—The St. Croix, after junction with the Namekagon above Riverside becomes wider. The Namekagon, a delightful smallmouth stream, offers many miles of excellent fishing above the junction with the St. Croix.

and would vanish. In a matter of seconds the line would be dragging way behind the boat with nary a bass within reach of the fly.

When I finally learned about current, I would drop the anchor away from those spots where I knew the fish would be, turn and throw my fly where it should go. Better yet, if the water were not too deep, I'd pull the boat on shore and wade out to the right position.

In a lake the problem of fishing bass changes, but we can readily adapt ourselves to the conditions. While the bass in a river strikes according to the current, this obviously is not true in a lake because there is no current unless we are fishing near an inlet or outlet.

Whether we are using a fly rod, plug rod or spinning rod in a lake, there is one important thing to remember about bass, both largemouth or smallmouth. It is the movement of the fly or lure that attracts them. You, the fisherman, must create that movement, for here you have no current to do that work for you. Stops and starts often bring hard strikes.

Lakes are likely to contain both smallmouth and largemouth bass. This is true of some streams, too, but the largemouth inhabits more sluggish river waters than the smallmouth.

I do not like to compare the fighting qualities of the two. This much I will say, though. The largemouth is not the trim,

230

fast fish that the smallmouth is. A bass that is forced to buck current all the time he is waiting for food to drift towards him inevitably acquires a strength and power that a bass in still waters doesn't have.

The largemouth bass of a lake is more sluggish in coming after small objects. He prefers larger morsels, so it is best to have larger lures for him than for the smallmouth. But once the largemouth strikes, he puts up just as good a fight as any other game fish in the lake. Considering the difference in weight, the largemouth outclasses the muskie, northern pike or wall-eyed pike when it comes to the struggle he can give the angler.

In lakes with lily pads, largemouth bass will often lie under the pads to feed on insects lighting upon the broad leaves and the damsel flies which go beneath the surface to deposit their eggs in plant stems.

Some insects use the underside of the pads to plaster eggs there. When these eggs hatch into larvae, they drop into the

Fig. 74.—The Element of Surprise.

When the boat is placed at U and the fly or lure is dropped alongside a bed of lily pads or weeds, large fish are surprised into striking from their cover. The first cast is made at number 1, then 2, then 3 and so on.

When the boat is at Z, it is much easier to cast the lure but you will have a following fish. A smart old fish will dash towards the lure but, as you bring it away from cover, towards the boat, in open water, he sees that it is a fraud and turns away. Bass, northerns and muskies have this habit, but the muskie has it to the nth degree.

231

water. Bass collect the larvae as food, even during the brightest days.

Some underwater insects actually cut a piece out of a lily pad, place their eggs on the hinged leaf and seal it. Then the larva bites its way out of the sealed, hinged leaf and completes its growth on the bottom of the lake.

What angler hasn't seen bass smack at the dragon flies, damsel flies and crane flies hovering over the lily pads?

Since the dragon fly is a faster flier than most birds, the bass must take him quickly or not at all. The damsel fly is a slow flier, bobbing around the pads before it makes a landing to crawl down a plant stem underwater to deposit her eggs. In its mating, if the day is at all windy, the male flies at the female and his weight, plus the wind, forces her into the water. Bass gather a harvest of these long insects when this occurs.

But it is the crane fly which affords me an opportunity to get the bass fighting mad. I tick the water again and again with my fly, perfectly imitating the behavior of the living, slow-flying crane fly. You've seen them dance in the air about two feet above the water, dipping down to the water repeatedly in practically the same spot. Their extremely long legs dangle like a "daddy long legs" spider with wings. I have counted as high as 23 such dips to the surface. It's just their after-end that touches the water, and every once in awhile you see a bass or trout smash at one.

The Slim Jim is a perfect imitation of the crane fly. If a bass makes a smash at the Slim Jim as I tick the water, I pull it away from him and continue ticking. Then, when I figure I have him so furious that I can almost understand what he is calling my Slim Jim, I drop it on the water. The rush with which he takes it, the feel of the hook and the intense play he gives me is really something.

Often I stand on a high bank to tease the bass in this manner. That gives me even more of a struggle when I finally let him take the fly. I grin to myself as I release him with the thought that he'll not touch another "dancer" for a week.

If you are familiar with the usual kinds of fly casts—the wet, dry, wind and roll—it takes but another 10 minutes to master this tick cast. It is merely a ticking of the water and a return of the fly over and over. This, incidentally, is a good way to perfect the false cast needed for working the dry fly on a trout stream, for it teaches perfect control of the fly. I might

FIG. 75.—Good Bass Water.

Whether the bulrushes are hard stemmed *(Scirpus acutis)* or soft stemmed *(Scirpus validus)*, they harbor much food for fish. They slow the wave action, much as a forest breaks a breeze. This is ideal lake water for the fly fisherman with his slowly worked cork bass bug and a high, quick lift.

Whether the fisherman uses a fly rod, a spinning rod or a plug rod with pork chunk, he must move slowly and quietly to get as close to the fish as possible. Long casts are useless here to avoid getting hung up. Early morning and late afternoon and evening bring best results.

also add that ticking often catches trout, too, although not as often as the longer float of a dry fly.

Whether you are fishing for large- or smallmouth bass in a lake, your knowledge of the water tells you that in the early morning, late afternoon and the evening hours you will use a popping lure which creates good disturbance in the water. As the evening grows gradually darker, the darker should be the lure you use for the bass see it better against the sky.

In the bright daylight sun, of course, you will have to go deeper for the majority of bass. Again, almost any lure will do the business, but it must be at the right depth and within the vision of the fish. Most fishermen fish a bass bug, fly or lure too fast—easy does it.

When there is an onshore wind, the bass are just as smart as the walleyed pike in knowing there will be food washed along with the waves. Here, almost on the wave-swept shoreline, you can work your bass bugs and wet flies to good advantage, as well as your spinning lures. Figure 75.

PANFISH DELIGHT THE ANGLER

The scientists place all bass in the sunfish family, *Centrarchidae*, but when I want to fish for panfish, I ignore the bass and try for crappies, blue gills and sunfish. These provide much fun with the fly rod.

I am amused whenever I hear a fly fisherman say, "Panfish, I wouldn't waste my time with them." That may be all right with him, but rather than sit around the resort listening to disdainful anglers arguing the contention, I pick up my rod and go forth for sport with the panfish.

If I can't shake the Missus and little Willie, I rig up a canepole with a worm for the "terror" and Momma uses her 8 foot fly rod, a 7½ foot leader and some nymphs and wet flies, sizes 10 for the small sunfish and 8's for the crappies and blue gills.

While they are busy fishing off the dock, I wander away with my 9 foot rod, tapered line and 9 foot leader. What a relief! No boat to bother with and no one to hand worms or flies. Momma and Willie are on their own, and although I'll probably get lonesome way down shore, I shall just have to suffer.

I come to a point of land jutting out into the lake. The underwater shoreline drops rather sharply near the point, and I examine the water through my Polaroid glasses. Close inshore I see blue gills, but I know that the nearer the shore, the smaller they will be. Still, just for fun, I tie on a size 10 orange body dry fly, wet it in my mouth to make it sink quickly, then draw it through the school of small blue gills. Fishermen in the South call them "bream."

Everyone of them rushes at the fly, so conspicuous with its brown and cream game cock hackles and tail whisks of golden pheasant tippets. Then I take it away and do it over again. Meanwhile, my leader is getting the soaking it needs for effective casting.

But wait! What's this? A bullhead comes swimming along with her brood of young. This I've got to see.

Rolling along in a ball, those little black babies hold together in that sphere. They look much like a basketball rolling underwater. The blue gills gather around, but keep a respectful distance from mother bullhead. They know she has been taking toll of them since they were first hatched.

Now the situation changes. One bold blue gill eases towards the black rolling mass and the mother protectively rushes to attack him. She no sooner gets after the retreating blue gill before another on the opposite side of the ball dashes in and grabs a bullhead fry. There is a scramble as several more blue gills each seize a fry.

The rolling mass does not break up, however. The fry just form more compactly. The mother returns and makes a complete circle. She can't count, and as the attack is repeated over and over she fails to realize her ball of minnows is getting smaller and smaller until I wonder how she can have any left to grow to good size.

Just to teach those carnivorous blue gills a lesson, I tie on a smooth black body fly on a size 8 long shank hook with a small bunch of hackle at the eye. The blue gills hurry to hit this poor little orphan that mother bullhead apparently forgot. How they turn and tug when they realize their mistake. Then I release each fish as I catch him and repeat the action.

All this, of course, is good diversion while I am giving my leader more soaking. Just to see how the stock of young bass is coming on, I tie on a black gnat, size 14 hook, the body of moose hair and the hackle black, tied dry fly. I wet it with saliva and it sinks slowly as a blue gill rises to get it. On the outer circle of blue gills, a small bass which refused to look at the orange body fly has taken it away from the blue gill, leaving him to stare dumbfoundedly with his mouth wide open.

Gently, I remove the hook and do it all over again, noting by the young bass I catch that they are healthy, with not a single parasite on their bodies or gills. I turn them back to grow into fighting foes.

Knowing the larger fish will lie in the deeper water, I snip the black gnat off with my handy gut cutter and tie on a mayfly nymph. To reach them, my nymph must be tied to sink quickly. I make sure the nymph is tied on a size 6 hook, with 2X stout wire.

Fifty feet of line and leader are soon out, and the saliva-wetted fly is allowed to sink well down. The rod tip is just over the water, and a slow stripping in of the line finds a whale of a fight on my hands. Back and forth goes the fish. Maybe it's a muskie. Giving it the bend of the rod, I tire it out and bring the fish to the surface. The muskie turns out to be a one pound crappie.

Were it evening, I would tie on a size 6 hook with a white chenille body and a wide silver ribbing, with down-tied white hackles sparse at the eye. The crappie, one of the heaviest minnow eaters in the lake, would think he had another easy victim, and would hit.

Where spots were breaking the water surface here and there, I would know the blue gills, sunfish and crappies were taking surface food. I would then tie on a gray body size 10 dry fly with game cock whisks for tails and a closely tied short hackle from the same game cock neck, with a brown hackle added. Worms and grasshoppers on a fine leader are eagerly taken by all species too.

But it isn't evening yet, so I keep on casting for panfish in the deeper water. I get many more, too, and release them all. Anyhow, the evening fishing isn't for me—not today when I have Momma and little Willie to think about.

I hear hollering. "Coming," I yell. Casting the fly as I begrudgingly walk toward Momma and little Willie, I pick up a couple more crappies, and a black bass.

Momma, little Willie and I stroll up to the resort. The gang, which could see no sport in angling for panfish and stayed behind to argue, hasn't even settled the fate of the nation by this time.

"What did you get, Nell?" someone politely asks.

Momma replies, "I caught about 20."

Willie shouts triumphantly. "I got 24."

The gang turns to poor neglected Poppa. "And what did you get, Sid?"

"Oh, I got fun looking after Willie."

Poor downcast Poppa, if they only knew it, he had more fun than a cage of monkeys, but do you think he'll tell them so? Let them find out for themselves what they are missing in not fishing for blue gills, sunfish and crappies.

CHAPTER XV

Muskies, The Fish of a Million Casts

LITTLE WILLIE, my obstreperous nine-year-old whose mother spoils him, refused to go fishing with us yesterday, which disturbed me quite a bit. Along about noon, when no muskie should be thinking about food, Willie brings the largest muskie of the week before the veranda sitters at the resort.

He had picked up an old rod that I wouldn't think of using. Tying on a hook that would hardly hold a sunfish, he put a gob of worms on the hook and threw it in the water at the dock. Something hit and Willie ran for shore, dragging the something up on the sand and then tromped on it. One muskie, such as Poppa would have given his eye teeth to land, lay prostrate on the beach.

Two days before that, I. B. Greenhorn, who didn't know the difference between a pole and a rod, nor a muskie from a sucker, was out with a guide. He hooked into something that nearly dragged him out of the boat. Greenhorn "drug" back and the horrified guide couldn't even reach for his gaff hook before Greenhorn had heaved the fish into the boat. No play, no science, just another prize muskie.

And then there was Schultz, from Milwaukee. He had come up to Hank Koerner's resort at Rest Lake, Wisconsin. The guides were all busy so Hank took him out. When Schultz tied into a big muskie, Hank hustled the boat into open water. The muskie dove and as his huge head and body came out of the water at the stern, he almost drowned the bewildered Schultz with the splash. Schultz paled and his hands trembled like aspen leaves. Hank yelled, telling him what to do, but out came Schultz's knife and he cut the line at the reel.

Hank almost cried. "Why did you do that? He was a prize winner!"

237

Fig. 76.—This lean 27½ pound muskie was caught on a Goofy fly, shown on the nose of the muskie. Caught in the spring, just after spawning, the muskie would gain several pounds before winter comes. The Goofy fly is of bucktail, heavy yarn body and a roughly tied head.

The Goofy Fly is two and three quarter inches overall, shown in the inset, was wound by Vic using a coarse yarn for the body, with a tag of the same yarn. He cut off some brown and white hair from a buck's tail, seated it over the eye with heavy thread and varnished the head. Every color of dyed bucktail and yarn is now used. Knot it to a two foot gut leader. Tie the other end on a dipsey swivel sinker of the weight to match your rod. Tie the line to the sinker and "heave" it to the fish.

Schultz leaned back on the seat and calmly said, "Vell dere is lots of muskies in der vorld but dere is only von Schultz."

Nothing like that ever happens to me. I have to go out and work for my muskies. I don't pretend to understand them and I have yet to meet a man who I think does. Sure, there are those who know where they are to be found, but as for men who can take you there and show you how to get legal size muskies any old day like they can lead you to bass or trout in public waters, there just isn't any such person.

Usually the muskie is the toughest fish to fool, the hardest fish to land and is the greatest prize of all our freshwater fish.

You'll find them mostly in the inland lakes and flowages of Wisconsin and from Canada to Kentucky.

Years ago I named him "the fish of a million casts," and rightly so, I think. If all your casts and mine and the other fellows' were added up, I am sure we'd find a million casts actually are made to each muskie landed. But little Willie, Greenhorn and Schultz got theirs on almost the first cast! Figure 76.

In 1938 I decided my lake and stream improvement work needed more facts about muskies. Otis Bersing, one of my co-workers, went with me to the Flambeau Indian Reservation in Northern Wisconsin to make some first hand observations. Our main objective was to find what sort of underwater soil muskies choose for depositing their eggs and to make chemical tests of the type of water they used. It may help your muskie fishing if you go along with me here while I relate what I found out about their habits, from egg to fry to prize winners.

John Lynch, a member of the Ojibway (Chippewa) Indian tribe at Flambeau, told me that the muskies spawned there in the river about April 24, but small ones only. John said the large muskies came along about the 7th to the 10th of May, and that there was only about three days difference in the time each year. From this I figured temperature of the water had little if anything to do with their spawning period. The large muskies laid their eggs on the same beds which the small fish had used some two weeks earlier.

Otis and I spent a whole day working in the cold water, wading in our leather boots and heavy wool clothing. We took the chemical tests of the water and found it to be *medium* water of *clear* transparency, with a temperature reading of 50 degrees. When Otis and I screened the silt and vegetation of the bottom soil, a glistening egg or two would show every once in awhile. The screening reminded me of the days when I learned to pan for gold near the Rogue River in Oregon 10 years earlier. Our search for eggs revealed they had been deposited upon the underwater roots of sedges, burr reeds and bass weeds.

At the hatchery we saw men stripping eggs from muskies which the state's netters had brought in. We noticed several large walleyed pike and northerns in a large tank. With them was a huge muskie whose eggs, too, were not yet ripe enough to strip.

I watched that muskie for a full half hour. The walleyes

239

and northerns just lay there, but the muskie wanted to get out. Extremely restless, she swam around and around the tank, and now and then she would rise on her tail and look over the cement rim of the tank, which was six inches higher than the water. Seeing nothing but cement floor, she dropped back and resumed her cruising around the tank. Had she seen enough water, I am sure that one quick lift of her powerful body would have brought her out of the tank and away to freedom. A muskie does not give up easily!

I reached that conclusion after creating a small pool along side of the tank just to see what would happen. She did not make her complete circle again until she had sized up that pool several times. When she saw there was only about an inch of water over the cement floor, she resumed her usual swing around the tank.

Wendell Anderson then had charge of the fish hatcheries of Wisconsin under B. O. Webster, Division Chief of the fisheries. They were trying to set a world record in muskie production. I saw them accomplish their goal.

One day Wendell took me across land to a lake near the hatchery where there was much plankton to feed muskie fry. In previous research he had noticed that when he fed plankton to the fry, they swallowed all the bugs but disgorged many at once. The bugs which were eaten were soft shelled water fleas, with no hard crust or shell-like coverings such as those of the Daphnia of the plankton. The bug they ate was Polyphemus (*Polyphemus pediculus*, Linne, 1761), as shown in Figure 7, Chapter 3 and was about 1/30th of an inch in length.

Those bugs, which must be available if muskie fry are to survive, are quite common in our northern waters. Under the miscroscope they show up as beautiful transparent insects of blue, orange and white gelatin. If you study them, they tell you much about the habits of the muskie.

When you drop a Polyphemus in the water, the fry will see it instantly, tiny though it be, but he seems in no hurry to go for it. He indicates no perceptible movement, yet his body has turned and is pointing at the bug with the same unerring aim that you sight your rifle. If you've never seen speed in a fish, you will see it now, for that seemingly dead stick in the water shoots forward like a bullet from a gun and just as surely hits its mark.

The first time I saw this I marvelled at the little inch long minnow that had so perfectly camouflaged his intentions, and wondered where he got such quick, tremendous power. It puzzled me as I continued to drop Polyphemus bugs and watched the speedy dart of the fry towards each bug. Finally, I saw that the muskie "breaks" its body just about at the middle. Unlike the other fish which put their entire body into their swimming, and unlike humans who keep their feet on the ground and get their swing for power from the waist up, the muskie forms a "Z" at his middle which can be seen very distinctly. He gets that one terrific thrust towards his target by using the full force of the entire rear half of his body.

Then and there I said to myself, "I know I sometimes reel in too fast for a bass, but I can see now that no plug of mine could ever move so fast that it could get away from a muskie in a mood to strike."

Strange things happen if you toss a small sucker minnow at a muskie fry which has grown to about an inch and a quarter in length. If the sucker lies still, the fry won't move. When the minnow starts to swim, the fry will turn and aim. Quicker than you can wink, the minnow will be held amidships by the fry. Sucker minnows come on just at the right season to furnish food for the fry. I have frequently seen fry eating their own brothers and sisters in this manner, too.

If the fry can't swallow the minnow soon enough after he has turned it to swallow it head first, he will force it down his throat by pushing it against a stick, stone or hard bottom, just like little Willie shoves the cake he has swiped, down his throat with both hands, making room for more.

Muskies, from fry to old age, gorge themselves like wolves, but once gorged, they will not look at food for quite a spell. Neither will they use up their energy cruising around. You feel like offering them a good cigar and an easy chair for more comfortable digestion.

And so I see the fry as a dead ringer for his parents who never hit anything which is not moving. Only to capture their prey in motion will they take aim and utilize the tremendous energy which is theirs. It may be that muskies are so skeptical that they regard only moving things as edible, but how early in life they learn it.

Should you catch a muskie with wide stripes, he will be a hybrid, a cross between a true muskie and a northern pike. The tiger muskie, long known in our waters, was the object of experimentation by Lyman Williamson at the hatchery where Wendell Anderson first fed the Polyphemus to the fry. Lyman, a

241

biologist, had stripped the spawn from a muskie and fertilized it with the milt of a northern. The result was hundreds of tiger muskies. Figure 77.

He was seeking to determine whether the hybrids could renew themselves, for no one could prove the claim that the tiger is barren, a "mule." I watched their growth increase every time I came through his territory. I am sorry to say that he was just within a short time of knowing the answer to his research when someone accidentally or maliciously allowed his hybrids to escape from the pond. All his work was lost! No one has resumed this experiment, as far as I know.

It was Lyman who discovered why a hatchery at Rest Lake did not produce. Examining a jar of walleye eggs under a powerful microscope, he found that they were being eaten by *Vorticella campanula*. This tiny member of the plankton, a ciliate protozoa, about one fiftieth of an inch long, swarmed over the

FIG. 77.—Tiger Muskies.

When well defined stripes are seen on muskies, I am inclined to judge them to be tiger muskies, such as the 52 inch muskie at the top and the smaller one below. They are the offspring of a muskie and a northern pike, a hybrid. If the lower cheek and lower gill cover is barren of scales, the dividing line being sharp and fairly straight across the scaled portion, then I am not so positive. Most tiger muskies I have examined have scales running down into the usually bare cheek and gill cover of the true muskie. There is no set pattern for tiger muskie scales, usually a V formation below the dividing line around the center. Muskie or tiger muskie, I can see no difference in their habits nor the strong fight they give the fisherman. No one knows yet whether these hybrids will renew themselves, or whether they are "mules". I feel sure that the muskie on page 238 is a true muskie.

eggs, inserted a stem in the yolk and absorbed the content. A filter was built and the trouble ceased.

The scientific name of the muskie is *Esox masquinongy*, but I wonder what name would be selected for this hybrid, the tiger muskie. Probably *Esox tigris*.

It is easy to distinguish a true muskie from a northern pike by noting the position of the scales on their cheeks. Except for the stripes, I have found that identification of a tiger muskie is more difficult because their scales often run down the cheeks. If you don't look critically you might mistake him for a northern. See Figure 78.

The muskie has a more powerful after end than the northern pike. The northern's body slopes more from the vent to the end of its body. A large muskie's body thickens much more there. This gives him his tremendous fighting power when he exerts it.

I am sorry that I can suggest no "sure fire" lure for muskies. My personal preference is a large bucktail with two pork strips added, or a feathered spoon. But I have never caught a world's champion muskie, so you had better use your own judgment as to what to throw at them.

In my lake and stream improvement work I had a committee in each community with whom I consulted as to their needs in that particular area. There were always a fisherman, a business man, and a resort owner on the committee, and I made it a point to enter all the information they gave me on my survey cards.

My notes on the lures which they reported had taken muskies tell me not one thing! The lures were so varied, from bucktails and spoons to wooden and plastic plugs, all the way to flies on a fly rod, that there is only one bit of advice I can offer the fisherman. NEVER FISH FOR MUSKIES. Make believe that your muskie lure is searching for walleyed pike, northerns, bass, or bullheads. Then if a muskie happens to hit the particular lure you are using, you'll vouch for it the rest of your days and probably never get another on that same plug. That is why we change lures so often, with our bucktails as first choice.

There is so much confusion among the fishermen that I hesitate to attempt submitting any cut and dried rules, for the muskies will cross me up, I'm sure. For instance, most muskie fishermen, guides included, tell you that the muskie is a shallow water fish, that he usually lies in water from two to 10 feet

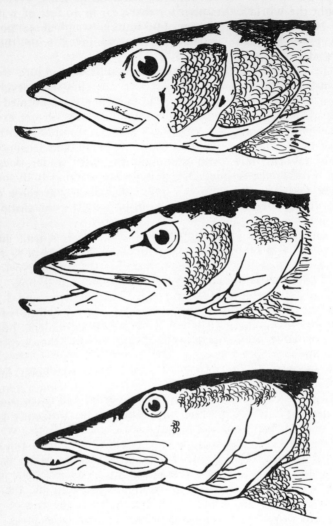

Fig. 78.–Pickerel, Northern Pike and Muskie.

While the pickerel never attains the growth of a northern pike or muskie, it has more scales on the cheek and gill cover, for they are completely scaled. Sketch at top.

The northern pike has the cheek completely scaled but the lower half of the gill cover is bare, as shown in center sketch.

The muskie has the upper part of the gill cover and cheek scaled but the entire lower portion is bare as shown in the bottom sketch.

244

deep. Yet in 1938 my friend, Gust Peterson of Irma, Wisconsin, caught the world's champion for that year in 30 feet of water in the Lac du Flambeau chain. His muskie weighed 52 pounds, was 52 inches long, and the scales I removed from the fish showed it was 15 years old.

I have seen muskies look with contempt at my lure 20 feet down in a *Very Clear* water lake. There they lay, several of them, as immovable as logs and so still that algae formed over their great backs. Under such circumstances I never get excited. What if my hands do tremble while I am fumbling with the tackle box? The dratted thing sticks, that's all, and I cannot get at my favorite lure. And supposing the wire leader does not snap on the lure at once. No, it isn't my shaking body or my quivering hands. It is the fact that I am looking at those enormous fish, hoping they will not be frightened by the shadow of my boat on that bright July day and go away.

Finally I allow the boat to drift away from them, and at 50 feet I use a high looping cast to get it down there to them. I'm ready to set the hook instantly at the first touch. No touch, and I comb that spot with everything in the tackle box.

Then I give the boat a little kick with the oars and I drift over the convention. There they are, the chairman of the board, the president, directors and the stockholders, but no greeters! With such a dead organization, how do they expect to do business?

Desperately I look at the largest bare treble hook in the kit and wish I weren't a good sportsman. I am almost tempted to lower the gang hook and snag the disdainful creatures, especially the 50 or 60 pound chairman. Well, at least I know they are in that lake, and that is something.

Each muskie in that convention is probably full to bursting, but I'll lay for them when a two day fresh to strong breeze comes up and churns the water so the lake "tilts." This is called a seiche. Then their appetites will quicken in the mixed waters of fresh oxygen which a seiche brings on.

I know they will start feeding then, for their digestion will be stimulated. In the ruffled waters the convention will break up and the muskies will be all over the lake. It is then that a floating, shallow diving plug worked as fast as I can make it operate often hooks them, for they do smash at lures during such periods.

Then the lake becomes calm, the sun gets its work in and their gorged stomachs will not digest their food until at least the third or fourth day after the "blow". The convention reassembles. I figure my only chance is to get the stray muskies which feed in the food trough near the shoreline food shelf from daylight until about 8 o'clock in the morning and again after 4 or 5 o'clock in the evening.

Another tried and true method of catching muskies is known as "drifting". It is peculiary adapted to the angler who is not inclined to exert himself, such as my good friend who had been working like a dog in the city and had taken his wife and four lively children up in the Hayward, Wisconsin area.

He was a confessed sleepy head and I showed him how to become a "drifter". As it turned out, he was a prevaricator, too, but he wasn't any bigger liar than I, who had given him the advice and had to back up his story.

All he wanted to do the first few days was to sleep and relax at the resort, but he couldn't get away with it. With four husky youngsters pulling at him and the Missus driving at him to go hither and yon, it was just too bad.

I had dropped in at Shorty's on Twin Lakes where he was staying and he confided his thwarted desire to me while I was making some water tests. "If you want to sleep", I suggested, "go fishing for muskies in this good *hard* water lake."

He looked at me with consternation. "But I don't want to fish", he exclaimed, "I just want to sleep!"

I finally convinced him to bring his tackle down to the boat. Looking over his tackle box, I selected a heavy sinking plug and snapped it on the wire leader of his 24 pound test line.

"Start the kicker, go west and a little north until you come to that patch of timber on the west shore", I instructed him. "Then shut off the motor, park yourself on those nice cushions and go to sleep. Don't worry, your boat will drift along easily towards the east and a little north."

I did add, however, that before going to sleep he should toss out the underwater plug and let it sink down to China. I also advised him to "take a few turns of the line around your wrist before you drift to sleep while you're drifting." This was a muskie lake, I told him, and with a gentle breeze blowing, who could tell?

I met him in town the next day where he had gone to have a huge muskie photographed for posterity. "For heaven's sake, don't say anything to Shorty", my friend implored. "I told him I saw a big swirl in the lake, threw my plug at it and landed this!"

246

I insisted that he give me the true story. "I woke up with something pulling at my arm as if I was going to be dragged out of the boat", he said. "I rolled the line off my wrist, picked up the rod and socked this muskie so hard I fell backwards He landed in the boat, and now Shorty has made me out as quite a hero."

As luck would have it, Shorty came down the street just then and rushed up to tell me how the fishermen were giving me the credit for picking the right plug for the big muskie. Then Shorty and my friend wanted to lead me into an ice cream parlor to fill me up on sundaes. As it was Wednesday, I went away from there before I became too much involved.

I relate this just to impress upon the beginning fisherman's mind how "drifting" on a good lake, under a bright sun, will take fish if you select the right lure. No casting, no rowing, no use of the motor, but sometimes a muskie, bass, walleyed pike or a northern!

Just let out enough line, according to the breeze, to allow the heavy underwater plug to ride along the 25 foot level, but not near the surface. You may tempt those large fish lying at that depth in *clear* water lakes on sunny days. If, in your "drifting", you "drift" off to sleep, let your alibi be fool proof. No one catches a large muskie without having to relate every move you and the fish made. Add to it right there and stick to it. Further additions only cause subtractions by your envious friends.

Although I may be frustrated in my summer muskie fishing, I return in late September when the lake is no longer in three layers. That is the time the muskie becomes the tiger of the waters. No longer is the muskie like the spring spawner whose appetite doesn't quicken until about two weeks after spawning. Neither is he the overheated, short-of-air summer fish whose digestion slows and who usually shows activity only on cool days or during moderate to strong breezes, 15 to 30 miles per hour.

In autumn the muskie stuffs himself during the cool days and evenings and the still colder early morning hours, just like a bear preparing for hibernation. Truly, the tiger in the jungle is no more carnivorous than the fall muskie.

Then is the time to look to your jumpy, splashing, diving lures, spoons, and large bucktails with two pork rind strips added. The waters are well mixed with oxygen, the temperature is cool, and those tremendous fighters, 10, yes 15 to 30 years old, are there, sometimes for the beginner on his first cast, sometimes on the millionth.

I like bucktails, spoons and plugs best because I can remove them from the muskie's mouth—just one big, bony, insensitive cavern—and release the fish without harming him. A muskie gets no chance to swallow such lures because when he strikes I set the hook with everything my 30 pound test will stand, and how constantly I check it for line fray.

But the live bait fisherman with his harnessed sucker lets the muskie, seize, crush, turn and slowly swallow the fish. He seldom sets his hook until 20 minutes or more have elapsed. Then he sets it with the hardest quick pull his line will stand. When a muskie has swallowed the bait and hooks in this fashion, there seems no point in releasing him. The merciful thing to do is to bring his life to a speedy end, but in Wisconsin the legal size for muskies is 30 inches, so we have a contradiction.

While I usually release a muskie, I would be tempted to keep the fish which Robert Malo of Port Arthur, Ontario, Canada caught when he "invaded" the U. S. in 1954. His 70 pound, 4 ounce, fish was over 30 years old. Along with her 8½ pounds of eggs the muskie was digesting a 5½ pound northern pike from Middle Eau Claire Lake, a hardwater lake near Gordon, Wisconsin. The 52½ inch fish was still hungry enough to strike at his live sucker on a 40 pound test line. A large 9½ inch lure such as shown in Figure 80 is a mere tidbit for a hungry muskie.

Once a muskie is on, it is merely a question of how good you are in playing and landing a fish. You can expect the strongest of lines to break, the reel is likely to fall off the rod, and the net often knocks the lure out of the muskie's mouth. You thought you had him firmly hooked, but he merely clamped down hard on the lure, opened his bony mouth and gave you back your lure. See Figure 79.

Some troll for the muskie with 90 and 100 pound test lines in both rivers and lakes. Here, too, hooked muskies are often lost. When those sharp teeth and powerful jaws clamp down upon a live fish it is curtains. The muskie hits his victim in the center and doesn't mind if he drops the fish for a moment. He can easily recover the sorely wounded fish. That is why I believe he so often releases our plug when he has hit, and clamped down with full power. Then, when we think we have a soundly hooked fish, he merely opens that "vise" and our lure returns to us so sweetly, and no fish.

248

Fig. 79.—The Bony Mouth of a Muskie.

If the hook is not set hard, the fish opens that cavernous mouth which has clamped down upon the lure, and the lure returns to a silent (?) fisherman.

When I get a strike, no matter how hard, I give the rod and line everything it will stand for a second setting of the hook. In this way I am often lucky enough to secure a firm setting. Let him who will use his light lines, but when fishing for muskies I'll still stick to my 30 pound test lines, for I am always hoping to land the chairman of the board in that lake.

This much I can say definitely. Any fish which eats about 30 pounds of other fish in the fall to gain a single pound in weight is no mean adversary for any angler. And when one is caught, once in a million casts, it is like winning a share in the Irish sweepstakes!

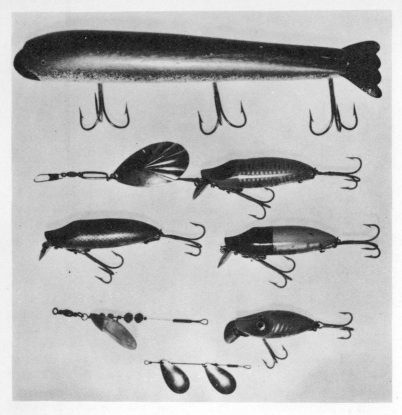

Fig. 80.—The top muskie lure is 9½ inches long, an imitation sucker which is worked fast in the water. The "tandem" beneath it is Jim Scheel's muskie lure which he claims was originated by the fishermen around Eagle River, Wisconsin. It is simply a jointed lure with a flange which allows the number 5 skinner spoon to be fastened to the flange of the lure. The feathered treble of the spoon is discarded in order to connect this 9 inch lure.

Below it are shown three plugs for wall eyes, northerns and bass, all about half size—just three of the hundreds we fishermen use.

The twin blade spinner, blades each one inch long, is used with various Aberdeen, Carlisle and other hooks from size 1/0 to 3/0 for walleyes. With night crawlers or minnows, cast or trolled, thousands of walleyes have been taken. Muskies, bass and perch hit it too. The spinners are nickel, brass or copper and each fisherman swears by his particular choice for his own waters.

The June Bug spinner has its advocate by the thousands for walleyes and northern pike. Used the same as the double bladed spinner, below, its advocates sneer at the twin spinner, particularly for trolling.

250

CHAPTER XVI

Northern Pike Rivals
the Muskie

THE NORTHERN PIKE, first cousin to the battling muskie, is worthy of any fisherman's attention. When taken from the same waters, he is just as good eating, and pound for pound, will in many instances put up just as good a fight. The muskie is the tiger of our waters. The northern pike is the wolverine.

The analogy is entirely apropos because the northern pike has many of the attributes of the wolverine, the meanest and most insolent animal on earth, hateful and destructive, contemptuous of human beings, a cunning destroyer and a killer as well. To my way of thinking, the northern pike is every bit as much a glutton and a killer. I reached this conclusion years ago after observing these fish, from fry to old age, for hour after hour.

They in turn have watched me. A large northern, almost motionless in the water, will gaze at you with the coldest, most baleful look in his eyes as long as you persist in staring at him. He seems to be saying, "Here's a brother killer—wonder what makes him tick?" You are always the first to move and then he is gone.

Time was when the wolverine was such an upstart in our northern forests that he taxed the ingenuity of our hunters and trappers to cope with him. With the ever-continuing advance of civilization, he has retreated far to the north in Canada, and very few are now caught in the United States. But the wolverine of the waters is still with us, offering many a thrill for anglers—men, women and children.

The northern pike, whose Sunday go-to-meeting name is *Esox lucius*, is often called great northern pike to distinguish him from the pickerel. In Wisconsin, some of our more rabid

251

muskie fishermen regard the northern pike with contempt. To me this is a peculiar attitude, particularly when they refer to him as a "snake".

It is the lowly mud, or grass pickerel, with the lofty scientific name of *Esox vermiculatus*, which confuses them. If there were no muskies in our waters, you can be sure the persnickety muskie fisherman would eagerly seek out the fighting northern for his quarry.

The muskie and the northern pike are so similar in appearance that it often is difficult to tell them apart. Frequently I have had opportunity to examine a fish which an angler was carrying, firm in the belief he had a small northern in his possession. One look at the cheek and gill cover told me he was fortunate that the warden had not caught up with him, for he had caught an illegal size muskie, not a small northern.

Muskie fishermen, in their contempt for the northern pike, too often forget that some muskies come to the net far more sluggishly than a northern pike. Also, they unfairly blame the northern pike for the scarcity of muskies, claiming they feed heavily on muskie fingerlings.

If they ever watch muskies in the rearing tanks, as I have, and observe the inch and a quarter muskie fry devour his brothers and sisters, one after another, possibly they would realize why so few muskies grow to legal size. It is true, of course, that northerns also eat numerous muskie fingerlings, but they haven't much on the muskies themselves, and possibly that is why both fish, when mature, are so canny. Muskies seem to lie only in certain spots where they drive all other fish away, including the northerns.

The northern pike is a great rover, more so than the muskie but not nearly so much as the walleyed pike, which, incidentally, is not even a near relative of the other two fish.

An extremely voracious appetite is characteristic of the northern. His gluttony is such that he hardly swallows one large fish before he grabs another. His big sharp teeth get such a firm hold on his victims that there is no hope of escape. He is more of a swallower than a crusher. Like the muskie and walleye, he lives almost entirely on flesh after his first year of existence.

He comes out of hiding with a rush and offers much greater sport than the muskie, not because he's a scrappier fish but because there are far more northerns to do the striking.

I have watched eight inch northerns lie near the shoreline

of a lake or under a tree-bordered bank and have seen them display fully as much speed as any muskie. When a large fly drops on the water or a spider is shaken loose from a branch, I marvel at the streamlined fish that travels so gracefully through the water at lightning speed in quest of this tiny bit of food. I acknowledge the muskie to be the speed king of the lake waters, but I consider the northern pike the prince of speed.

If I loop a plug, spoon or other lure through the air, a large northern may be there to meet it when it hits the water. Yet he was 15 feet away when the lure was still sailing through the air. Here, then, is no near-sighted fish like the wall eyed pike. This fellow is an aerial observer as well as an underwater sleuth.

With his eyes set right on top of his head, he seems to have the vision of the whirligig beetle, *Gyrinidae*, which in effect has one set of eyes for underwater and another for aerial observation. The northern, with but two eyes, seems to use one for the water and the other for the air. Woe betide any small bird which comes too close to the surface. I have seen many a hapless duckling snatched by a northern in his relentless quest for food. How we duck hunters despise him for this trait!

In the *soft* water lakes where the food is so scarce that the bass and pan fish cannot obtain enough nourishment to grow to good size, the northern pike is a blessing. Cannibal that he is, he keeps the balance of nature by thinning out the hundreds of over-crowded smaller fish which eat the food that would grow larger fish if there weren't so many hungry mouths to fill in the acid water lakes.

Northern pike thrive best in the *medium* to *hard* water lakes. In my old home waters at Big Bay de Noc near Gladstone, Michigan, I have taken many at depths of 30 feet in its rich, crystal *clear* water during sunny August. Like all other fish. the northerns seek the depths in hot weather, but when the bay was windswept, I have caught many by casting a mid-water lure.

In a trout stream northerns are a real menace to trout, and should be kept at a minimum. They seek the wide and warm portions of the stream, taking terrific toll of those trout which migrate up or downstream in the various seasons.

In a stream, northerns can be fished from the banks, from a canoe, or by wading upstream. Often they can be seen by paddling the canoe slowly upstream, or by carefully approaching likely spots along the banks.

When casting a spoon or a plug so it works toward the resting fish's mouth, it is advisable for the angler to keep out of sight. Some times the northern follows the lure but doesn't take it, especially if he sees the fisherman. He will then either retreat to his resting place or will disappear under more protective covering.

If he goes back to his resting place, it pays to keep casting. He may eventually decide to grab a different lure than that which was first offered. Should the pike disappear, it is best to work other waters and come back later. He may then have assumed his former stance and this time may strike the lure immediately.

Northern pike spawn in the spring about the same time as the walleyes, but a little earlier than the muskies. For this reason they begin their heavier springtime feeding sooner than the muskies, offering earlier season sport to the angler. The northern is generally responsive to lures throughout the summer, but to a lesser degree. In the fall he becomes as active as in the spring. The northern offers good winter time fishing through the ice, too.

It is surprising how often you can catch northern pike from a dock, especially if it is rather long and is built upon a rock foundation. They like the darker water under the dock if it rests on piling, or else they hide out among the rocks. In fishing for them, don't cast straight out from the dock. Cast alongside the dock and reel your lure towards you so it follows the edge of the rocks or the dock.

As a rule, anything you throw at the northern pike is apt to be taken. There is no one "best" lure. Spoons, plugs, minnows, bucktails and even large bucktail flies, all are hit with ferocity if the fish decides to strike.

The northern can be extremely exasperating when he follows the lure but does not choose to hit. There is a possible remedy for this frustrating situation, however. As the lure nears the tip of your rod, lift it with a sudden jerk, and then slam it down on the water forcefully. The northern may then, in his fury, grab it.

Since northern pike grow to a good size—some as large as 30 or 40 pounds—you must always be prepared for an all out struggle. Even the smaller northerns strike viciously, often leaping out of the water and then carrying on with the struggle underneath the surface. The fish may soon give up, however. Then you have but to reel him towards you. But be not disillusioned if you think your northern has given up too quickly.

Many muskies sometimes behave that way. Always be set for a final flip of his tail and a mad try for freedom as you bring him to net. His extremely sharp teeth will cut a line if you haven't taken the precaution to fish with a wire leader.

In some waters the northern pike take on an algae flavor, quite objectionable if they are served up that way on the dinner table. All summer northerns should be skinned and cut into filets. Then there is no unpleasant taste and they are highly appealing as food. Their forked bones must be carefully extracted.

To the beginning angler who wants to do battle with the northerns, I again emphasize that he must know his waters, as explained in the first eight chapters of this book. There he will find a pattern in which to judge the northern's haunts and, if he works the waters in the manner applicable to nature, he should have little trouble getting his limit.

Who am I to say? If he persists in fishing only for northerns he may tie into a muskie large enough to mount in his den, for the muskie hits the lures intended for northerns and the northern hits the lures for muskies. Then everyone is happy but the poor fish.

CHAPTER XVII

Wall Eyed Pike, Here Today There Tomorrow

WHEN MOMMA AND POPPA and little Willie, that angel-faced villain of ours, want an enjoyable day, we go fishing for walleyed pike. Poppa goes a trifle reluctantly for he knows what he is in for.

Momma will catch the biggest fish, little Willie will catch the most and Poppa the smallest and the "leastest". Then Momma ribs Poppa about fishing. She doesn't call him Poppa as dutiful wives should. She patronizingly refers to him as "the expert".

Each of us has a long bamboo pole for still fishing from the boat and each has a casting rod. The "expert" starts the motor, hunts up a reef, drops anchor and rigs up the bamboo poles, with minnows for bait. There they are, sticking out of the boat like porcupine quills. Then he rigs up Momma's casting rod, fastening a double-bladed size 4 copper spinner to the leader on her 10 pound line. Little Willie all but upsets the boat clamoring for a nickled spinner with his wriggly night crawler, the bait they both use for casting.

The "expert" finally manages to get a deep-going spoon on his own six pound test spinning line, and just as he is about to search the side of the reef for a walleye, comes a frantic yell from Momma. Calmly, and with all the restrained poise he can muster, the "expert" tells her what strategy to use, but Momma isn't calm.

The chore of netting her fish, placing it on the stringer and baiting her hook is almost over when little Willie has a strike. Hollering like a Banshee, he brings his walleye towards the boat. The "expert" again holds the net, scoops in the fish and then loses some of his equanimity when he sees Momma's bamboo pole bend almost under the boat.

257

Do you think that walleye would hit the "expert's" boat pole? Never! Now she says, "Poppa, please handle it for me, I just had a strike along the weed bed." Then little Willie's boat pole—not the "expert's"—has a fish. Ten minutes go by and in unison Momma and little Willie yell, "They've left here, let's move." The "expert", all but bushed from moving around the boat like a blind dog in a meat market, yields to the command. He looks sadly at his spinning rod and begrudgingly pulls up the anchor.

Deciding it is time to get in a bit of fishing himself, he starts the kicker and heads for another spot in the lake he knows. He'll let the boat drift while he casts with his spinning rod. As the boat drifts along, little Willie hooks a walleye, and promptly the "expert" tosses overboard a sealed can with a cuttyhunk line and a heavy dipsey swivel sinker to mark the location of the school of walleyes he knows must be there. He takes the oars and works the boat back and forth around the tin can "buoy." Then Momma's casting rod gets a fish, also her boat pole, and to complicate the situation, little Willie also connects with one. Soon the yell goes up again, "The school has moved, take us to another good spot, Poppa."

And so on, *ad infinitum*. Oh, happy day! We arrive at the dock and my beloved urchin shouts for all to hear, "I got five, Momma got seven and Poppa only got one."

But the walleyed pike is well worth fishing. It offers great sport in many lakes and streams throughout the United States and Canada. The fish is especially favored by women and children, although men enjoy catching this species, too, for the walleye puts up a fight and is a delectable dish on the dinner table, its flesh firm and well-flavored.

Belonging to the same family as the perch, the walleye's scientific name is *Stizostedion vitreum vitreum*. Sneeze it, don't pronounce it. In Canada he is also called doré. The name doré has likewise become very common in Upper Michigan. Some of the fish's other names around the United States are Jack Salmon, pike perch, blue pike and blow fish.

Like perch, the walleyes travel in schools and that often is their undoing. They are far more clever than the muskie or northern pike in finding smaller food by taking advantage of every whim of nature, but they are more foolish in allowing the angler to take one after another from their school.

Walleyes are fish eaters from the time they are large enough to swallow. In the hatcheries they show this propensity as soon

258

as they are out of the egg. If they aren't removed from the incubation jars as soon as they "pop" from the eggs, they start eating the tails off the fish ahead of them while the ones behind are eating their tails. See Figure 81. It's a vicious circle of cannibalism, even if they cannot, as yet, swallow one another.

Because of this cannibalistic trait, hatchery raised walleyes must be rushed without delay to their place of stocking, or there won't be anything to stock. One good sized walleye will swallow another almost as large as himself. I have, on many

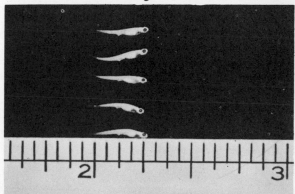

Fig. 81.–Walleyed Pike Fry. Length one-quarter inch.

Just out of the egg, these fry must be planted at once or they devour the tail of the fry in front of them. Meanwhile the fry in front is doing the same thing to the one ahead of it.

occasions, seen a walleye try to swallow another fish too big for him to get down his gullet. Sometimes both die, for the feeding fish cannot let his quarry go after its head is stuck in his gullet. He can't gulp him down because the body is too large to slide through his mouth and the dorsal spines prevent the release.

Walleyes produce many eggs at spawning time, nature's way of making up for huge losses due to cannibalism. A 10 pound female walleye will spawn as many as 250,000 eggs each spring-season.

I believe that nature does a better job of perpetuating wall-eyes than our hatcheries. In my early spring surveys I often saw windrows of walleye eggs washed up on shore by an ice push, for they often spawn before the ice is gone. Those great masses of white eggs looked like snowdrifts. I have examined their underwater eggs and invariably have noted that

90 per cent of them were eyed, fertilized by the male. That is always an indication to me that in such a lake nature is doing such a good job in keeping up the supply of walleyes that, in spite of the waste, it is needless to stock them.

It is very, very wrong to stock *soft* water lakes with walleyes. They seldom grow to legal size there, yet they will eat every bass in the lake they can swallow. Then the lake is ruined for any kind of fishing, for there is soon not enough fish food to the acre to nourish the hungry walleyes.

Only in *medium* to *hard* water lakes should walleyes be stocked. Even there, it is generally a needless effort unless, of course, walleyes are being introduced to those waters to add to its variety of fish.

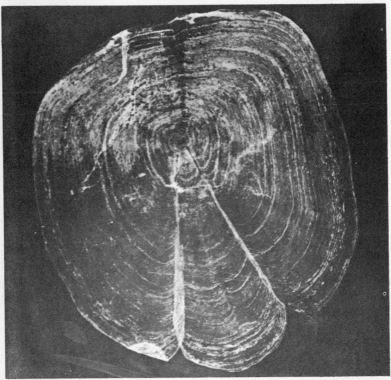

Fig. 82.—Reading The Age Of A Fish By Its Scales. (Greatly enlarged).

I judge this walleyed pike to be in its eighth summer. The close divisions show the winter period of much less feeding. Note the great growth between the second and third year. These rings, like the rings on a tree, show the age of every fish, from muskie to panfish.

260

While walleyes, as a general rule, prefer to eat only other fish, they do hit night crawlers, spoons, plugs, spinning lures and large flies. Were this not so, much of the fun of fishing them would be lost.

The big secret of successful walleye fishing is knowing how to find them. That's where your knowledge of the water and behavior of the fish comes in.

You've heard the old saying, "When the wind is in the East, the fish bite the least." That's not so in Lake Winnebago, the largest in Wisconsin and one of the richest in the United States in fish food. There we citizens of Oshkosh and Fond du Lac and such nearby cities as Appleton, Neenah and Menasha, on the West shore, welcome a big "blow" from the East. It's our signal for unusually good walleye fishing. These cities represent a population of about 100,000, but it seems to me that when there is a two day "blow" from the East there are about 102,000 fishermen on hand for the fun.

The second day of the "blow" finds me on the West side of the lake in the city of Oshkosh, a short walk from my home. It is then that the walleye schools arrive along the shore from the other side of the lake and from the deeper waters as well. I need no boat, for I cast with my plug rod from shore into the breeze. I am fully armed with heavy spoons, sinking plugs and certain large flies.

Since this is a "blow," the East wind kicks up great waves, for the lake is only 21 feet deep in its lowest spot. As the walleyes move toward the shore, they are in quest of the minnows, giant mayfly nymphs, crayfish and all other bottom food stirred up by the waves. How eagerly they feed in those agitated waters! How vastly more successful your fishing now becomes on the shoreline that on other days yields a walleye only now and then!

Whether I cast into the wind with an underwater plug or spoon I will now take walleyes. I can also tie a Goofy fly, or any other kind of large fly, to a leader with a dipsey swivel sinker and catch them with spinning rod or plug rod.

If you are a beginner, or a stranger to this special type of walleye fishing, you won't catch any until you apply your fish and water sense, regardless how expert a caster you are. You'll see the man next to you taking fish with a red and white copper-backed spoon. Next to him will be a woman using an all brass spoon and she will be catching walleyes. Someone else

261

will be casting a green and white spoon and still another will be using a plug, all with similiar success.

We have a little "secret." It's the action of the lure we use and knowing where and how deep to work it.

The walleyes are not in the trough of the waves and certainly not near the top of them. They are feeding on wave-washed minnows, crayfish, and nymphs just far enough off shore so the waves cannot roll them against the bottom. Your lure must be of just the right weight to work their feeding places.

Too light a lure will ride the waves and not go beneath the trough. Too heavy a lure will sink to the bottom in the shallow water. You would soon get hung up among the boulders and be compelled to break the line to start fishing again. This sometimes happens to the best of us. Many a good rod is broken by those who use great force with the rod instead of working the lure loose by pulling on the line with the hand only.

It pays a newcomer to observe the casting methods of a successful fisherman on Lake Winnebago. If you talk with him, he'll more than likely tell you what lures he is using for this kind of walleye fishing. Chances are you haven't got the right kind of lures with you, but that's no problem for you are fishing in the city park at Oshkosh. You just jump into your car, head for a downtown tackle shop and in ten minutes you are back with the lures the fisherman advised you to buy.

Then, as your casting and reeling ability improves, so can you keep your lure at just the right depth—not too high, not too low. You switch from spoon to spoon, plug to plug, or fly to fly. Soon you will be giving advice to some other newcomer who envies your string of walleyes.

You're hungry now, so you leave your stringer in the water, hike up to the park stand, order a hot dog or hamburger with hot coffee, and return to find your stringer and your fish intact. Who knows but that someone in Oshkosh hasn't added a couple more to your string while you were gone. It sometimes does happen, strange as it seems. But then, an East "blow" yields a bountiful walleye harvest, and the cup overfloweth with kindness.

"Bigosh, we who live in Oshkosh like to get out of town once in awhile, too." We do that by going over to the East shore when there is a two day "blow" from the West. We have the same success catching walleyes there. Northern pike hit also, and occasionally we get bass or a muskie. If you have a sturdy boat and have someone with you who can handle it in the rough water, you also get fish by working the reefs which only an old resident can find in our 38-mile long lake.

I hope you do not get the idea that it is only on Lake Winnebago where strong winds provide excellent walleye fishing, nor that it is only the East or the West wind that sends them on the feed. All winds, North, East, South and West, churn the waters over reefs and shoreline during a "blow." And in all larger lakes with walleyes you can expect the same good fishing as on Lake Winnebago. The same goes for bass, northern pike and muskies when you have an onshore "blow."

Some years ago when my fishing friend, Vic Plouff, tied up a bucktail fly to use on the river and along the shoreline in Oshkosh, I looked at it and said, "That's a goofy fly." The name has stuck ever since. It was crude and rough and could be tied in just a few minutes with yarn and bucktail, but we gave it a try.

That "monstrosity" amazed us. It took walleyes with the fly rod and both the casting and spinning rods as well. In case you think it is a "bluffer," convince yourself to the contrary by looking at that huge muskie in Figure 76, caught with the "goofy" here in the city of Oshkosh.

Up in my old home town, Gladstone, Michigan, we also have excellent walleyed pike fishing. Fifty years ago, before there was any thought of conservation, I used to spear them with a "jack light" in Bay De Noc at night. This Bay was listed in *Life* magazine as being the best spot in the United States for walleyed pike fishing.

Up there the fishermen troll almost entirely, getting splendid catches off the banks in 18 to 25 feet of water and over the reefs 10 to 12 feet below the surface. The few anglers who cast use night crawlers and spinners on treble hooks, also many different kinds of plugs and spoons.

The walleyes at Gladstone are called dorés, and are much larger than those in Lake Winnebago. They range over an extensive area in Lake Michigan, and down as far as Green Bay in Wisconsin.

When walleyed pike are in the deeper waters of a lake, you must apply your knowledge of transparency, temperature, oxygen and three layer lakes. You'll have to get your bait, plug or spoon down to the level where they are resting during the daylight hours. In the early morning and evening, of course, surface lures will get them because like other fish, they

263

go on the feed at the food shelves. In all events, you'll have to get your lure near the fish, for the walleye seems to me to be a very near-sighted fish. His large wall eyes plainly show this. Movement attracts him much quicker than anything else.

Walleye fishing can be good in winter, spring or summer, but if you really want to get them, try September and October when they gorge themselves.

264

CHAPTER XVIII

Spinning Calls For Reading
of the Waters

THE EARLIEST REFERENCE to spinning that I have found is in an old book in my angling library, "Salmonia," written by an Englishman, Sir Humphrey Davy, and published in 1828. He tells about spinning a "bleak for salmon" in the year 1810.

The first demonstration of spinning by a fisherman that I saw was in 1936 when I visited at the summer cottage of one of my fishing friends, Paul Snyder, at Plum Lake in Northern Wisconsin. Paul, a pianist of considerable attainments who has played in the leading concert halls of Europe as well as those of our own country, had just brought over his friend, Geoffrey Luard, a secretary in the House of Lords in London. To my great delight, he, too, was an angler.

While I was tying up a few of my favorite nymph patterns for Geoffrey to try out in England, Paul asked me to get out my plug casting rod to show his guest my style of casting. We went down to the little dock, and naturally I tried to "show off" the American way of striving for accuracy. I pointed the rod tip towards a small deadhead about 85 feet from the dock for a target, and as good fortune would have it, I laid the plug "right on the nose" at every cast.

I thought that Geoffrey seemed quite impressed. Then he spoke casually about spinning as practiced in England. Like other Englishmen I have met, Geoffrey was quite diffident and very polite. When he modestly agreed to show us some of the fine points about spinning, I was most eager. Although I had heard much about that style of fishing, I had never had the opportunity of seeing anyone use a spinning rod.

Geoffrey looked at us with an air of apologetic confidence. "I shall endeavor to hit that spot out there," he said.

I focused my eyes on the deadhead with the thought of comparing his spinning rod accuracy with my plug rod. To my astonishment his lure didn't even come near it. I turned toward Geoffrey and saw him coolly reeling in his Devon minnow.

"What spot are you aiming at?" I asked, as if harboring no thoughts of poor marksmanship.

"That small clump of rushes there," he replied.

I failed to see any clump of rushes near the deadhead.

"Out there," said Geoffrey as he shot his lure gracefully over the water. It sailed and sailed, 65 feet beyond the deadhead, and hit the water right beside a little cluster of soft-stemmed bulrushes. With the same deadly accuracy, Geoffrey repeated the performance several times.

I looked increduously at Paul. "How do you like that!" I exclaimed. "The English have a saying for that, don't they—carrying coals to Newcastle?"

Geoffrey's rod was nine feet three inches long, and I think it weighed about 12 ounces. He told me he used it for everything from salmon to trout. Englishmen, he said, like spinning rods from five up to nine feet three inches.

Strangely enough, American anglers were slow to follow the English in the adoption of this fascinating method of fishing. It wasn't until about 1950 that fishermen in the United States took up spinning to any appreciable extent. But once the idea took hold, it spread rapidly and soon established itself as a favorite method of casting with many anglers.

On my travels around the United States I saw the spinning rod used for saltwater fishing in Florida and California, and on freshwater all over the country and in Canada as well. I noticed that a great number of fishermen used the spinning method on Pacific Coast waters, including such streams as the Klamath and Eel in California, the Rogue, Deschutes and the Umpqua in Oregon, and on up into Washington and British Columbia.

In Ontario I saw men in a canoe using the spinning rod in the Nipigon River off Don Gapen's Point, just above the spot where the world's record brook trout was caught. This 14½ pounder was taken by Dr. W. J. Cook, of Fort William, Ontario, in 1916. Dr. Cook used a Cockatouche. I believe it was our minnow, the Miller's Thumb, which is about five or six inches long and belongs to the Sculpins, *Cottus bairdii*. We also call it the Muddler. Figure 83.

When spinning first gained favor in the United States, most

of the spinning reels were imported from England, France, Italy, Sweden and Switzerland. These countries also made most of the rods and lures. By 1952 American manufacturers generally began catering to the growing demands of the sportsmen.

While the spinning rod will not take the place of the dry fly rod for surface fishing, the wet fly rod for nymphs or our plug rods in cluttered waters, it does have a great many uses on lakes and streams.

The spinning rod begins where the fly and the plug rods leave off. We will soon see the manufacturers bring out the sort of rods and reels for handling large fish in log, stump or down tree infested waters and heavy weed beds. They will be heavy duty rods of various lengths. The reels will allow us to bring the fish out in the open water to make his fight. The new equipment will have to be a compromise between the heavy saltwater spinning tackle and the light rods and lines which we now use in our freshwater spinning. The rods may go to 12 and 15 feet in length.

Spinning can best be compared with plug casting, although it is by no means the same. One thing I must emphasize, how-

Photograph by Seegar Swanson.

FIG. 83.—The Nipigon River, Ontario, Canada, just a few feet above the spot where Dr. Cook caught his 14½ pound brook trout. It still holds the world's record.

267

ever. Once you have mastered the technique of casting your spinning lures, you must let the water tell you how to catch fish, just as it does when you cast with the fly rod or the plug rod. The water tells the same story to all. If you give heed to its information about transparency, the food shelf, underwater plants, temperature, oxygen, current, drainage and seepage lakes, and three layer lakes, your spinning rod will produce at times when nothing else will.

So many claims are made for spinning that some of them must be taken with a grain of salt. It is the fashion to claim that one can learn to cast in just a few moments. While this is true to a great extent, it requires many hours of fishing to drop that lure exactly where you want it to go, just as it does with fly or plug rod.

For anyone accustomed to fishing with a fly or plug rod, learning to cast with the spinning rod will be harder than for a person with no previous casting experience. A girl or boy, or any other beginning fisherman, will take to spinning quickly and will enjoy fishing with this equipment immensely. Learning to cast easily with the spinning rod requires a little more time than with the fly or plug rod.

Since your spinning reel does not revolve, it cannot backlash. This is a great blessing, whether you cast overhead or use the side cast. Just an easy flip of the wrist will give the rod a backward bend, and by shooting it forward at once, allowing no pause, you will achieve accuracy. Side arm casting does not lend itself to accurate casts.

One of the main advantages of the spinning rod is that it enables you to cast greater distances than with the other types of rods, and with the lightest of lures. Whether your lure weighs but one tenth of an ounce or as much as a full ounce, your spinning rod will handle it with ease.

On the streams you will get more fish if you change your lure as you encounter the different kinds of water. When you see a piece of water ahead that is only a foot deep, you snap on your lightest lure. If you have learned to handle your spinning rod properly, you can place the extremely light lure right where you want it in that shallow run of water.

As you approach the deep pool at the end of a rapids, the light lure is not the one to use. You switch to one that weighs half an ounce. If your cast is accurate, that lure will sink toward the bottom of the pool and should appeal to the fish.

In the rapids you may find a quarter ounce lure is best,

and in the long, quiet reaches you may try a slightly heavier one, depending upon how deep the water is.

If a bass or trout stream has too many deep holes for wading, you can walk along the bank to work the waters. No matter how cluttered the bank may be with trees or other vegetation, you will find that you can fish the likely spots with your spinning rod.

Oxbows are the bane of a fly fisherman. One cannot but admit that the spinning rod has it all over the fly rod in taking large trout from such water. See Figure 84.

Stream fishing from a canoe with the spinning rod offers ideal sport for many. Whether the canoe is being slowed by branches or is drifting lazily along, you can reach most any spot on a wide stream. For variety, the canoe can be beached and the water thereabouts can be easily and thoroughly covered for as much as 100 feet or more, although your average cast in a stream need not be much over 45 feet.

The fisherman who casts his spinning lure downstream and works it upstream does not get nearly as many fish as the one who casts upstream.

The fly rod fisherman, casting his wet fly or nymph upstream, must penetrate the fast upper currents of all rivers. His fly must drift along in that much slower current which friction with the bottom always creates in a stream.

Similarly, the angler with his spinning rod who casts upstream, or up and across, penetrates those two fast upper layers immediately. Whether his lure be one-sixteenth or one-half ounce, the bass or trout in the quiet bottom layer sees the lure coming downstream towards him in a natural drift, not swimming upstream.

On a lake, as you sit in a boat, the bass are smashing at the minnows along the shoreline. You snap a quarter ounce lure on the leader, one that stays close to the surface after you cast it with your spinning rod.

After fishing for the shoreline bass, you turn to deeper water and fasten a ⅓ ounce plug or spoon to the swivel to get down under. Out in the open waters 100 foot casts are readily made with the spinning rod. The very fine line, scarcely visible, that goes off your reel fools the fish into striking quicker than when they see the heavier line you use with your plug rod.

When you come to heavy weed beds, down timber or stumps in the water, the spinning rod is not of much use until further advances are made by our manufacturers. You must then turn to the plug rod with a heavy line—12 to 30 pound tests—depending upon the fish there, bass, walleye, northern pike or muskies. You work those cluttered waters closely if you expect action.

There need be no mystery about the lures required for spinning. Figure 85.

On streams you let the water and the fish tell you what is needed to reach and search every type of water—rapids, riffles, pools and quiet reaches. You carry lures in various weights for this purpose, and care not too much about the patterns.

FIG. 84.—A Perfect Oxbow.

One seldom sees so perfect an oxbow. On the Mecan, a hard water stream in Wisconsin, it offeres a challenge to any fly fisherman, for oxbows are exceedingly hard to fish.

Wading down stream the silt and sand you stir up warns the fish in the undercut banks and deep holes. Wading upstream prevents one from offering his fly in a natural drift as the holes change your course. The bank fisherman has a chance if he fishes slowly in the manner shown in chapter XI, fig 63, page 189.

The fisherman with his spinning rod and long, almost invisible line finds this ideal water to work with small spinning lures. Every heavy tread on the bank is felt by the trout along their lateral line, those open pores along the middle of a fishes' body, from head to tail. These are his "ears" which telegraph our presence much as we feel an earthquake tremor.

Stream improvement, planting of alders and red-osier dogwood at the water's edge by individuals or groups of fishermen, would be most practical here. It would stop erosion of the stream banks and become the home of very large trout. The trout would range upstream and downstream during their feeding times and this spot would never be "fished out".

270

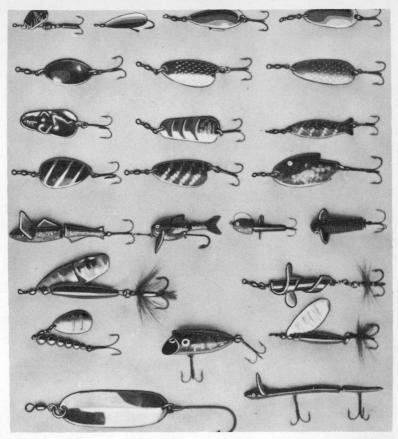

FIG. 85.—A few of the hundreds of spinning lures now on the market. All are about half size. The little 1⅞ inch spinner with treble hook, top row, number one, left, has accounted for hundreds of trout in Wisconsin.

The same goes for the lakes, where the water indicates whether you should use a surface lure, a light weight type to work the waters at a depth of only a few feet, or a heavy lure to go deeply.

The varied weights of the lures require you to put just the right amount of pressure on the cast or you will miss your target by a "city block."

Just as the rod and line are the most important factors in our fly fishing, so are they most important in our spin fishing. The reel in both methods is secondary.

271

My favorite spinning rod is 6½ feet long. It is of hollow glass construction, with a plain cork handle and reinforced butt. The action comes down nicely into the hand as it must in all fly and plug rods. This action enables the all around angler to turn from fly rod to plug rod to spinning rod with ease, comfort and accuracy, without "pressing."

Spinning rods are made in lengths from 6 to 7½ feet for the average lake and stream. For salmon and steelhead, single and double handled rods ranging from 7½ to 11½ feet are conventional adaptations of this type. They may well prove to be the answer for the yet unfilled gap in equipment for muskies.

I believe the all around fisherman will like the 6½ foot length best, especially now that some manufacturers began wrapping in extra glass to reinforce the butt section. The 6½ footer handles weights of one quarter to one half ounce lures nicely, yet one can easily cast lures as light as one sixteenth of an ounce.

Each rod can be forced to cast lighter or heavier lures than their maximum efficiency. However, if that fresh water can be searched properly with lures ranging in weight from ⅛ to ⅓ ounce, the medium action rod is the better all around choice.

Spinning rods range from $4.50 to $30 in the solid glass while the hollow glass ones start at about $9 and run up to about $35. The solid glass rods do not have the smooth action of the hollow glass rods, in my opinion, nor the durability either. Bamboo rods can be had for almost any price from $5 up to the finest hand made rods at $75.

Cork handles are on all glass rods and the reel seats are of the fixed type or the adjustable "loose" type. I much prefer the "loose" type for it holds the reel firmly but allows me to adjust the balance to suit myself, something which I cannot do with the fixed reel seat.

When casting a heavy lure, I like the reel "up forward" since this allows me to handle the half and five eighths ounce weights more smoothly. In casting the very lightest lures, I adjust the reel so it seats farther back. This adds to my accuracy as well as ease and comfort in my casting.

As soon as one gets thoroughly familiar with the particular rod and reel he is using, he gets the feel of it. He need but test the weight of any lure in his hand. Almost unconsciously he will seat the reel where his rod will give him the smoothest action he needs for that lure.

The reel, while not the most important part of one's spinning outfit, becomes a matter of one's purse strings. There is something in the pride of possession. If you have more money than hair on a dog, you can buy a spinning reel for $60. Then there are some as low as $4.95. Good reels can be had from $12.50 and there is no need to go over $30 if you wish a most excellent reel.

I prefer an open spool reel because the makers of the open spool have so much experience back of them, and I have learned to handle mine nicely. There are over 80 reels on the market today, with more coming along, I presume. I use but two in my fishing. If one looks for a conventional design, good workmanship and good material, he will have no trouble in his spinning.

Reels are not made to be oiled. They are made to be greased. If one cares for his spinning reel as he does his plug casting reel, he will get very good use from it. Grease it when it becomes wet or sanded and clean it thoroughly at the end of every season. It is important to use an occasional drop of oil on the bail pick-up mechanism, especially in salt water areas.

The bail type arm has displaced the finger type pickup. The manual type pickup will eventually find its place with the fisherman, just as the anti-backlash, level wind reel has come into popularity with our plug casting.

I make no claims at being at all expert as a spinner fisherman. When it comes to using the right line, I look at the water. I feel that I should know what sort of fish I should find there, and use the weight and type of lure I need to search for those fish.

When fishing *brown* to *dark brown* waters, I long for a simple dye that will color my 100 yard spools of monofilament. It goes without saying that it is as important to have invisibility in dark waters as it is in clear waters.

One day I was chided by my neighbor, Dick Talbot, who makes the famous line dressing and fly dressing, Silicote. (Adv.) Dick lives across the street from me, and saw me out in the yard throwing a lure with an 8½ pound test line. He didn't know I had gotten tired of yelling at little Willie every time I saw him picking on one of the kids in the block, always, you may be sure, on someone much smaller than he. I was practising for extreme accuracy. All I intended to do was to sit out in one of the lawn chairs, pick up the spinning rod and nail that roughneck of ours any place in the block, and his anatomy. Then only little Willie and Momma would be doing the hollering.

Dick looked with ill-concealed scorn at the heavy line I was using and what he thought was a light lure. He didn't know it was a solid chunk of lead. "Man, do me a favor and use a light line with that light lure," he pleaded. "We are never going to nail that little pest trying to throw a light lure with a heavy line." Now, this was an important point and should be heeded by all beginners. Always select the line, conditions permitting, for the weight of the lure you are casting; not the size of the fish you hope to catch.

There are so many lines on the market that one is apt to be greatly puzzled when he first takes up spinning.

I live in an area where I may be fishing trout on Monday, but walleyes, northerns or muskies on Tuesday, and what not on Wednesday, etc. Noah forgot to remove a lot of water before he made his landing of the ark and left much of it around my home in Oshkosh, Wisconsin. That is why I use a six pound test line most generally, and carry two extra spools in my pocket, one of four pound test and another of 8½ pound test.

Naturally, and quite contrarily, the muskies hit the lures when I have the four pound test spool on the reel and the crappies and perch hit when the 8½ pound test line is on the reel. That is why I usually start out and finish with the six pound test line. In this manner I always have a good alibi.

The best line, in my opinion, is the monofilament line for general fishing, up to 8½ pound test. If I fish for muskies in the flowages and have to "horse them out" from deadheads and heavy weed beds, I carry an extra spool of braided monofilament of 12 pound test.

Nylon spinning and casting lines braided without a core are the least desirable. Without a core the diameter is smaller, but it is so soft that it does not slip off the spool as easily as the monofilament. Anything over 8½ pound test, braided, tends to become too springy and this makes it hard to control. For the beginner, it is easier to learn to use the braided monofilament as it does not pop off the spool.

Nevertheless, the beginner should not "baby" himself. He should learn the hard way, by using the plain monofilament line of four pound test. His success will depend greatly upon the visibility which no plug casting line or heavy fly line, slapping the water, can possibly give him.

A monofilament spinning line, in effect, is like a 100 foot gut leader. In our fly fishing we seldom use a leader longer than 9½ feet, with 7½ feet the most common. Thus we frighten many a fish with our heavy lines, while the spinning line makes the fish much less wary.

Hardly had spinning taken hold in our country before the line makers came forth with a new wrinkle. It converts any spinning rod to a fly rod in less than five minutes. They sell a 14 to 20 foot length of "spin taper" fly line which you fasten to the end of your six pound test monofilament spinning line. To this added fly line, which weighs a quarter of an ounce, you tie on your regular fly leader and attach the fly you wish to use. The addition of the torpedo taper allows you to cast overhead or underhand, shooting the line off the reel for long casts. This does away with the necessity of using plastic bubbles to cast a fly. My experience has been that this is a poor substitute for a regular fly rod, primarily because of lack of control.

For spinning a fly with a tapered line you use a light plastic case, referred to as a "casting bubble." This is tied directly to the end of the line and, as a dropper, tie the fly about four feet from the bubble.

Some casting bubbles must be filled with water to get distance. Others, of heavier construction, contain an air chamber for flotation. These offset the type of plastic bubble which must be filled with water to cast your fly and dropper properly.

The spinning lures I show here are just a few of the many hundreds to be had, with new designs coming on the market almost daily. I can make no recommendation other than that the angler must use his own judgment when he learns how to read water and the behavior of the fish. Spinning is merely another method of searching the water for fish, and in that respect is not one whit different from any other fishing.

CHAPTER XIX

Choose Your Tackle Wisely

POLITICIANS of opposing factions argue too much. We who pursue the gentle art of angling are mild, even-tempered gentlemen, which is as it should be, until we gather in the fishing shack and start discussing our tackle.

It is then that the novice, sitting dumbfoundedly in the corner, decides the politicians are mere babes in the woods, insipid in their puny arguments. With anglers it's a battle to the finish, brother against brother, buddy against buddy, each to do his own dodging so the verbal missiles leave him unscathed. The weight of a fly rod, the length of a casting rod, the knot for a fly and the translucency of a Hare's Ear are argued with passion and downright vehemence.

Then everyone shakes hands and goes at it again. But look who's preparing to enter the debating arena, the old timer himself! And let me warn one and all, you are going to be backed into the corner until I get in my two cents' worth on this tackle business.

For the beginning fisherman, it's my opinion that the problem of rods, lines, reels and leaders can be quite complicated and needlessly expensive unless he uses good judgment.

In order to become an all around angler he should own a fly rod, a casting or plug rod and a spinning rod, along with the necessary reel and line for each rod.

If he lives in an area whose waters are mostly streams—cold enough for trout in the upper reaches and warm enough for bass in the lower reaches—his fishing will be mostly with the fly rod. Here he should buy the very best fly rod and line that he can afford, for it should last him his lifetime.

If he now and then fishes ponds and lakes and is able to travel and try out various waters, he should add a low priced spinning

277

rod and a low priced casting or plug rod. He can find very good action in the medium priced rods of these types, but his reels for both should be of good quality.

When he becomes acquainted with water and feels he should acquire more costly equipment, he can sell or trade his first rods, or better yet, let members of his family use them or have them on hand for spares while teaching some friend the grand art of fishing.

The beginner will allow the water and the fish to tell him whether he has the right tackle and will add to it when his own experience tells him what to buy. In a season or two he will find that everything he owns will serve him well. He will not be cluttered with a collection of useless tackle, for he will put every article to good use.

In his fly fishing he will be astonished at the ease and accuracy the right rod, reel and line will give him. Each day he fishes he will drop his fly but a few inches from a boulder, a log or the bank of the river, and take more fish.

With his plug rod he can sit in the boat and, with just a motion of his wrist, drop his lure alongside a lily pad or an open spot in a weed bed 50 to 75 feet away.

A little practice with his spinning rod will allow him to reach out 50 to 150 feet with ease on lake or stream.

Casting with any or all of the three rods is easily mastered.

More than half a century ago, when I first began fly fishing, a 10½ foot bamboo fly rod was considered ideal for our wet fly angling. We knew nothing about dry fly or nymph fishing then. In reality, our rods, soft in action from tip to handle, were far from ideal. Today those "weepy" rods would be laughed at.

When, along about 1911, we stream fishermen took up dry fly fishing, the rod makers had to change their ideas entirely. In order to handle the tapered lines with their heavier weight in the belly, the bamboo naturally had to have more power. The rods have consistently been improved since, with the result that today's fly rods are indeed potent weapons on our waters.

Back in the 1920s I had my own ideas what the ideal fly rod should be, and decided to have two of them custom made by F. E. Thomas of Bangor, Maine, one for the dry fly and the other for wet fly fishing. I also had ideas about a plug rod that would best serve my purposes.

For the dry fly rod I gave Mr. Thomas the following specifications: Length, 9½ feet, weight 5¾ ounces, cork handle 8 inches long, tapered from 1-1/16 inches at the thumb to 13/16

278

inches at the reel seat. All nodes to be staggered and the action to be in the upper two-fifths of the rod. Windings to be only at the guides and the ferrules, and the ferrules to be waterproof and serrated. One guide on the butt joint an inch below the female ferrule, five good sized guides on the middle joint and five guides and tip top on each of the two tip joints, for easy shooting of the line. The rod must handle an HCH double tapered line with ease. The reel seat to be made to carry my imported Hardy trout and salmon reels.

I requested Mr. Thomas to build the wet fly rod according to the same specifications but to make it a little "softer in the hand." The action was to be not quite as stiff as in the dry fly rod but it must handle a heavy line, a C level line at the least.

Ever since, those rods have had hard usage up in Canada and out on the Pacific Coast, as well as on the lakes and streams of Michigan and Wisconsin where they have been used in many a battle with large, scrappy fish, everything from fighting steelheads to muskies. To this day there is not as much as a trace of a set in the rods, and they still act as if they were doing the casting, which, of course, they are with only the scant help of my wrist.

When I was testing the Maine waters chemically about 25 years after I had received the rods, I stopped off at Bangor for a little visit with Mr. Thomas. I am sorry to say that he had died, but his son, Leon Thomas, looked over my rods critically and said, "All these rods need is to have the windings gone over." I left them there and received them in New York City later. They looked every bit as good after the tune-up of the windings as the day I had first seen them.

As far as my own views on fishing are concerned, the specifications I submitted to Mr. Thomas back in the 1920s are still the ones I look for whenever I sample the action of a new rod in a tackle shop for some friend.

In 1928 when I was on the Pacific Coast to fish the waters there, I decided to go up into British Columbia. During my change of trains at Seattle, a porter, not realizing the valuable cargo he was handling, ran over my rod case with a loaded baggage truck. I had that inner urge—he had smashed one of the tips of my dry fly rod and also one of the wet fly rods. But I controlled myself, and later cut off six inches of the broken tips, glued and fitted the tops of the tips and they looked as good as new.

That porter really did me a favor, although I was in no mood to realize it at the time. For years I have used the shorter dry fly rod tip for throwing bass bugs and the shorter tip of the wet fly rod for offering flies to walleyes and northern pike. Thus, with the other two tips still intact, I have had the use of both a 9 foot and a 9½ foot rod for the dry fly and the wet fly.

The demand for shorter rods came on as more women became interested in fly fishing and a new generation of anglers was coming along. Fishermen began using rods all the way from 7, 7½, 8, 8½ to 9 feet in length. I tried them all and decided that for me an 8 foot rod was as short as I cared to get. My wife preferred that length, too, and found that she could use it without tiring.

When trying out the shorter rods I look for the same action as in my 9½ footers. If a fisherman can afford two fly rods, my advice is to buy one 8 foot model along with his 9 to 9½ foot rod. There are times when he prefers the lighter rod for smaller streams and uncluttered waters.

Today almost every bamboo rod maker staggers the nodes of the bamboo, even in the low price class. Apparently today's anglers also prefer action in the upper two-fifths of their rods because practically all rods now have their action there. Bamboo rods of fair quality can be purchased for as little as $15, while the better hand-made rods, such as those built by Thomas, Orvis, Leonard, Payne, Dickerson, Uslan and Paul H. Young cost up to $100.

Steel fly rods came on the market in the late 1920s. These gave fishermen a fair rod at lower prices and little care was required for their upkeep. Shortly after World War II, before the 20th century turned its half way mark, the glass rod appeared on the scene and has all but made the steel rod obsolete. The glass rod also seems inclined to make the bamboo rod a thing of the past for the masses. Only those of us "old timers" who appreciate the craftsmanship and the excellence of bamboo, and a few of the younger men, are still insisting upon hand made bamboo rods.

There is much to be said for the glass rod. It needs hardly any attention. You can put a glass rod away while it is wet and it can be dropped in the water and no harm comes to it. No varnishing is needed and you can buy a rod of good action for a modest sum. No fisherman need deny himself the pleasure of fly fishing, for there is a glass rod for every purse.

Many anglers do not know how to judge a new rod. Picking

up a fly rod and flipping it like a buggy whip tells nothing of its quality.

It is not necessary to rig the line, leader, fly and the reel to the rod and try it out on the water. I grasp the cork handle with my thumb resting on the top and my fingers around the handle. Then I shove my elbow firmly against my body above the hip bone. With my elbow and forearm directly in front of me, I *do not move* them. They merely serve as a vise for the rod. Using only my wrist, I start swinging the rod from side to side—never up and down—making certain not to move the elbow and the forearm at all. Now, with an almost imperceptible movement of the wrist I cause the handle to move the rod back and forth, back and forth until the rod gets swinging so that you can see its true action. If the rod bends mostly in the upper two-fifths, doesn't dither, and you note power there, along with good action "down in the hand," it will handle your fly, streamer or bass bug nicely.

The surest way to make a man disgusted with fly fishing is to give him the wrong line for his rod. The right line and rod will, under competent instruction, make him a good caster in a few hours. Remember, I said hours, not days.

I charge my "customers" 15 cents an hour. If they aren't fair fly casters in three hours, I pay them 50 cents an hour for their "lost" time. Just to make it interesting I lay down a 5 dollar bill and make them put up a nickel. Then I wager I can teach them the roll cast in five minutes. I have never failed to take their money. If I only had enough "customers" I'd get rich quickly, except for that awful income tax.

If the line is too light for the rod, one might just as well cast with grocery twine. If it is too heavy, that will be almost as serious. The wrong kind of line can make a man a dub caster all his fishing days.

This is a vexing problem. The best way to solve it is to borrow a line from a friend, since no dealer can be expected to open a nicely packed line for purely experimental purposes. Try your friend's line on your rod at the waterside, not on the grass or driveway. You may find your friend has a line of the desired weight. If so, your casting will improve immediately.

Lines run in level sizes from AAAAA, B. C. to size I. Their diameters in hundredths of an inch are from .80 to .022. Your choice should be in the sizes C, diameter .050, or D, .045, or E, .040. Nylon lines run a little lighter in weight than silk ones for the same diameters, but fly fishermen consider nothing but diameters from A, B, C, D and E, using F. G. H and I for tapering only, in either silk or nylon.

I use a nylon level fly line but prefer a silk line for my double tapered fly line. Until the nylon line makers get more weight and less stretch for the same diameters, I shall always use silk.

I do not advise the dry fly angler to use a level line. It will not have the delicacy, the accuracy and the ease of casting your dry fly, for this style of fishing demands many false casts before you allow your fly to drop upon the water.

A torpedo taper line is not good for dry fly fishing and should be bought only after you have had much experience with wet fly and nymph fishing. Then you can try out the various torpedo tapers of your friends from sizes GBG, GBF, GAF and GB2AF until you find the right weight that your own rod will handle. These torpedo tapers allow one to make extremely long casts on wide rivers and lakes where accuracy is not of such moment as distance.

The double tapered HCH or HDH lines allow you to cast 50 feet nicely. At 20 feet the heavy belly of the line C, .050 in diameter, comes beautifully into play and the tapering down to H, .025 diameter, gives you opportunity to drop your fly lightly on the water. There will be no pull of the fly and leader on the water such as with a level or a torpedo line, and the greased fine part of the taper will ride along lightly even in broken water. Very seldom does a good dry fly fisherman reach out for more than 40 feet. A 50 foot dry fly cast I regard as a very long one.

We are on the threshold of the greatest fly line development of a century. My double tapered HCH silk lines have served me faithfully through all my dry fly days. Now the manufacturers are bringing out lines of everything from fiberglass to dacron to nylon and silk combinations of these materials.

Casts of 90 to 100 feet can be made with the same ease I cast 60 feet with my double taper or level silk lines. Those of us who cast with a "heavy" hand, a "light" hand or bring out the easy "medium" power of our rod can now fit our line to coordinate with our individual wrist and forearm action.

The reel to buy is one that has a spool large enough to carry at least 150 feet of light 12 pound test nylon fishing line for backing. Your level line and double tapered line will each run 25 to 30 yards. When you fish such turbulent waters as the Soo Rapids between the American and Canadian locks at Sault Ste. Marie, or any of the wide steelhead streams in the West, you may require 100 yards of backing to let your big fish run.

A torpedo taper line is good here. I use 30 yards of such line at the Soo. It is nothing unusual here to have a large rainbow smash at the fly and take the whole line and almost the entire 300 feet of backing as well.

Some anglers prefer an automatic reel, and I have no quarrel with them on this score. Personally, I find an automatic reel is very heavy and does not give me enough room on the spool for the backing I like to use with my fly line. The lack of room ruined the finish of a $12 imported line I had way back when, and $12 was important money then. Yet many of my friends use an automatic reel on the creeks and rivers which are not too wide, and will use nothing else.

Buy as good a reel as you can afford after you have had some experience on the stream. Your first reel—a single action—can be had for 5 or 6 dollars. You can use it later for fishing exclusively with the level line, going into a better quality of about $10 for

Small rainbows in Wisconsin's Brule river are great leapers.—Fish and photograph by Seegar Swanson.

your double tapered dry fly line with the extra backing line you will need.

Leaders for fly fishing can be as complicated a problem as the fisherman wishes to make them. He can take much of the grief out of this problem if he learns to tie the barrel knot for the strand and the perfection knot (sheepshank) for the loop. For the fly to leader knot I use the Major Turle knot.

Nylon leader material is considerably cheaper than gut of the silkworm, known to fishermen as Spanish gut. The same knots will tie both materials, although there are so many leader sizes available that the angler can buy almost any length, level or taper he desires.

A level six pound test nylon leader, six feet in length, is my staple wet fly, nymph and wet-dry fly leader. On windy days when I fish for bass, I shorten it to about four feet for easy handling of the wind-resisting bass bugs. On less windy days I use five feet for the bulky bass bug, going back to six feet when it is calm, for both bass and trout fishing with the wet fly.

For dry fly fishing, I use tapered leaders seven and one-half feet in length. In my leader box are several tippets of gut and nylon in various pound tests. It is but a matter of minutes to tie tippets to the staple leader and make it as long as I wish, for the knots are easy to learn.

This staple leader is tapered from a 12 pound test gut at the fly line to a three pound test at the fly. When I fish very *clear* water in which the trout are apt to see me if I fish close, I add one and one-half feet of tippet which tests two pounds. This gives me a nine foot leader which is ample for almost all of my *clear* water angling if I keep out of sight of the trout. I use this length, too, for fishing with small flies from size 20 to 14.

When I meet up with fairly fast water I go back to the seven and one-half foot leader by cutting off the extra one and one-half feet. In this manner I am not fumbling around to drag out various size leaders, for it is so easy to add to my staple leader. At night I use the same leader but cut off one and one-half feet of it for dry fly fishing. The next day I look over my leaders and tie the tippets back on again, so that once more I have all leaders tapering from a 12 pound test to a three pound test. I prefer Spanish gut for dry fly leaders, but now and then I use nylon tapered leaders.

When I look at my nylon or Spanish gut leaders in *dark brown, brown or tan* waters the sun shows them up as plainly

284

as a white bean in a black cat's flank. I dye them just one color for these waters, brown. In *clear* or *very clear* waters I use the natural or mist color. Thus I fish with confidence through the range of water colors.

PLUG RODS

It is confusing to call our 4 to 6¼ foot rods by so many names, such as bait, casting and plug rods. This type is used to cast weighted flies, plugs, spoons and other lures in addition to bait. I prefer to use the name "plug rods" and trust I shall be forgiven for using this term in my discussion.

In buying a plug rod it is best to select one at least five feet in length. Five and one half feet is better for anglers who use the best reels and light lines. My three 6¼ foot Thomas bamboo rods are of various weights. I want ease and accuracy in casting, trusting to my ability to play a heavy fish without breaking the line. My three Meek reels, made to match the rods, give me all this to the highest degree.

I have no idea how many hundreds of casts I make in one day of fishing. The less I have to work my wrist and arm to throw a lure, the happier I am. With the longer rods one can hit an opening in the weeds, and lay a lure along side a stump or in any pocket with little effort.

There are many glass plug rods with nice action which can be bought for as little as $3 and up to $20. With a five and one-half footer and any smooth running reel the fisherman can work any waters.

But the angler who intends to specialize in plug casting should buy as good a hollow glass rod as he can afford in a five and one-half foot length. He should stretch his purse to the limit. He should own a muskie rod, too, a heavier rod with stiffer action, five feet in length and of good quality. It must handle the large lures he will need for this species of fish.

A five and one-half foot rod with a line no heavier than 10 pound test of braided nylon is best for bass. For northerns and walleyes a 12 pound test nylon is better. But for trolling, a stronger line, at least an 18 pound test, is advisable to withstand weeds and other obstructions.

The line for muskies must be strong, no lighter than 24 pound test in cluttered waters. Muskies are so often found in waters from a foot or two to more than 10 feet deep that we must be prepared literally to drag them away from dense weed beds, down timber, waterlogged stumps and other cover, or they will break the line and vanish.

A muskie, like a northern pike, makes a short run, but sometimes he fights with fury. No light line will drag him out to the open water where he can be put at a disadvantage. In unobstructed waters an 18 pound test will hold any muskie, and is much easier to cast than the heavier lines. Wire leaders should always be used for northerns, walleyes and muskies.

The angler who specializes in muskie fishing should own a low priced fly fishing outfit and a low priced spinning rod and reel to enjoy the days when muskies will look at nothing he offers. A change of pace to a bass lake or trout stream is always welcome when cast after cast for muskies yields naught but frustration.

There are so many excellent plug casting reels in the shops that it is impossible to select any one particular model as the one and only. Buy the best you can afford for it will last for years with just a little extra care.

The level wind, anti-back lash reel is, of course, the most comfortable to use. It is just the thing for early morning and late afternoon and evening fishing when a "bird's nest" on a reel without the level wind would ruin the few good hours the fish are hitting.

I always carry an extra reel so that if anything happens, I can reach into the tackle box and be fishing again in a few moments. This spare can be one of the lower priced reels and is always good insurance, for the best of us get hopeless back-lashes now and then.

CHAPTER XX

Casting Is Easy To Learn

THE YOUNG FELLOW shook his head in bewilderment. I heard him say, "Guess I better quit right now. This fly fishing business is too complicated for me."

Who could blame him? The "expert" who was teaching him to cast was showing him some 12 to 15 different casts. Four are enough, and with these he could fish with the fly on any lake or stream in the country.

Most any man, woman or even a child of 10 years can become an efficient caster of the fly, plug or spinning lure in such a short time that each will be pleasantly surprised at the ease of it.

The "ease of it" tells all. Casting, truly an intriguing art, does not require brute strength, nor does it call for concentrated brain power. Rather, it is a coordination of your muscles that spells success.

How often we see someone pick up the rod and work like a Trojan to cast the fly, plug or spinning lure. Then, when he begins to tire, he discovers that a sort of lazy, easy and smooth action of the forearm and wrist carries the fly or lure far beyond where he expected it to go.

What really happens is that the embryonic caster becomes too tired to put all his strength into the cast. He finally uses the rod instead of his arm and body to get the lure out. And that is all that casting is, allowing the good action of the rod to have its rightful place in every cast we make.

When I am asked to teach a beginning fisherman how to handle his fly, I stress the four essential casts, the wet fly, dry fly, roll and the cast to get the fly under branches.

As my time is worth money, I put up a five dollar bill and make him wager a nickel against it that he will learn the fundamentals of all four, in less than an hour. Soon he walks

FIG. 87.—Casting The Wet Fly.

Dr. Meilicke, "Mike" to his fishing buddies, uses 35 feet of line and leader on the water. He raises the rod slowly until it is in the position shown. Then with one quick sharp lift the rod is brought to the position shown below at left, elbow at side, thumb pointing straight up and all the power of the rod goes into the upper two fifths of the rod. Never point the thumb one inch past "straight up." This is the back cast.

A slight wait until he feels the tension telling him that the line, leader and fly has exerted its greatest pull on the rod. (about as long as you can count one, two, three). Now, not losing that power, he snaps his wrist forward, without changing his position. Following through, he lets go of the line in his left hand. It shoots through the guides and the fly lights lightly upon the water. This is the forward cast, really a "throw" of the rod tip.

Casting The Dry Fly.

This is done in exactly the same manner as the wet fly cast except that the rod is kept going back and forth, smoothly, easily and with the same

288

away with the knowledge and fair casting ability and I go some place and squander his nickel gleefully.

The first lesson is in throwing the wet fly. I have him pay out about 30 feet of line and leader on the water. Then I have him take a "healthy" strip of line off the reel. This gives him about five feet of extra line to hold in his left hand, assuming he is right handed.

With his right elbow held firmly against his side so that he can use only his wrist and forearm, he points the rod tip at the water just over the surface. To start the fly out of the water, he raises the rod tip until the fly has moved very slowly towards him in the water. Now a quick, sharp lift of the rod tip takes the fly, leader and line out of the water and they shoot over his shoulder. He stops the rod tip when it is pointing straight at the sky overhead. This is called the back cast.

He holds his thumb right there, pointing at the sky, while he says to himself, "Hold and cast." This gives the line, leader and fly just enough time to straighten out behind him and bend the upper two-fifths of the rod in a backward bow to give him the power he needs for the forward cast. See Figure 87.

After a few attempts, he will get the feel of the tension on the tip and the upper part of the rod.

Before he loses that tension, his thumb on the cork handle and his wrist use a fast forward "snap" which he stops at a point half way between the sky and his waist. Here he releases the five feet of line he has held between the thumb and finger of his left hand. The line shoots through the guides and kills the full power of the forward thrust. The fly falls lightly upon the water, followed by the line and leader. Really, that is all there is to it.

It isn't long before the beginner gets the feel of this cast, the timing needed to sense that back stretch of line and leader which will tell him when to make the forward cast. Right

power but the fly is not allowed to drop on the water until it is pointing at the spot where he wishes it to light. To get more distance the line is stripped off the reel with the left hand, in good healthy strips, not "picky" strips. After a few moments, when you get the feel of this cast, this will come to you easily. Then you will soon strip line from the reel, shooting it through the guides on both the backward and forward casts. Smooth casting avoids the "wind" knots in your leader which weaken the gut and lessen your accuracy. On your back casts turn your head, not your body, and you will soon learn to get the perfect timing on your back casts so that the line and leader will not dither, for your eyes will tell you when to "throw" with the rod tip.

then he has the fundamentals of the dry fly cast and the cast for getting under branches a foot or two above the water. In all casts the idea is to allow the rod to do the work. The wrist and thumb are merely "directors." Women learn this more quickly than men. They have a better sense of rhythm and not so powerful a wrist.

To learn the dry fly cast, the beginner does exactly the same as with the wet fly, except that he does not immediately allow the fly to drop on the water. He keeps it in the air until it reaches the spot he would like it to drop so it will float down to him. When he sees the fly is about to touch the water, he brings it back by using the ordinary back cast. Repeating these backward and forward casts, he strips off more line from the reel with his left hand while the fly is kept in the air with the false casts. When the fly has reached the spot where the angler wants it to go, he releases the line from his left hand and it "kills" the cast. His dry fly lights upon the water as daintily as a living fly.

Thus, dry fly casting is merely a series of wet fly casts backward and forward, backward and forward three or four times in the air. The rod hand never allows the cork handle to point anywhere but at the sky at every back cast.

I'm afraid that if it took you 15 minutes to get fairly good with the wet fly cast it will require another 10 minutes to get the knack of the dry fly cast. Twenty-five minutes gone. Quit worrying about the nickel. It is as good as in my pocket.

We old timers taught a novice to cast by making him hold a handkerchief against his right elbow all the time he was casting. In this way he had to use the power of the rod and not his upper arm if he expected to hold that handkerchief in place. When he had learned to feel the pull of the line behind him and could manipulate his rod, line, leader and fly, we allowed him to wade in waist deep water. Here we let him raise his elbow just as he would in fishing from a canoe.

The under-the-branch cast is basically the same as the wet and the dry fly cast. The only difference is that the rod is held over the water all during the cast. This cast is especially advantageous when the angler is working against a rather stiff wind. The fly is worked horizontally over the surface of the water, where the wind resistance is practically nil. While other fishermen run home in a 15 mile an hour breeze, stay with this cast and you'll have great sport.

To execute this cast, imagine that you are casting with the

FIG. 88.—Getting Under The Branches.

This is the same action as the wet fly or dry fly cast, except that the rod is held over the water. Note how Mike holds his wrist firmly, to give the rod the right timing for the backward cast. Note also the action he gives the rod on the forward cast to allow the rod to do the work. Observe also how the rod is kept in the same plane over the water. To make the dry fly cast he merely extends the line until he sees that it will reach under the branches. Then he "shoots" the spare line held in his left hand and the fly and leader curve under the branches.

rod held over a plank which is six feet long and about level with your hip over the water. Assume there is another plank six inches above this one. Your casting technique calls for keeping your rod in the imaginary groove between the two planks, as shown in Figure 88. You work the rod with backward and forward casts, the same as with the wet and dry fly casts except that your rod is now in a horizontal rather than vertical position.

To get your fly under the branches, you begin with the false casts of the dry fly, extending your line until you see that the fly will light under the branches hanging a foot or two over the water. When you think you have the right distance you release the extra five feet of line in your left hand. The fly and leader will curve right under the branches in a left hand arc. When you cast with your left hand and release the line with your right hand, this makes a right hand curve.

This horizontal cast is also important because it enables an angler to curve a leader around a stump or boulder in the water.

No one should cast exclusively with his right or left hand all day long. It requires only 15 minutes to learn to cast with the "wrong" hand. Casting 15 minutes with the "wrong" hand each hour you are on the stream soon makes you expert with either hand. How you can "lay into" a breeze after a few minute's practice!

I wish you would quit worrying about losing that nickel. The money is practically mine for you have only to learn the roll cast. If I were with you on a stream I'd guarantee that you would learn it before you could read these instructions. Just two practice casts and you'd have it for the rest of your fishing days.

The roll cast is merely half a wet fly cast. With 35 or 40 feet of line, leader and fly in the water, you bring the rod up slowly towards you until the tip is pointing straight up at the sky, exactly as shown in Figure 89. The line will be lying in the water, not moving towards you, for you have brought the tip up slowly.

Now, give it a fast downward motion until the rod tip is about half way down to the water as shown in Figure 89a. Stop the rod tip right there for about a half second. Then follow through with the rod hand until it is in position 89b. The line, leader and fly will roll out of the water and over

292

FIG. 89.—The Roll Cast.

I wouldn't take a "million dollars" for the satisfaction I have had over the years with this cast. Mike offered me a prescription for halitosis in payment for it. Said it would cure what I said about his golfing, under my breath.

At left he has brought in the 35 feet of line which was lying in the water. It is bellying at his feet and the rod motion is stopped dead. Without bringing the rod backward one inch from the position shown, rod pointing straight up in the air, he gives it a fast downward snap but stops the rod tip at the position shown for one second. Then he immediately drops the rod tip over the water as shown at bottom. It is the stopping the rod with the follow through action that will amaze the beginner in the way the line "rolls" out.

293

to any spot you aim at with the rod tip when you start the roll.

While I am picking up my ill-gotten gains, your precious nickel, let me explain why this cast is one that you MUST use With no room for a back cast, it will enable you to stand with your back against a solid wall of stone or tree branches and roll your wet fly, dry fly or nymph 30 to 60 feet across the stream. You need never be concerned about being hung up behind because in using the roll cast you never bring your rod a single inch backward over your shoulder.

You will use the roll cast continually in your dry fly fishing. After the dry fly has floated over the water which you have worked nearest you, pick it off the water with the roll cast and resume fishing without bothering to strip in a lot of line.

When you get proficient with this cast you can often release a fly which has been caught in a log, stump or other obstruction in the stream. You strip off a great deal of line until you have a very slack loop in the water, then throw a roll cast. The line will roll along and back of the fly. This will cause a pull which releases the fly if you give it a lift at the very end of the roll. Be very careful with this release pull, for you can break a rod tip until you learn to handle the cast with ease. Practice it first out in the stream with about 30 feet of line until you get the timing and the knack of when to pull and free the fly.

In all of your casting never forget that it is the upper two-fifths of the rod that does all the work. Give the sweet power of the rod a chance by not pointing your thumb over your shoulder on the back casts. This kills the back cast, for you do not allow the line to go straight back and put the power into the tip for the forward cast.

Learning to cast with a plug rod requires a little longer time than with a fly rod. The reel and the rod do the work in plug casting. Until one learns to handle both rod and reel smoothly, without brute strength, he will never gain the ease and the accuracy needed for skillful fishing.

There are two necessary casts in plug casting, the overhead and the underhand. The overhead is the smoothest for accuracy and for the safety of those around you in the boat or on the dock. The underhand, often called the side cast and the side-swipe, should have no place in your casting unless it is used solely for getting under branches or other obstructions over the water.

294

The plug caster cannot get distance or accuracy if he has a poor reel and a line that is too heavy. Today most casters use a level wind reel or a self caster. Some few, like myself, have used the old fashioned fast reels without the level wind or the anti-back lash features for so many years that we will never change.

Assume that you wish to learn the overhead cast with a five and a half foot plug rod. The rod action should be fairly "whippy." You have an easy running anti-back lash level winding reel and a 10 pound test line. Tie a ⅝ ounce plug to your line. This weight will allow for proper thumbing of the line. The spool will revolve nicely with the proper use of your wrist, and you should get ease and accuracy with this outfit.

Place a clock facing you at your left. Take up a position with the rod extended over the water at about 2:30 o'clock. With the upper arm close to your side, and kept there throughout the cast, swing the rod up to 11 o'clock. You are now in position to begin the forward cast.

Start with a slow movement, but increase it to very fast by the time your wrist is at 12 o'clock. Then bring it sharply forward to about two o'clock, reducing the pressure of your thumb somewhat at about one o'clock, but do not take your thumb entirely off the line and flange of the reel from start to finish.

The plug will leave the rod tip at about two o'clock, but you follow through with a graceful, easy motion of your wrist until the rod is at three o'clock. Then you check the line with a heavier application of your thumb, which at no time has been entirely removed from the outgoing line and the flange of the reel.

Sounds simple and easy, doesn't it? It will be simple, very simple after an hour's practice. But many things happen to the beginner, and they happen fast. If you put too much pressure on the flange and the outgoing line with your thumb, the plug lands in the water at your feet. If you use too little pressure you have a tangle that we call a "bird's nest" or back lash.

The side or underhand cast is executed the same as the overhead, except that the rod is held over the water during the cast.

There actually is nothing to learning how to cast the plug, although at first you will become so tired you'll want to throw the "whole works in the drink." Don't give up. When

295

you are so tired that you are in despair, make another cast. Then it will dawn upon you that it is the spring of the rod tip plus just a little help with your wrist which sails the plug out so smoothly in a looping arc. From then on you'll wonder why you hadn't realized that an hour sooner.

CHAPTER XXI

Fly Tying Is
a Wonderful Hobby

MOMMA WILL STUFF that reprobate of ours, little Willie, all day long with everything from doughnuts, candy, mashed potatoes to onion sandwiches. "Children will eat anything," she tells me.

In her abysmal naivete she has the same idea about trout. "Fish will eat anything," she says. "Tie me a light and dark pattern for my dry fly fishing and one pattern for my wet fly fishing. Just give me enough of them, that's all I want."

I can handle Willie any time with the knotty wooden club I keep in the corner. Momma outweighs me; I merely argue with her.

Very carefully I select the patterns I shall need for my day's fishing. With Momma, it is, "Just give me my flies," and she is set. She carries them in two ordinary penny match boxes, and how I shudder for fear she will matt those beautiful dry fly hackles.

Of course she takes fish: brooks, browns, rainbows, bass and blue gills—sometimes more than I—but it isn't because she is a good angler. It is due solely to the exhaustive research Poppa has done on her flies.

With the wet fly pattern I explained very carefully that it was an all around pattern. Consequently, she always says, "Tie me up some more Rounder flies."

The pattern I tie for her makes a great deal of work as any fly tying husband will tell you. Two minutes of the artist's time, but somehow I've got Momma believing that each fly requires a half hour of intensive work. I figure this develops greater appreciation of my product.

I tie a body of orange yarn, rib it with fine gold wire and wind on a grouse hackle at the head. To make the hackle flow away from the body, I tie a fat body. I tie a thin body to make the hackles cling around the body.

When she takes trout with the Rounder fly, she wants to know why. I show her how the thin body causes it to look like a nymph coming up to hatch. See Figure 90. Then I drop the fat body fly into the water and explain how it looks like our orange body mayfly when it has drowned. I also tell her the fat body fly imitates the opening and closing of the wings of many land and water-bred flies when the current has its way with it. Thus, I explain, the Rounder fly serves three purposes, which is the reason she catches so many fish.

"H-m-m. A three-way stretch, just like my gir----." But I listen no more. What with feathers on the floor, fur in the magazine rack, and fish hooks where company sits down, to

Photo By The Author.

Fig. 90.—Alan N. Miller selecting herl from a peacock feather to imitate moving gills which most species of mayfly nymphs have along their sides. Alan photographed about 98 per cent of the pictures in this book during the many years I was gathering the material. I am quite proud of his excellent work.

FIG. 90a.—Peacock Herl And Mayfly Gills.
At left (much enlarged) is shown the underside of a mayfly nymph.
The majority we imitate have seven pairs of gills. Peacock herl is excellent to imitate their fast moving gills. Teased muskrat fur or a saddle hackle with barbs cut, not torn, are also very good. Some nymphs drift up to the surface to hatch, with legs folded under the body, as shown. For dressings of my imitation, see "Rounder Fly" in the fly tying chapter.

say nothing of orders to get myself and my whole fly tying kit and caboodle in the basement, I sometimes wonder if I'm right when I insist fly tying is a wonderful hobby. It most certainly is!

Anyone, no matter how clumsy he may think his fingers are, can sit down with a small vise and learn the very few knots necessary to tie flies.

If he has the right materials—feathers, furs and yarns—and the varying sizes he should have in his hooks, there is no imitation he cannot produce.

The fly tying tools are simple. All you need besides the vise are two small pairs of scissors, hackle pliers, a razor blade, a bodkin, thread, some wax and a small bottle of quick drying varnish.

Now that we have another fly tyer in our midst, what does he proceed to do? Without a doubt, exactly what I did 40 years ago. I sat down and tied the most utterly foolish contraptions. They weren't flies, they were monstrosities. But they took fish!

Immediately I flattered myself that along with being a good

fisherman, I was now also an expert fly tyer. Things were different then, however. Trout were far more plentiful, and that old saying of "hide behind a tree to bait your hook or a trout will grab it out of your hands" had some semblance of truth. No wonder they took my freak flies.

My efforts as a fly tyer improved rapidly when I began tying imitations of the flies and nymphs I found in the stomachs of the fish. I was highly elated when I noted for the first time that peacock herl looks almost exactly like the gills on millions of the mayfly and beetle nymphs in all our lakes and streams. My feeling that I had then become an observant angler was quite understandable.

In my opinion, Charles Cotton was easily one of the most observant anglers of his time in all England. This is clearly reflected in the 13 chapters he added to Izaak Walton's immortal classic, "The Compleat Angler." At the time I made my observations about peacock herl, I did not know about Cotton. Years later, when I read his chapters, I found he had used peacock herl for many of his fly bodies.

More than 250 years ago Cotton tied the Coachman fly. It is right there in his list of 66 flies, and his explanation of how he covered the wet fly field, tying all his flies without the use of a vise.

I almost fell out of my chair when I read this paragraph by Cotton: "There is also this month a fly called the PEACOCK Fly. The body is made of the whirl of a peacock's feather, with a red head (red brown hackle) and the wings of a mallard's feather."

If that isn't our Leadwing Coachman, I'll eat it, hook and all. More than 200 years later this same fly was tied by Tom Bosworth and has since been known as the Coachman, for he was Queen Victoria's carriage driver.

Some anglers in England refuse to fish with the Coachman fly for they write that "it resembles nothing on earth." I've read that same statement in magazine articles in the United States, too. How wrong they are! This is what they should say about the Coachman fly:

"There is no fly, of all the thousands of fly patterns, which so closely resembles the mayfly nymph coming to the surface to hatch. How plainly visible to the fish are the gills of the rising nymph when its wings and body are half withdrawn while its shuck is still in the water! See Figure 90a. With its peacock herl body, how closely the Leadwing Coachman

300

imitates the dull winged species and the Coachman the white winged species. Millions and millions of our mayflies hatch like this, their bodies ranging from one fifth of an inch in length to three quarters of an inch. Small wonder that the Coachman fly catches fish, whether the hook sizes be as small as 20 or as large as 8. Look at the Royal Coachman too, and note the "gills" of peacock herl.

Again Cotton showed me that my "discovery" was ancient history when he wrote: "We have also another, made of a peacock's whirl, WITHOUT WINGS." Here again he was discussing a fly that imitated a mayfly nymph. In this instance, however, the nymph was not rising to hatch, but was in its underwater stage. In this stage, too, the mayfly nymph has gills along its body, perfectly simulated by peacock herl.

Scoop up a few mayfly nymphs from a stream with the palm of your hand. You'll see for yourself the fast movement of the gills along the bodies of the nymphs. Or, look at the photograph of the nymph and the peacock "whirl" in Figures 90 and 90a.

It is a simple matter to tie imitations of these mayfly nymphs. If you are not a fly tier and cannot buy them in a tackle shop, purchase some Leadwing Coachman flies, or the standard Coachman fly. Cut off their wings to a short stub and trim the hackles a trifle. You will then have good nymph imitations that will take many trout or bass when fished wet.

How well Cotton knew the tiny mayflies, such as our little *Caenis*, those flies which have four generations in one year in all our streams here. I tie them on hooks size 18 and 20 and have caught hundreds of trout with them. See Figure 95. Cotton's conversation with Viator clearly tells why.

Viator said, "This is a very little hook," and Cotton replied, "That may serve to inform you that it is for a very little fly—for as the case stands it must be a little fly and a very little one, too, that must do your business." Figure 36, Chapter IX, shows how right he was.

Long before I ever dreamed of looking at the bodies of the caddis flies with my little hand lens, Cotton knew that millions of them had rough bodies. He imitated them with fur spun on a thread and wound around the shank of a hook. To imitate the Green Drake, the largest mayfly in English waters, he mixed FOUR different furs to make their bodies.

Although I like to think that I have done quite a bit of research with water-bred flies, the more I read Cotton, the

301

more I feel like a pupil in kindergarten. The few instances I have cited here of his great knowledge of insects in his home and how to imitate them bears me out on this.

Sometimes I get so exasperated with the English when they run counter to American views that I could buckle on the old broadsword and have at them. But in my later years when I bought and read their fishing literature, from Walton and Cotton to Ronalds, Halford, Skues and Tavener, I offered up a silent prayer for the souls of those venerable fishermen, modest men all.

The run-of-the-mill fishermen and fly tier will never know the full pleasure that is experienced by the few anglers in a thousand who study nature to guide them in tying their flies.

The serious-minded fly tier sits at the streamside, his rod and reel forgotten, and watches the nymphs rise at his feet. He seizes one in the water and places it in a small bottle. He captures the dun of the mayfly as it comes out of its nymphal shuck. The next day, when he looks in the spider webs, or at the insects flying in the air, he sees how the dun of yesterday has turned into the "spinner" of today. He observes the "spinner" when it has mated and drops its eggs upon the water that same evening and dies, a spent fly.

Right there, he is an authority on fishing with that particular species of mayfly. He goes home and sits at his fly tying bench. The entire life cycle of the fly is before him—the nymph, dun, spinner and spent fly—and he even knows the color of the egg sacs which affects the body color of the fly.

He may not know the order, the family, the genus or the species, and its Latin name may likewise mean nothing to him. But, when he sits at his bench and goes through his materials he doesn't need to be an entomologist. It is the color of the body, its length, the color of the wings and how much wing spread the fly before him has that is of concern.

When he looks at the imitation he has created, no one can tell him that his is not a good fly to use in his home waters. Didn't he see it hatch by the thousands? Isn't he sure that it will be there year after year, from nymph to drowned spent fly, all eaten by the trout? Away from his home waters that species may not be in the rivers, but he cares not.

Every moment at his bench brings production of patterns he knows are good. He spends no time tying a lot of "dream" flies, vagaries and hallucinations that are not based on the true flies of nature. He does not run to the vise every time he reads or hears of the "latest" creation of some new type which has no basis in nature and will have its day and then be forgotten.

He knows that fish and insects were on this earth millions of years before man and that the real flies of old are still in our waters. Gradually he collects the flies which hatch in May, June, July and August, his fishing season. Soon he has an authentic list of dark, medium light and light colored bodies. He ties but a few general patterns for his fishing but he ties them on hooks all the way from size 20 through size two. His fly box compartments are filled with good imitations and he knows from his observations how to work them. He has seen how they act in the water, out of the water and on the water.

The naturalist, the good caster and the fly tier soon develops into an expert fisherman who takes his hat off to no one on his home waters, and that, my good sir or madam, is what makes an all around fisherman.

The prime requisite in all fly tying must be the lasting quality of the fly you tie. If the fly will not stand hooking and playing many fish without having it look like somthing the cat dragged in, your workmanship is poor.

One great fault of flies not being able to take punishment is the half hitch which so many use. The half hitch is as obsolete to me as the horse and buggy. It loosens immediately. The "Scotch hitch", on the other hand, will hold your work and should be used on every size hook from size 20 to the largest hooks we use. I first learned of it from Herb Van Horn, of Gladstone, Michigan, the best fly tier I know of in the Upper Peninsula of that great fishing state.

The "Scotch hitch" is merely the old half hitch with one more "pull through" of the thread before you have made the half hitch. This extra "pull through" locks the work much more permanently. It also saves the more complicated work of making the whip finish.

The next thing which makes for permanency in our fly tying is the foundation. This means wrapping the bare hook shank of all flies with the finest thread you can handle. Then, no matter how many fish hit the fly, the materials will not roll and work loose on the shank.

The next step is to use lacquer on all your work. The foundation should be lightly covered with a good dope that is waterproof and lasting. Every time you tie off your material—tail whisks, body and hackle—use one little drop of dope there.

303

FIG. 91—Fly and Mayflies.

It is all very well to strive to tie a "pretty" fly, but examine the wings of the mayflies shown above. Countless numbers of each type are on our waters all season long. Types like *Baetis*, bottom, have wings that ex-

This does not mean drenching your work with the varnish and thus having a hard fly which will feel too solid in a fish's mouth. Remember that all nymphs and waterbred flies have soft feel to a fish. Some may have a little tougher upper crust but all have a soft belly and our hook shank is hazard enough.

To imitate the buzzing wings of the mayfly we use only hackles, but "pretty" dry flies that do not stand up are not desirable. We often fish anything short of a rapids with our dry fly and sometimes we even fish smooth spots in the rapids, therefore, a good dry fly *must* dry quickly and have an upright appearance. Everything we do to hamper its quick drying qualities and upright appearance is wrong tying.

Tieing off the thread behind the hackles corrects this fault. It also enables you to angle a few of the feather barbs just over the body, thereby giving the fish the illusion of wings extending over the hook shank. By looking at the wings of many of our mayflies, you will note the wings lie back along the body as in Figure 91.

Tieing off the thread ahead of the hackles causes them to train backwards after the wetting of them and several false casts. Then you have a wet fly, one that will sink quickly after every cast on fairly fast or broken water. Here our efforts must be to tie so that our wet flies and nymphs will have a quick entry in the water. We want them to hold that water and not drop on the surface dry, in our casting.

All our stone flies, caddis, gnats and midges, as well as most land flies, have wings which lie flatly over the body, or slightly roof-like. Note the wet flies shown in Figure 92. As designated in fishing catalogs, they are supposed to represent wet mayflies. Yet no matter under what names they may be listed, these are not only of the mayflies, but are good imitations of the roof-winged caddis flies.

No fly tier should neglect the nymph. It offers such a big

_____

tend all along their bodies and beyond the body. Types like *Stenonema*, center, show a long, barren body to the trout, looking up from below. When you tie off the hackles from behind, this allows you to lie down several of those good game cock hackles over the body as shown in the orange body fly at top. This gives a semblance of the extended wing type, helps floatation in the dry fly and when fished wet-dry fly carries the "wing view" to the trout. The fly at top is tied with golden pheasant tail to help it sink. Use the best game cock hackle tail whisks to help it float for a dry fly. Observe the wings of both flies. In one, we have a right to tie light wings; in the other dark, mottled, wings can be shown to the trout, for the color and the venation differs in many species.

FIG. 92.—A Mayfly Becomes A Caddis Fly.
Weber lists these patterns as two mayflies and a black gnat, at right. Cut off the tails and you have an excellent imitation of the roof-like wings of our light and dark caddis flies. Actual size of the imitation flies is 18 mm.

field for observation and imitation. I tie them from the small hook sizes to the large, and find them all effective in my fishing.

I greatly enjoy the writings of G. E. M. Skues, England's greatest authority on nymphs. What surprised me most when I first read his works was that he tied and fished nymphs in small sizes exclusively. His hook sizes, ooo, oo, o and 1 corresponded to our sizes 17, 16, 15 and 14. In the *very clear*, weed-cluttered chalk streams of England, Skues caught many large trout on his tiny nymphs, trout as large as three and four pounds.

The nymphs Skues used are shown in Figure 36 Chapter IX. Compare these with our mayfly nymphs in Figure 35 Chapter IX. Note that some of ours are also in the same small sizes as those of Skues, but that they also run as large as hook size 1, exactly one and one half inches. You are right in imitating nymphs in this much greater range of sizes because within this range millions of nymphs hatch in our streams from Canada to Mexico.

Your nymph flies must be tied on heavy hooks, 2X to 4X stout, if you wish to take fish off the bottom. For fishing when nymphs are coming up to hatch, use hooks of regular wire. For rapids, use heavy hooks which can be tossed and tumbled down among the trout which lie ahead of or behind the obstructions on the stream floor. Regular wire is the thing for long reaches of quiet water.

I never judge a wet fly or nymph from the fly tying bench or in a tackle shop. Not until it is dunked in a wash basin with the water running about two feet per second can it be judged rightly. Then you get the true movement of the body, tails and wing materials as they will act in the stream, for water is just as much a part of your fly as the material itself.

306

Who can look at his imitation shrimp or mayfly nymph in his hand and visualize the great mobility of the fur until it is seen in the water? Neither can a winged wet fly or a wet dry fly be appraised for its quick sinking or general effectiveness while in the hand. Only water will tell you whether you have achieved the purpose for which the fly is intended.

With your dry fly patterns, floating them on the water film proves whether the hook, body material, hackles and whisks will give you the long, buoyant floating quality you must have.

Any of these factors, if wrong, will render your fly useless. It is up to you to learn this before you go into production on any pattern, or buy it in quantities in the tackle shop.

One of my favorite dry fly bodies with good floating and lasting qualities is made of the shaft (rachis) of any hen or rooster saddle hackle stripped of its hackles (barbs) and wound on like moose hair.

This nicely tapering body material was brought out by the English authority H. C. McClelland in his excellent book, *How To Tie Flies For Trout*, published in 1898. McClelland wrote, "A friend to whom my first acquaintance with this material was due, makes a very beautiful red spinner of the shaft of a saddle feather of a dark red game cock."

The color range of "shafts" in the various breeds of poultry enable me to obtain the color of any dry fly body I desire to tie. I also use his idea for making the gills of mayfly nymphs but I do not then strip the barbs off the rachis or quill. With a fine scissors I cut off the hackles but leave a tiny bit of the hackles down each side of the rachis. For instance, Plymouth Rock cut barbs, wound around the body gives me a sturdy and lifelike nymph in sizes 16 to size 10. When the hackles are too dry, soak them in water and they will wind without splitting.

Too often, however, we look only at the fly, paying too little heed to the hook. After all, the hook is the thing, for the hook really catches the fish. The fly is merely something with which we hope to fool the fish. With me, the hook comes first, then the fly, for of what use is the most closely imitated fly or nymph if the hook won't hold the fish when he hits, or if it is not of the right weight to present the fly properly?

Successful fly tying manufacturers know that the iron in the hooks must be of the very best. They spend much thought and money on this phase alone.

If the gape is too narrow the hook is not good. If the point is too long and the barb too small the hook will enter the fish's flesh but will not sink home beyond the barb. The fish throws the hook and you have lost him. An angler must hook, hold and land every fish which strikes to get the most out of his sport.

Hooks are a problem to me, and I am afraid I can discuss them only from my viewpoint and experience, a one man opinion. The sizes and weights I use are based upon the flies and nymphs I find in the trout's stomachs. Those I see on and in the water, and those which I capture with a sweep of my hat in the air or take from the spider webs or trees are all considered.

As a fly tier, I try to cut down on the hook sizes but I find that I must have some of each of the following sizes, 20, 18, 16, 14, 10, 8, 6, 4 and 2. Thus I am able to eliminate only sizes 22, 12 and 1 in the entire range from 22 to 1.

I never use a sneck or offset bend, preferring round bends, whether they are called Sproat, Viking, Model Perfect, Gallic Supreme, Round Bend or Limerick. I use Limerick only for my 2X or 4X· stout or strong wire hooks.

For dry flies I use as light hooks as I dare, all 1XF, a fine or light wire, in sizes 14, 10, 8, 6 and 4. In the 20, 18 and 16 sizes I use the regular wire as I prefer this strength for so small a hook, and my materials float them nicely. For near the surface and for midwater fishing of the wet fly and the nymph, I use regular wire hooks from size 10 to 2.

But for fishing the bottom waters and in rapids and deep pools I insist upon stout or strong wire hooks. These are Limerick hooks from size 10 to 2, made by Mustad. The number is 3123 B with a turned down ball eye, short shank, 4X strong, when I can get them. Otherwise I will use 2X stout or strong wire hooks.

For these Limerick hooks I prefer the ball eye, as the mayfly and stone fly nymphs have large heads. In imitating nature, I also get the extra weight the ball eye gives me for the bottom waters.

While the caddis flies have smaller heads, I use the same ball eye hooks for my wet and wet-dry fly imitations, too. May nature forgive me, but I need the quick sinking and deep riding quality these hooks provide. How otherwise would my fly go through the fast upper layers and drift along in the slow bottom layer of the stream?

The beginning fly tier should start out with size 10 hooks of 1XF and Regular wire, and size 8 in 4X strong wire. With these three weights he can go to the stream and allow the water, the fish, the nymphs and the flies to form his own opinion instead of using mine. River current will soon tell him he must never be a "one weight, one hook" fly fisherman.

I offer for what they may be worth, the dressings of a few flies which I use extensively, and some of which I have "discovered". I carry others, too, when I go fishing but these I list are by all odds my favorites because they are the result of long observation of the waters, insects and trout habits.

Here are the dressings:

FLY DRESSINGS

Figures 93, 94, 95

As I am just a run-of-the-mill fly tyer, I hope that you will not regard my patterns as the final word for the naturals I try to imitate. When you examine the live nymphs and the flies which hatch from them in your own waters, you can surely equal my patterns. After a little practice, your own artistry should beat mine all hollow. More power to you!

SID'S GIANT MAYFLY NYMPH
(*Hexagenia*)

Hook: Size 8 to 2. Mustad 3123 B. Balleye, 4X strong wire.
Body: Pale yellow or ivory yarn for belly. Overlay of stripped peacock herl, ribbed with silver tinsel to show segments.
Tails: Two very small hackle tips from neck feather near head.
Gills: Thinnest strip of muskrat belly fur with hide.
Legs: None.
Thorax: Muskrat dyed black from a "Hudson Seal" coat.

After winding the hook shank with fine silk or nylon thread and varnishing to prevent body from rolling, tie in yarn, herl and silver ribbing. Lay on hook shank and bind all with thread to a point opposite barb of hook. Tie in hackle tips for tails.

Wind yarn from barb of hook half way to eye of hook but do not cut off. Tie in muskrat hide with fur. Wind muskrat over itself for two turns, tie and cut off. Resume winding of yarn to back of eye, leaving ample room for tieing in peacock herl, wing case and tinsel. Tie off yarn and cement tie off.

Bring bunch of herl tightly over yarn and fur gills, arranging fur so that half will be on each side of body. Tie off and rib with silver tinsel to make segments. Spin dark fur on thread and wind thickly to make wing case and head.

There is a little trick to cutting the hide so that the fur will not be scraggly, missing here and there. Use a furrier's knife

309

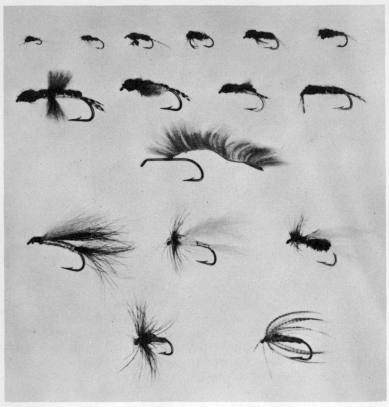

FIG. 93.—Nymphs and flies. Tied by Author.

For dressings, see end of chapter.

Top row: Reading left to right, six small mayfly nymphs. Hooks size
20 to 10.

Second row: Reading first three, giant mayfly nymphs, 3, 2, and 1 year
old sizes; fourth from left, the "Bucking Bronco."

Third row: Showing where to tie in muskrat fur for gills.

Fourth row: Three wet flies: Reading from left to right. General Immell
Bass Fly; White Calf Tail, yellow and silver body; White
Calf Tail, black chenille body.

Fifth row: Drowned mayflies. At left grouse hackle wound all at head
with a fat body. Right, same type but with woodduck or
mallard breast feather.

310

or a single edge razor blade. The hide is held with the left hand and the blade is used with the right while the edge of the left hand keeps the hide tight. Your furrier will teach you this in a few minutes.

Look at the gills of the live nymph and you will have the right proportion. As this nymph swims with its legs folded tightly to its sides, omit the legs. This staple nymph in size 4 hook is good wherever the large mayflies hatch on lake or stream. As good for bass and walleyes as it is for trout.

THE BUCKING BRONCO NYMPH
(Formerly *Baetis*, then *Chirotenetes*, now *Isonychia*)
Hook: Sizes 8 to 4. Mustad 3123 B, 4X strong wire, ball eye.
Body: Gray and dark brown yarn or fur spun on thread
Tails: Two of the very smallest hackles at a cock's head.
Legs: Short, of grouse hackle.
Food Basket: Tie in a medium hackle feather of cream color or white to represent the "basket" of the front legs. Trim hackle to size needed.

This nymph has plate like gills along its sides. Make body of gray yarn, then wind over with dark brown angora yarn or dark brown fur spun on thread, exposing the light underbody by open but rather close ribbing as shown here. This should be one of your staple nymphs too, tied on a size 6 hook.

THE SMALLER MAYFLY NYMPHS

While there are millions of mayfly nymphs in our streams and several hundred species, I feel that two general patterns will represent the small nymphs very well. As some have prominent gills and others show very little, if at all, I tie but one pattern of each type. I use a wide range of hooks so that I can cope with hatches of the very smallest to the largest which the trout may be taking at the time.

When the nymphs are coming up to hatch into mayflies, then I use a hook of regular wire to keep my imitations in their close-to-the-surface-feeding. The rest of the day or evening I use heavy hooks to search the bottom waters with my nymphs.

SMALL "SMOOTH" MAYFLY NYMPHS
(*Baetis* and *Caenis*)
Hook: 16 and 10, regular wire. 16 hooks will answer for 18 and 14 sizes of the small nymphs, while size 10 will take care of the others.

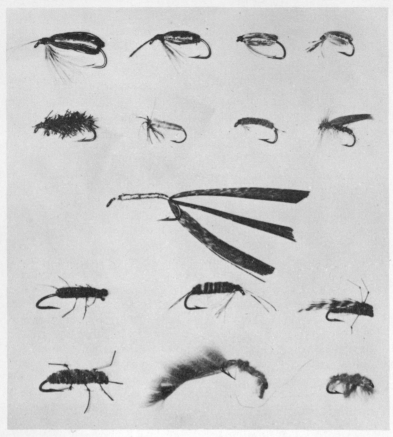

FIG. 94.—The Wet-Dry Fly And Nymphs. Left to Right:

Top row: The Swanson wet-dry caddis flies. Underwater egg layer.

Second row: Paul Young's Strawman, *Eruciform* larva coming up to hatch. *Thysanuriform* larva (fantail). Caddis dry fly.

Third row: Silver body with turkey tail to form wings for wet-dry fly. Hook size 4.

Fourth row: Two stonefly nymphs with stone fly, wet fly.

Fifth row: Dragon fly nymph. Muskrat body completed for shrimp. Dangling strip of muskrat fur to tie under body. Gold tinsel to bind the swimmerettes to the body.

All tied by author, except the Strawman.

Body: Natural Muskrat belly fur, tapered to wing case and head. Rib with fine gold wire buried in the fur. Sometimes I omit the gold wire and rib quite closely with dark moose mane over the muskrat but exposing some of the fur.

Thorax: Muskrat dyed black, from a "Hudson Seal" coat.

Tails: Three, of mallard or teal.

Legs: Not more than a turn and a half of small hackle from brown hen or Plymouth Rock hen.

Medium Size Mafly Nymphs
(*Blasturus*, *Heptagenia* and *Stenonema*)

Hook: 10 to 6 with size 8 my staple. Mustad 3123 B, balleye, 4X strong.

Body: Two strands of unstripped peacock herl for gills at rear, then muskrat fur spun on rest of hook shank to thorax (wing cases).

Tails: Mottled duck feathers or Plymouth Rock. Three strands.

Wing Case: Dark Brown fur spun to make large dark thorax or wing case. The large ball eye of the hook makes a fine head.

Legs: Pheasant tail.

Sometimes I wind peacock herl, unstripped, over the muskrat body in open spiral turns for the prominent gills. For brown or roiled waters I rib with narrow gold or silver tinsel.

THE "ROUNDER" FLIES

These flies have been tied by the Irish, Scotch and English for centuries, but they call them "wet flies". The first fly represents a nymph coming up to hatch, about as well as any fisherman can expect. The second imitates the wetted swaying wings of a great number of drowned land and waterbred flies.

THE NYMPH

Hook: 16 to 8. Regular wire when the nymphs are emerging, heavy wire otherwise.

Body: VERY, VERY thin body of dark brown yarn or gray muskrat fur. (Make the body short or the hackle will not cling to the body.)

Hackle: Grouse feather, ruffed, sharptail or prairie.

Leave hackle tip of feather jutting out over the eye of the hook, as shown in photograph. Tie feather down tightly back of eye after stroking the feather back evenly all around the hook shank.

313

FIG. 95.—Dry Flies. Tied by Author.

For dressings, see end of chapter.

Top row: Dry flies from size 20 hooks to size 16.

Second row: Dark bodied mayflies. One pattern will suffice. The fly on
the right was tied by Jim Deren of The Angler's Roost in
New York City. Called the Fifty Degree fly, my photo does
not do justice to the grand dun hackle, the sharply barred
wings and the perfect body.

Third row: Three medium color bodies. Hackles red game badger
and dun.

Fourth row: Left, the orange body wet-dry fly. For dry fly fishing I
substitute game cock whisks for tails. The golden pheasant tails

314

THE "ROUNDER" WET FLY

Hook: 8 to 4. Mustad 3123 B, ball eye 4X strong wire.

Body: Light, medium or dark colors with or without gold or silver ribbing.

Hackles: Grouse, wood duck or mallard.

Tail: None.

Wind on a fat body of fur or yarn and bring it up *fat* right to the eye. Leave only enough room to wind on hackle in the manner described for the nymph. Thus the hackles are forced out and away from the body to swing widely whether fished upstream or down. Size 6 hook is my favorite in all rapids and deep pools. Use the patterns whose color, light, dark or medium best imitate the drowned flies of the moment.

Stone Fly Nymphs
(*Plecoptera*)

These are nymphs of every rapids and reach of well oxygenated water. Two patterns should be enough to cover the waters of the U. S. and Canada, I believe.

The Large Stone Fly Nymph
(*Pteronarcys dorsata*)

Hook: Size 4. Mustad 3123 B, 4 X stout wire, ball eye.

Tail and Feelers: Very thick and tapering. Use pheasant tail.

Body: Fat, of dark brown angora yarn. Do not tease out fur. This yarn will imitate body and undergills.

Thorax: Several extra windings here to show the prominent wing case.

Legs: Well scattered and heavy. Use dark brown turkey tail strands. Figure 97. For the wet fly, simply tie two Plymouth Rock feathers over body. This nymph changes very little upon becoming the real fly.

---

will drown any dry fly quickly. The dry fly in center has light yellow body and the dry fly at right, a white body of bleached muskrat.

Fifth row: Keene's Giant Mayfly. Note body tied on needle, then tied on bare hook shank. Tied by Herb Van Horn of Gladstone, Mich.

315

Fig. 96.—Fly Tying Cabinet.

This wooden cabinet, 12½ inches high, 10 inches deep and 8 inches wide, outside measurements, has been "on the road" with me for more than a quarter of a century. It holds an enormous amount of material in the 7 drawers, along with the two compartments in the lid.

Small To Medium Stonefly Nymphs
(Perla)

Hook: 10 to 6. Mustad 3123 B, 4 X strong wire. Size 8 is best.

Body: Light yellow angora yarn. Overlay bunch of stripped peacock herl for the dark, upper body.

Thorax: Very "fat" wing cases. Pack on yellow angora yarn. The overlay of dark herl, tied down, will be sufficient then.

316

Legs: Thick and scattered. Brown turkey tail.
Tails and Horns: Moose hair tips or stripped peacock herl.

DRAGON FLY NYMPHS
(*Odonata*)

There are so many species and sizes of dragon fly nymphs that I imitate but one general pattern. This does well on trout ponds, springholes, streams and every lake. The colors range from green, dead brown to almost black. I imitate the numerous green nymph.

Hook: Size 6, Mustad 3123 B, 4 X stout or strong wire. Ball eye.
Body: Soft shade of olive green yarn or olive color chenille wound over fat round body of floss.
Legs: Long, of bent hen hackle with barbs trimmed closely.

Damsel FLY NYMPH
(*Odonata*)

This long dark nymph is imitated closely enough with the "Bucking Bronco" mayfly nymph, *Isonychia*. Very good in pondweeds where the damsel nymph lives in numbers.

FREE LIVING CADDIS NYMPH
(*Trichoptera*)

This *Thysanuriform* larvae, the "fantail" caddis nymph is found in great numbers in every stream. Floods, freshets, disturbance by wading feet makes them easy prey for trout and bass. Sometimes they come out of their homes, tunnels in the moss, leaves, sticks and among rocks and hang in the water by a thread which they spin.

Hook: Size 10. Mustad 3123 B. 4 X stout.
Body: Any brown green fur to match color in your streams.
Tail: Make the fantail of cut neck hackle.
Head: The ball eye hooks make the black head but tie in just a few VERY short grouse feather barbs behind the eye of the hook. Trout seldom see the light caddis nymph which is so often imitated, unless they are hatching. They see this species all the time.

HOUSED CADDIS NYMPH
(*Trichoptera*)

This eruciform larva, the caddis nymph which builds and lives in its house, abounds in every lake and stream. I use but one imitation to serve for them all.

Hook: Size 10 for small and size 6 for large nymphs.

317

Body: Gray muskrat fur spun on body. Gray yarn can be used as well. Wrap entire body with wide white quill stripped from outside of white goose feather. Taper the body.

Legs: One turn of medium size grouse feather to imitate the fast moving oarlike forelegs of the nymph swimming to the surface to hatch from its pupal shuck. The eye of the hook represents its protruding head. Use only for caddis coming up to hatch.

O'Gara's Shrimp
(*Gammarus*)

The best shrimp I know for brooks, browns, rainbows, bass and panfish. Named after a friend, Bill O'Gara.

Hook: 10 to 6. Mustad 3123 B, 4 X strong wire. Size 6 best for streams.

Body: Spun muskrat belly fur.

Ribbing: Very fine but strong gold or silver wire.

When tieing in muskrat hide with fur, tie it off under the body just opposite the barb, or a very little way past the barb. Train fur to jut out at rear and under head. Rib hide and body with gold wire to resemble legs and swimmerettes.

Fig. 97.—Stone Fly Nymph To Stone Fly Wet Fly. (Size 6 hook).

When you have tied a half dozen nymphs of the stone flies, tie another half dozen of the same patterns and add wings as shown on the stone fly above. Select two matched plymouth rock hen feathers and tie them over the body of the nymph and fish them wet when the stone flies are on the water. There is so little change between the nymph and the fly that, except for the wings, one can hardly tell the difference.

318

DRY FLIES
(*Ephemeroptera*)

THE KEENE MAYFLY
(*Hexagenia*)

J. Harrington Keene brought out this fly in the 1890's. His book, "Fly Fishing and Fly Tying," is the first American book to describe dry fly fishing, as far as I know. The flies shown of this pattern were tied by Herb Van Horn, Gladstone, Michigan.

Hook: Size 10 or 8, 1 X fine wire.
Body: Deer hair flank, natural, tan, white or dyed yellow.
Tails: After ribbing on body, trim off ends leaving a few for tails.
Hackle: Best game cock hackle obtainable.
Wings: Van uses veined wing material for his patterns. I prefer to tie mine without wings.

Place a needle in vise. Tie on deer hair and rib with thread. Slip body off needle and seat on hook shank. Wind on hackle after coating body with rubber cement.

SMALLER MAYFLIES
(*Ephemeroptera*)

One can buy good dry flies in many tackle shops. Select three types: light, medium and dark colored bodies in size 16 to size 2. Avoid those which have woodduck, mallard, golden pheasant or other tail whisks which have a tendency to allow the water to creep and sink the fly. Game cock hackle whisks, or old rooster hackle whisks help a fly float for they have no barbules.

SID GORDON DRY FLY
(*Baetis*)

I consider this fly to be my best all around dry fly. In Wisconsin and Michigan we have a bright orange body mayfly, a raspberry orange mayfly and a duller orange mayfly. The bright orange seems to answer for all.

Hook: 14 and 10, 1 X fine wire.
Body: Orange dyed muskrat fur or bright orange yarn, ribbed with gold tinsel.
Tails: Good game cock whisks—at least eight or ten of them.
Hackles: Best sharp hackles of cream game or white wound at eye and tied off behind the hackle. Sharp brown (red game) cock hackles wound off behind the hackle, with some lying

slanting over the hook shank. This resembles many wings which lie along the body of living mayflies.

For wet-dry fly fishing: Use yarn body with golden pheasant tippets to help it sink well. Use heavy hook in size 10. Wet with saliva and fish sunken.

SMALL DRY FLIES

There are thousands of gnats, midges and tiny mayflies on the water all through the fishing season. While only the mayflies have tails, I use but one type, all with tails to help flotation.

Hook: 20, 18 and 16. Round bend.

Body: Dark moose mane when the black gnats and dark bodied mayflies are on the water. I rib the dark mane with light colored moose mane when the striped bodied midges are on the water.

Hackles: Gray and brown mixed, black and gray mixed, all gray or all cream according to the wings—and my fancy.

LARGE MIDGE DRY FLIES
(*Chironomus*)

Hook: 10 and 8. 1 X fine wire, round bend.

Body: Dark Moose mane ribbed with light moose mane.

Tails: Cream color to keep them inconspicuous. Midges have no tails, but we need them for flotation.

Hackles: Plymouth Rock with a few turns of red (bright brown) game cock to aid the softer Plymouth Rock hackles in floating.

.CADDIS DRY FLY
(*Sedge Fly*)

Hook: 10 and 8, 1 X fine wire, round bend.

Body: Gray muskrat fur—small hackle, wound palmer over body.

Wing: Cut small piece of mallard wing. Roll with fingers and seat on body.

Hackle: Best game cock hackles you can obtain. Mix brown with gray. Good on all waters, easy to tie and a splendid floater when oiled. Everything will hit this staple fly.

THE SWANSON WET-DRY FLY
(*Trichoptera*)

Hook: 10-8-6-4 with size 8 the most staple. Mustad 3123 B. Ball-eye 4 X strong.

Body: Fat body of white mercerized floss. Rib solidly with plain or embossed silver tinsel 1/16 inch wide.

Wings: Three separate sections of turkey tail feathers.

Horns: The antennae can be omitted or use moose mane, two long strands if you insist.

Legs: Extend turkey wing feather and trim to suit.

Make foundation of silk thread on hook shank. Varnish. Wind thread over floss, tinsel and turkey together down shank to a point opposite the barb of the hook. Wind floss, then wind tinsel to cover floss. Loop and tie one-third of turkey feather under hook shank. Complete by tying down surplus turkey feather for legs and thin out.

Note that the rooflike wings of all caddis flies taper from almost nothing at the head to very wide at the end of the wings Your aim must be to see that the silver shines through at every turn of the fly in the water to imitate the shining bubble around the live, swimming insect.

Pucker or loop the turkey feathers of each section to get that taper and allow the fly to flash in the water. Soon you will be able to judge the right amount of feather to use for each size hook you wish to use.

To imitate the fast moving legs, working like pistons as the fly swims down, tie off but do *not* cut off the turkey feather at the eye of the hook. Carry those strands down below the eye for legs and then trim out the surplus. This will make a strong anchor for the feather loops over the silver body, thereby preventing the fish from tearing the body loose.

THREE GENERAL WET-DRY PATTERNS

1. The dark brown turkey tail described above. Hook size 6 and 4.
2. A mottled tan feather of turkey wing, size 10 to 6 hooks.
3. Mallard wing feathers, hooks size 10 and 8. All hooks 3123 B.

THE GENERAL IMMELL FLY

Hook: Size 4. Mustad Limerick 3123 B. Balleye, 4 X strong wire.

Body: Yellow yarn, ribbed with wide plain or embossed silver tinsel.

Tail: Polar bear hair, dyed bright red.

Wing: Black bear hair, topped with white polar bear hair.

The hair must be well soaked with varnish while tieing head. A long tapering head with no hackles as the fly must swim and drift with the current.

White Calf Tail

Family *"Erroneus"* but it accounts for many trout.

Hook: 10 to 4. For floating, 1 X fine wire. Wet fly, 4 X strong wire.

Body: Black Chenille for evening. Bright days, yellow chenille with lower half of body bright silver tinsel.

Tails: White calf tail, curly.

Wings: White calf tail curly. A new born calf has the most curl.

Hackles: Wound dry fly style with Plymouth Rock. Oil fly for floating. Wet with saliva for sinking wet fly.

STRAWMAN FLY
(*Trichoptera*)

This fly was tied by Paul Young. I am not at liberty to give the dressing. It imitates the caddis house of the Platycentropus species almost exactly. Figure 94.

THE HOOK PROBLEM

The reader might judge that I am extremely partial to hooks made by Mustad. There are other hooks as good as Mustad. The reason I list Mustad is because I can always depend upon getting a supply of their hooks in any size and weight I need and their quality is good.

When the beginnner becomes thoroughly familiar with the various speeds of a stream, he is not "lost" when he sits down at his fly tying bench.

Knowing the good holes and reaches of his own stream he can tie result bringing flies for his own waters. That long reach where the current is fast in the center but loafs and eddies all along the undercut bank, demands a quick sinking fly. Just so does the bottom water in the center need a sinking fly.

Upon learning which materials will help a fly sink, or float, to the best advantage and give the trout a good imitation of a real insect at the same time, he develops a "weapon" for each piece of water he intends fishing. He does this without leaving his bench.

Soon he knows by experience what every hook in his kit will do. From then on he ceases to be a novice and becomes expert in his tying as well as in his fishing. Hook weights are SO important but how little attention the average fisherman gives them.

CHAPTER XXII

Stream Improvement
Betters the Fishing

THE MAN WHO SPECIALIZES in lake and stream improvement inherits a fancy title. He's called an ecologist.

Most any fisherman can become an ecologist if he will but grasp the simple fundamentals of improving the waters and put these principles into practice. As an ecologist he will not only surprise others with his work, he will also astound himself with the results he will accomplish.

The basic idea of lake and stream improvement is to restore or provide homes, food and spawning grounds for the fish. If waters already have these advantages in sufficient abundance, there obviously is no need for improvement. It is the run-down waters, those which do not measure up to their fish producing potential, that command attention.

All fishermen are more or less familiar with the long, barren, sandy stretches of many of our streams. "Poor water, no fish". they mutter, and hurry on to the more inviting pools and rapids.

Looking at the same piece of water, you as an ecologist, say, "What good water"! You've checked it and know its temperature can be lowered and its oxygen content increased. In your mind you visualize what stream improvement will do to attract trout there.

You build a trout nursery, hotel and grocery store for the fish. This you do within a few hours with the help of other fishermen in the construction of a V Deflector, one of various types of stream improvement devices. See Figure 98.

That deflector, installed at the beginning of the sandy 150 foot stretch of the stream, provides a good spawning bed by creating a current that sweeps the sand off the bottom and deposits it behind the structure. Spawning trout can henceforth

323

Fig. 98.—V Deflector. (Construction and Photograph by William O'Gara)

This V deflector on the Clam River transformed a quiet, shallow, dead stretch of water into a fine upstream pool, a long spawning bed below and a nursery, hotel and grocery store for trout.

fan off the newly exposed gravel, deposit their eggs, cover them and retreat to the hotel the new current has built for them in the quieter side waters 100 feet downstream.

The fast current you have created over the gravel aerates the water every moment, summer and winter. No silt, sand or debris will cover that gravel and smother the eggs because the speed of the water will now carry it all away. Under the clean gravel the eyed eggs go through the various stages in Figure 99. Within 90 days the food in the yolk sac has been consumed and the fry work up through the gravel. They are now in search of food.

This they find in the nursery your deflector has provided. The fry get to it by riding up on the escalator, the eddying current created by the V Deflector, to the quiet water behind the V. In the nursery you have provided a smorgasbord of baby food of such good variety that the fry need only open their mouths to dine on the delicious tidbits. It's in the form of plankton, the almost invisible specks of plant and animal life in water. While taking air from the water with their gills, the fry

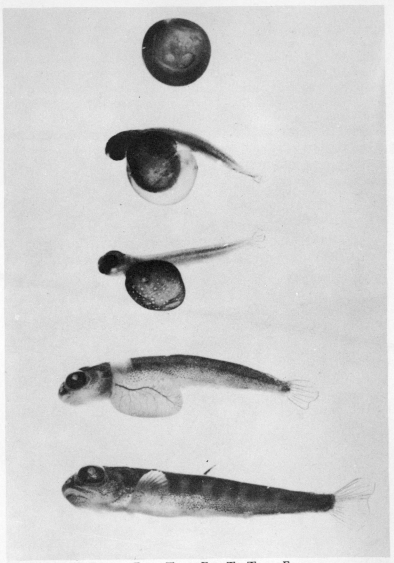

FIG. 99.—From Trout Egg To Trout Fry.

A brown trout egg, spawned in November and hatched in December. Living upon yolk-sac in January. Still under gravel, living upon yolk-sac in February. In March, a free-living stream trout fry. Soon it becomes a fingerling. If conditions are good—food, cover and temperature—it will be legal size by late fall. We call it a "yearling" when it spawns the next year, in November, although it will be 19 months of age then.

325

sift the plankton into their gullets with their gill rakers. "As I live and breathe," the fry would say in fish language.

In the nursery each tiny fry is quite safe from being devoured by his own Momma and Poppa residing in the hotel downstream. They'd be quite happy to eat their own offspring, which they wouldn't even recognize by sight. Here, in the brush cover, the fry is also safe from kingfishers, blue herons, bitterns, mink, otters and other water feeders constantly in search of a good live morsel.

Let us therefore pin a medal on you for the grand work you

FIG. 100.—A Y Deflector.

Here we needed a long, straight shot to prevent high water from hitting a bridge bank below. Made of logs and chinked with gravel, it did good work. Do not build a Y deflector where a wing or a V deflector will bring the result you wish. A Y deflector means double work, time and material.

have accomplished so far with your V Deflector. Having introduced trout to a hitherto barren stretch of water and having provided a spawning ground and nursery to perpetuate them, you are no longer just an ordinary trout fisherman. You are now a "private first class".

But there are other honors. Let us see if we can further decorate your manly chest.

Along the gravel and rubble stones you have exposed on the stream bottom with your V Deflector you have stocked a supermarket with ample supplies of food for the parents of the fry. Where there is gravel, there you will find nymphs, and these are a *piece de resistance* for hungry trout the year round.

A mayfly, dipping to the water, "spins" her packet of some 2,000 fertilized eggs. They scatter like particles of flour in the water and sink to the bottom. Each tiny egg has a gluish substance which causes it to adhere firmly to any piece of gravel, rock or log it touches. Sand, which previously choked this stretch of water, would roll the egg, crush it or smother it. Now it stays right there on the meat counter to hatch into a nymph and eat the slime, its vegetables, which grows on the gravel, sticks and stones.

The insects are continuously stocking your store when weather permits. The caddis flies, dropping their eggs upon the surface or swimming down very fast to "paint" them on the gravel, are just as numerous as the mayflies dropping their eggs. The stone flies, dragon flies, damsel flies, gnats, midges, beetles, crane flies and many other kinds of water-bred flies are also there in vast numbers, contributing to the underwater food shelf, the newly exposed gravel.

Were it not for that gravel there would be few if any eggs in that stretch of water hatching into nymphs.

The gravel also attracts snails and small clams, and these, too, are eaten by the trout as food, as rich to them as oysters are to us. Some clams deposit as many as two million eggs in one season, so you can see how important it is to provide gravel for them so they'll stick around.

The underwater fish food must also have something to eat in order to grow. Here again the gravel enters the picture by holding algae, which the fisherman call slime, thus providing the "hay" which every nymph, snail or clam must have for nourishment.

In the quieter waters above or below your V Deflector many species of minnows mate, hatch and feed. Aquatic angleworms

FIG. 101.—A Beaver Dam.

As a naturalist, I admire the beaver. As a fisherman I must admit that no brook, brown or rainbow trout can leap over beaver dams such as this to go upstream to spawn. Nor can they get below to renew the stock in the main rivers.

I have found dams to run as many as five to a mile of stream—excellent fishing for a few seasons, then ruined unless the dams are removed.

burrow in the bottom silt behind the deflector, sifted and carried there hourly by the eddying currents you have created. The giant mayfly nymphs live in the rich soil with them. And then there are the crayfish which become so numerous.

What a delicatessen you have furnished for the fish! Step forward while I pin this medal on you, Corporal!

But wait, in creating this eddying, fast-shooting current you have caused the sand to be lifted off the bed and swept behind the deflector so it doesn't go on down stream to create an additional barren stretch of water. Soon rich silt forms over the new sand bed. What's more, you have stopped further erosion along both banks of the stream.

It is said, and I firmly believe it, that a river whose current flows six miles per hour has a transporting power to move objects 300 times as great as one flowing two miles per hour.

Small wonder that you have caused the vastly accelerated current to dig this five feet of sand off the beds in just a few hours after the completion of your V Deflector.

How nicely you have flanked that gravel-bottomed channel with quieter waters on either side, and at the end of the long, deep run. No trout prefers very fast water continually. He goes there to feed, but then will lie and rest in the hotel rooms you have constructed so close to his supermarket in the channel.

Step forward, Sergeant, while we pin another medal on your chest.

It is not enough, however, to build a small hotel on a site where you hope to attract an ever increasing number of guests. In this day and age if you wish to accommodate crowds you must also build motels. You will therefore construct fish covers wherever the formations of this new pool tell you they should go. See Figure 118.

Lieutenant, you have skipped a grade through your earnest efforts!

Now that you have built covers in the fairly deep water where the trout can rest, and given them easy access to the deeper, faster water for quick and heavy feeding, you must provide some natural homes.

Notice how skimpy the natural growth is along the eroded banks of the sandy stretch in which you have constructed your V Deflector. You must do something about that.

Go downstream below the sandy stretch and allow nature to tell you what is best. Observe that clump of Red-Osier Dogwood (*Cornus stolonifera Michx.*) growing at the bank. Note how its many roots, trunks and branches protect the bank against erosion. Under its leaves and branches growing out over the water you will find excellent shelter for a large trout.

He gets much food from the land flies, caterpillars, spiders and ants that drop off the leaves and branches with every gust of wind. Here you have another hotel and grocery store, but not a supermarket. You'll invariably find a fighting trout there, even if there is but one shrub. He will allow no other customer to patronize that place until a mightier fish comes along and bunts him out of the choice location. And should this trout be caught by an angler, a new tenant will soon move in, because such an apartment has a waiting list of tenants in every stream.

Now that you have planted Red-Osier Dogwood along the eroded banks you can feel certain that with the aid of the V

329

Deflector you have protected that bank from further erosion during every flood and freshet. We know not how many years the stream has been tearing the sand from those banks, burying the spawning beds and filling good trout holes.

Major, you have accomplished much in giving the trout that long cover, a double promotion for you.

Look next at the barren bank on the opposite shore. It is a little lower there and needs better protection. Downstream, at the very end of the run you have created, you will see a small clump of alders *(Alnus incana (L.) Moench.)* This Speckled or Hoary alder is natural to this soil and climate. It likes wet soil and its trunks curve over the water. Some even lie in the water. If you can get these alders started at the upper end of the rehabilitated reach they will gradually spread downstream. We always plant upstream to encourage the plants, shrubs and trees to produce more of their kind through their spreading roots and floating or wind-blown seeds.

Fig. 102.—A Beaver Flowage.

Only the original stock will be found in a beaver flowage. Soon all the spawning gravel is covered and the trout cannot renew themselves. They are soon caught out or die as the ever widening shallow waters warm to a "death temperature" for trout.

Now that you have succeeded in getting a good stand of alders along that bank, Colonel, note the great benefits you have wrought. While the Red Osier on the other bank will furnish food for the sharptail and ruffed grouse, snowshoe hare and cottontail rabbits, we must not sneer at the alder. It furnishes food for both grouse and deer, the buds for the birds and the branches for the deer.

I have frequently sat in the water and silt under a long stand of streamside alders for the sheer joy of watching numerous woodcock probing for giant mayfly nymphs, aquatic angleworms and I presume small clams and snails, in the silt beneath the branches. How industrious they are in their searching!

Observe how the pull of the water holds the alder trunks on and near the surface, but see how their need for sun gradually straightens the trunks skyward. Here in the crooked cover of the alder is a $30 a day hotel room for the trout, American plan, since meals are included and no tipping required.

No otter, mink or predatory trout can seize the fish that chooses this kind of cover. One dash and the fish are safe among the tangle of trunks and branches.

Many spiders, caterpillars, and what not drop from them with every gentle to strong breeze. Aphis and ants are there from spring to autumn.

Unquestionably each alder clump is a hotel and grocery store for every trout which chooses to abide there. I shall not tell you the one very best fly to take them from their room and board unless you vow to keep it a secret. (All right, all right, it's a giant mayfly nymph tied on a size 6 hook, 2X or 4X stout wire. But keep this to yourself or we shall lose many tenants.) I well remember—say, are we fixing up a crick or are we fishing?

So now, in one brief season, you have made a complete new home—from kitchen to drawing room to master's bedroom—for the trout. The fishermen, the trout, the birds, the animals, and the insects, all are in your debt. The river will love you, too, General!

You have in the churning of the water through the structure you built, removed her cancer and given her new life. You have reduced the temperature, and have made at least 10 or more parts of oxygen right there where the hot sun thinned the water and drained the oxygen from the sandy bed, this former warming oven. You have torn the deathly blanket of sand from her bosom

331

and she is now fair to look upon. No longer is she drab, still and moody. Now she is purling with joy.

Spring has come again, so let us hasten to see that from a worthless, sandy stretch of the stream there now has blossomed a wonderful length of water for fishing trout. The General is elated. "My deflector performed a miracle in just one season. If I hadn't done it myself I never would have believed it could have changed the stream so much. Know what I'm going to do? I'm going to buy a 40 right here and I'm going to build some of those other types of structures you've been telling me about. I want my children to have good fishing."

The grocery store varies greatly in a river. The fast water we create will produce large quantities of certain types of nymphs and larvae. The wonderful short or long reaches, up-stream above the deflectors, grow great quantities of other types, while the types of the rapids will be in much lesser numbers.

A canny fisherman will greatly enhance his fish taking ability when he conforms to nature. For example, he will find large mayfly nymphs in the reaches but will observe that large stone flies abound in the rapids.

Critics to the contrary, lake and stream improvement is the means to better fishing, especially in this era when the march of civilization has wreaked such havoc with our once bountiful waters.

Fortunate is the Conservation Club which can call upon a fisherman who can guide it in a worth-while program of water rehabilitation. He will know there is more to the idea than constructing and installing devices. Above all, he'll know *the current must be managed correctly*, or else the devices will do more harm than good, or fail to perform properly and your work will be wasted.

I feel that I have presented sufficient facts in this book to give the average fisherman at least a fair knowledge of water so that he and his friends can build one or two of the devices in the water they fish. I shall now discuss the methods my men and I used on streams during the years that I worked for the Federal Government and the Wisconsin Conservation Department on a lake and stream improvement project that covered most of the counties in Northern Wisconsin.

If you will follow these methods, applying your common sense and your knowledge of the current, I am confident that you can benefit your fishing immensely.

Before you undertake any construction, however, I strongly

332

FIG. 103.—Sometimes Nature Harms.

Showing how nature ruins food beds and spawning beds when she falls a tree straight across a stream. A nice hole is built at the log, but the sand is carried on to form a bar, sometimes an island, which splits the current as badly as an A deflector. I have seen this type of work advocated by many and built with logs or rocks. Such work may do for rocky streams with rocky banks but never—NEVER—on sandy streams.

recommend that you consult an area biologist, telling him where and when you would like to build your devices. Some states even require that lake and stream work must have the sanction of the Conservation Department. This seems to be a good requirement because streams usually are public fishing waters, and as such they should not be damaged by the use of wrong "improvement" methods.

Perhaps you may wish to deviate from the methods I offer. But first, show your biologist what you propose to do. Who knows, it might be something practical, and if he passes upon it, we may all profit through your ideas. It is my advice, though, that it is better to stick by tried and approved methods until you have learned much about current and the awesome power of water in flood.

Whenever possible, improvement work should be carried on downstream, making it convenient to float materials for structures to the place of installation. The disadvantage of working upstream is that the deflectors, covers and other devices installed will deflect the current ineffectually towards the previously completed structure, thus decreasing the value of the downstream device. If you build two or more deflectors, it is impossible to judge current unless you begin your work upstream and continue on downstream with the next deflector.

Under no circumstances should currents be deflected into soft banks. Every effort must be made to protect banks that already are eroding.

The material for constructing the devices should never be obtained by cutting willows, trees or anything whatsoever on or near the banks of the river. Well-rooted trees, shrubs and grasses prevent erosion and provide needed shade for the stream. We plant, but *never* remove anything from the banks!

I know whereof I speak. Many times, during my lake and stream improvement years, I was falsely accused of cutting trees along the banks. For the record, I would like to state here that neither my crews nor myself were ever guilty of such ignorant practice. All I can say is that my accusers could not tell the difference between beaver-cutting and axe-cutting!

The trouble was, lake and stream improvement work was a new idea and required time to gain acceptance. It was inevitable that there should be critics but today this work is widely sought by conservation clubs in Wisconsin. The state conservation department regards lake and stream improvement as one of its important projects.

As conditions vary in each stream, it is best that a stream survey be made prior to the installation of improvement devices. What is necessary in one stretch may be unsuitable in another.

To insure successful improvement I gathered information relative to current, cover, spawning beds, food supply, immediate shore soils, temperatures, depths, stream widths, fertility and other pertinent factors, but I had to train and lay out the work for several hundred men.

The individual, members of Conservation Clubs, 4-H Clubs, Future Farmers of America and Boy Scout leaders who wish to improve a stream in their immediate vicinity need not go into such intensive surveys of the waters they wish to help.

They need only take temperature readings of their stream during the hot months of July and August. They should learn the highest water levels in the spring and the lowest in the summer. This will indicate the average height at which to build the deflectors, so they won't be so high in the stream that they look like forts. Deflectors a few inches above the summer water level will do a grand digging job all the year around.

If the stream has trout in it, above and below the stretch you

334

wish to improve, their presence will tell you that there is no pollution there and the temperature is right for them. The trout could not live there unless conditions were right.

You need make no chemical analyses of the water unless you wish, because trout will live in all waters, *soft* or *hard*, if conditions are right. They will not have the large amount of fish food in the *soft* water stream, but with your structures you can substantially increase this for a great amount of food grows on the structures themselves.

Sometimes a seemingly good gravel bed is so bound with clay, marl or sand that the trout cannot "fan," move the gravel for making nests for their eggs. Digging with your foot or a shovel will tell you whether raking with a coarse rake will loosen it sufficiently. Some beds may have to be spaded to loosen that thin "cement" coating.

If you find the temperature is too high in the summer months—80 degrees or higher—leave the river alone unless you can lower the temperature by removing beaver dams and opening springs which have been choked along the banks or behind them. While it is true that by improving sandy stretches here and there you can lower the temperature in those stretches, it would require too much work to reduce the temperature of an entire stream with structures, from the headwaters down.

Before you attempt to build any kind of stream improvement device, go to a very narrow brooklet about two feet wide and spend about an hour learning how to judge current. An outlet from a fast flowing spring or any running "trickle" will do. Follow my suggestions, step by step, and you will gain fundamental knowledge that will show you how to build deflectors on any stream if you use the methods shown in the sketches.

Bring an ax and a saw to cut off a few branches, or carry four pieces of split stove wood. If there are plenty of rocks near the two-foot stream you could forget the branches or the stovewood, but for the purpose at hand, let's use 16 inch stove wood.

Shove one piece of the wood into the bank on each side of the stream in the position shown in the V Deflector, Figure 104. Do not bother chinking them. By shifting the wood you will see just how closely to pinch them at the ends to get the most power out of the current. Observe that when you have the proper angles, the current created by the deflectors will dig so fast that you will marvel at what you can accomplish by right manipulation of the sticks. If the ends are too far apart the digging will be slight. Five minutes of experimentation will show you how to get the maximum power out of the water. You can tell when you have achieved this by looking at the churning and eddying sand.

Spend another five minutes with the stove wood V Deflector if you wish, and then turn to Figure 106 to note the Wing Deflector. Here is something which will be a little harder to learn, but once you have it, it will be yours forever.

Place one stick firmly into the bank, just as you placed

Fig. 104.—A V Deflector. (Showing upstream and downstream construction)

Built by Richard Thom and one helper at his summer home on the Pine. This is an example of what a riparian owner can do to help the fishing at his front door. When the rock deflector is chinked with gravel, it will speed up the current much more and will perform like that in figure 98.

the sticks for the V Deflector, so the current will not cut in there and get behind it. You will note that a wing is merely half a V Deflector. but you use a director log to guide the current. Observe how the single piece of wood picks up the current slowly at the bank, but notice the fast current it creates at the end of the stick.

That fast current is the secret of proper construction of every Wing Deflector, and here is the way to get it once and for all:

Study this faster current very, very closely. Note how it reaches out into the stream and then loses its speed almost at the end of the stick. It slides on almost straight downstream there and does nothing in the way of digging and does very little eddying.

Your object must be to turn that fast current into such great power that it will scour the river bottom, dig the sand off and throw it behind the Wing you intend to complete. Place that piece of stovewood where you see the current is fastest off the Deflector you have sunk in the bank. Add it to the Deflector at the angle you see in Figure 106.

Rightly placed, this director log will dig immediately. You will see the water eddying behind the completed Wing now, carrying the newly dug sand with it and depositing it right there. Then the faster current digs a long, deep channel downstream. It does this every second of every hour when your director log "directs" the current properly.

All the words in the English language cannot describe what the current will show you in less than five minutes with your sticks. After you acquire the knack of "directing" the most current the farthest and fastest, you will have no trouble building a large one on any stream. Spend at least another 10 minutes manipulating those sticks until you can spot that fastest current instantly.

Now turn to Figure 100 for the Y Deflector. You can readily see it is merely a V with two wings. It is also merely two Log Wings placed closely together. You already have learned how to handle a V, and also a Wing, so with the four sticks of stove wood go ahead and build a Y without hesitation.

I like a Y Deflector for a long, powerful shot to turn the water straight on down so it will not wash out a bridge which the river shows me might happen in a flood or freshet. Many culverts, sad to relate, are wrongly placed on our streams.

The Y Deflector shown in Figure 100 was built on the Brule River to throw the current away from a bank near a bridge, to

337

wipe out a large mat of thick weeds and silt and to build a long, deep hole for the fish at, and above, the wings of the Y. As you can see, it served a three way purpose.

Do not build a Y Deflector if a V Deflector will do. Also, do not construct a V Deflector on a wide stream where a Wing Deflector will serve, because this involves a tremendous amount of labor. A Log or Rock Wing will suit the purpose with much less effort. Rocks are always better to work with than logs. The construction is simple and much easier to keep in repair.

Now that you have spent a half hour or so building model stove wood deflectors, spend another half hour constructing the "things" shown in Figures 107 to 114. These "things" will teach you quickly how silly it would be to build such types on any

Fig. 105.—Rip Rapping.

A very nice piece of rip rapping where material is plentiful. Where it is not at hand, a wing deflector starting at the foreground would protect the bank with probably one tenth the material used here. Supervision and photograph by Wm. O'Gara.

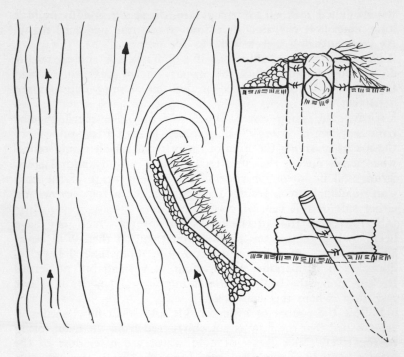

Fig. 106.—Log Wing Deflector.
Rocks are always preferable, if available.

HOW TO CONSTRUCT A WING DEFLECTOR

The upper section, the deflector log, is most effective at an angle of 45 degrees with the current. One should build and stake the deflector log before attempting to fit the director log. The principal purpose of the director log is to catch the thrust of water from the deflector log to create digging power and a backwash which deposits the sand behind the structure. No one should attempt to judge the placing of the director log until after the deflector log is *completed!* A director log placed parallel with the current is useless as a digging log. Wing Deflectors are ineffective in extremely quiet waters. All details of construction as well as the incorrect methods can be seen by the drawings.

stream. Their lack of current action, digging and eddying will warn you never to waste your time or materials on such "tripe." As your supervisor, if I were to see one of those "things," I would be derelict in my duty if I did not ask you to tear it down and start anew with the proper kind of Deflector, or add a wing or a V to that which needed only more work to make it perfect.

Clear, cold spring water, like a cold brook or creek, gives a river a "shot of energy" all summer long. Often springs are the means of saving the lives of many trout which would otherwise perish during the high temperatures in July and August. Trout will lie in long formation to take advantage of the cold water spilling into a reach. They would die a foot or two on either side of this vein of cooler water.

Search every foot of the banks for springs which may have been choked off by the river. Open them so there will be as ample a flow into the stream as possible. Sometimes I have reduced river temperature by opening very small but numerous trickles along the bank, consolidating several trickles into one nice flow where this was possible.

Follow the source of every trickle and small flow until you are satisfied that the flow is not obstructed from the main spring to the river. Nice flows of cold water are often lost to the main stream by being shut off above the bank, through "ice push" in the spring of the year. By following up a trickle you sometimes find that nearer its source it is a large flow that has been dammed by fallen trees, rain-washed debris and other obstacles. Like a beaver dam, these obstructions cause the cold water to spread out and be warmed considerably by the sun. When this heated water finally gets into the river it increases the temperature instead of cooling it. In your fishing, open these obstructed springs from time to time and more trout will be saved.

Beaver dams are a menace to good fishing on trout streams. They build one dam which holds the water back. Then they build another and another. Soon there is a series of small ponds, and how we fishermen love to get in those "secret" places to fish for the landlocked trout there. If we don't catch them, they will finally die because unless the dams are broken up, the heretofore cold water held back by the dams warms up to temperatures as high as 85 and 90 degrees, see Figure 101.

Most anyone will tell me that I am *non compos mentis* if I do not rush my child to the doctor when he has a fever of 104

340

Unsatisfactory Methods of Building Deflectors

Never use any of these. The same amount of time and labor will accomplish far better results when utilized to build the right types.

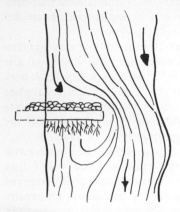

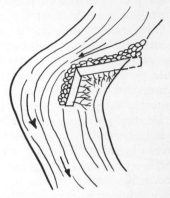

FIGURE 107. Single log or rock deflector not effective—tends to cut opposite bank and spreads sand downstream rather than behind structure and does not create a spawning bed.

FIGURE 108. Director log has no purpose when it is parallel with the current. This so often happens because the builder did not study the current after installing the deflector log.

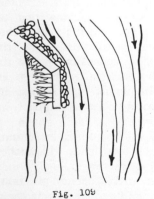

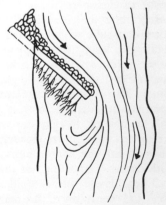

FIGURE 109. Built on side of stream away from current where it does not catch the main force of the water. The director log, lower log, obviously directs no water.

FIGURE 110. Does not deflect current properly. Catches debris and acts as a partial dam. Spreads sand on downstream. Makes sand bars and forms islands. Erodes opposite bank.

341

degrees. When the beaver, through their dams, have raised the temperature of a good feeder stream to 80 and 90 degrees, that stream also must have a doctor at once.

The beaver, however, has many avid defenders. These animals are termed "nature's greatest engineers." Trappers love them for their hides and the furriers love them, too. The naturalist devotes columns extolling the amphibious rodent.

Yet beaver "burn down" a trout stream by overheating the water. If his own house were ablaze, not one lover of the beaver would fail to yell "fire." And how welcome the firemen would be when they came to the rescue. Can they then blame the trout fisherman if he, too, yells "fire" when he sees how the beaver are causing the ruination of his fishing waters?

During my work with stream improvement, I could understand why the trappers resisted my efforts to have beaver in trout streams moved to other waters not inhabited by trout, but strangely enough it was five years before even a minority of the trout anglers finally agreed with the action. I eventually concluded this was because few fishermen had stopped to analyze how the warming of the waters by beaver dams not only harms the area above the barrier, but below as well.

The first year after a beaver dam is built there are small flooded, ice-lifted shrubs drifting over the bottom of the old stream bed. Then silt begins to cover the gravel which the trout used for spawning. The next year small trees are lifted off by the ice. These fall into the stream bed, covering the silt and shrubs which buried the spawning areas the year before. Then the larger trees fall in the beaver pond, so we now have three layers of debris over what once was trout water and spawning beds. The pond gradually becomes full of long, green, slimy filamentous algae, and soon the whole area around the beaver waters is the sorriest looking mess you can imagine.

The beaver, having cut off the timber for food, go on upstream to raise more beaver, cut off more timber, build more dams, ruin the water above, and now we have still another filthy mess, and so on, *ad infinitum*. Figure 102.

That bright, clear, cold brook or creek henceforth pours WARM water into the main stream and reduces its temperature dangerously. What's more, no trout can get above the dams to those once good spawning beds and no fry can get down to the main river from above the barriers.

In Wisconsin, where trout fishing had become practically nil on some of the state's best streams because of excessive tem-

FIG. 111.—The boulder on the left, downstream, does better work than the "things" on the right bank. This is merely half of a wing. While the construction is good, it does nothing for the stream. If a director wing were added to the deflector wing or the stream were pinched with a V deflector, you would see current action as in figure 104.

peratures resulting from beaver dams, I had to remove approximately 3,000 barriers before I could get the cold waters running into them again. Eighteen hundred of these were in one county alone. Once the stream temperatures were lowered, the trout began to come back. They had access to their spawning beds again, and the fry had their nursery water in the brooks and creeks.

The trout fishermen were enthusiastic about the comeback of their favorite streams, but the beaver advocates weren't so elated, and they didn't hesitate to say so in rather strong language. I still insist, though, that if you wish trout fishing in streams which are just on the temperature border line, have the beaver trapped and removed to other non-trout waters, kick those dams out, but be prepared for protests from the beaver lovers.

To insure permanency of stream improvement structures, sound construction is a vital necessity. Emphasis must be placed upon the value of sturdy stakes and logs, securely wired and so constructed that the structures will withstand the effects of ice,

343

drifts, jams and current pressure. Whether your work is done with logs or rocks, good chinking is a necessity.

In very few instances are dams desirable improvements in trout streams which flow through sand and clay soil. See figure 103. Dams are effective, however, in some rocky or mountainous streams where the runoff is rapid, but they should have a small opening for fish to go up or downstream. Detrimental features of dams as improvement structures are the warming of the confined waters, the creation of excessive sand and silt beds and the resulting undesired change in the character of the water. The free movement of fish during the spawning periods is stopped, with the result there must be continual stocking by the Fishery Division.

Although many different types of stream improvement structures are in use throughout the country, those effective for most conditions are the V Deflector, Wing Deflector, Y Deflector, Boom Covers and Bank Covers. They should be built

FIG. 112.—Another "Thing".

Here we see another "thing." It is not only useless but dangerous. It forces the current to continually wash out the opposite bank, forcing sand down stream to cover spawning gravel, pile up and warm the water below. Farther down we see another of the same type. An excellent V deflector, as in Fig. 98 could have been constructed with the materials of both. The man hours would have been the same.

344

Fig. 113.–Here we have another "thing." A useless piece of sheathing work. Great power and great good would have been attained if a duplicate of this were completed on the opposite bank. Then we would have current action and eddying power such as created by the V deflector in figure 98.

of rocks, but I show the log deflectors here to give you the angles you must use for current. Furthermore, rock is not always available.

The general purpose of the various deflectors is to create spawning beds, dig trout holes, and expose gravel on the bottom of the stream to enhance the amount of fish food. The sand and silt swept from the stream bed is deposited behind the deflectors to harbor an abundance of vegetation and insect food. This bar becomes a natural nursery for the fry. Their food, the plankton, multiplies fast and is not swept away.

The deflectors reduce the temperature of the stream by narrowing and confining wide flat stretches. This adds to the depth and oxygen content of the stream.

The proper use of deflectors by an expert workman will enable one to control and manipulate the stream in any manner desired.

There are many important points to keep in mind when building improvement structures.

Deflectors *must* be built at 30 to 60 degree angles with the

345

current. Installed at these angles, proper handling of the current will be achieved.

On all V and Y Deflectors the opening must be large enough to allow the passage of boats and canoes, but not so large an opening that it defeats the purpose by failing to create an acceleration of current.

It is desirable to place brush on the downstream side behind the deflectors, as shown in Figure 115.

Use solid material. Waterlogged material is preferred for the main logs of the structures. Build all devices solidly. All logs should be approximately the same size, if possible.

For the larger devices I recommend stakes four to six inches in diameter, and six to eight feet long, depending on the type of stream bottom. Smaller devices, more easily installed by two or three fishermen, also serve adequately in many waters. Stake sizes for these can be reduced accordingly. Larch, tama-

Fig. 114.—Another "Thing."

This is called an A deflector. The point of the A is upstream. Digs a hole at the head and along the side but throws the sand behind the deflector. The builder has foolishly planted willows in the bar behind the A. He has created a stable "island" in the center of this small stream. Every flood and freshet will now deflect the current to the banks, widening the stream and sending more and more sand to kill the food beds and spawning beds below. The only credit one can give the builders here is the good job of fencing to keep the livestock from eroding the banks.

346

rack, is best for stakes where it can be obtained, for tamarack will not rot in water.

All stakes should be driven at an angle and cut at an angle, as shown in the drawings, to reduce the possibility of catching ice, driftwood and debris, and pulling out of their beds. To prevent splitting, the tops of the stakes should be wired before driving. After the logs have been wired to the stakes, the stakes should again be driven to insure secure tightening of the wires.

Stakes should not be driven close to the ends of the structure because the stream will tend to undercut there and the staking would be ineffective. The number of stakes shown in the diagrams, and even more, should always be used in the building of these structures. You need no stakes when building rock structures, Figure 104.

Logs used as deflectors should be well seated in the bank and every precaution taken to prevent the stream from cutting into the bank and around the log.

The wings of the deflector should be made as water-tight as possible. This is done by placing rock and gravel on the upstream side of the deflector in order to prevent any possibility of undermining, whether logs or rocks are used. When more than one log is used, the irregularities should be removed from between the logs so they will fit tightly.

The top of all structures should be slightly above normal water level. If they are built too high above, there is great danger of destruction or clogging by water jams and debris. The relation of the normal water level to the structures should be as shown in the drawings.

Where rocks are available, they should always be used in building deflectors in place of logs. Rocks and boulders are easy for one or two men to handle and are every bit as good as logs. These should be carefully laid and chinked with gravel to make them watertight. Other principles of rock and boulder construction are exactly the same as in log construction, but you need no stakes with rock deflectors and they are more easily kept in good condition.

Inspect your structures each year. A stake pounded down here, a little wiring there or a few rocks replaced or added will cause them to perform admirably for many years.

347

V DEFLECTOR

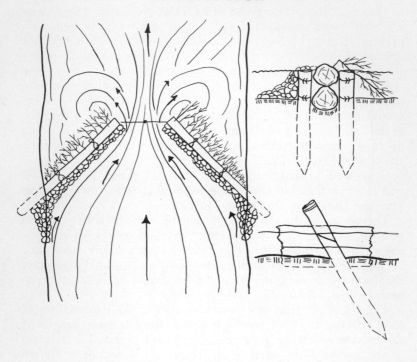

FIGURE 115.

Construction Plan   *Front Elevation*
                              (Without Chinking)

The value of a V Deflector is to increase the speed of the current, thus creating conditions favorable to trout life. The V Deflector is essentially a Y Deflector without the directors. It is generally desirable for use in shallow, slow moving portions of the stream where acceleration or direction of the current is needed. Details of construction are shown in the drawing.

Y DEFLECTOR

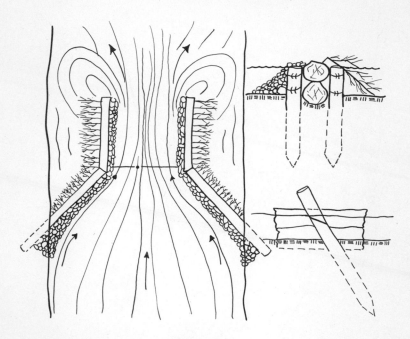

FIGURE 116.

The influence of the Y Deflector is effective further down the stream than the other types due to greater concentration and acceleration of the current. Construction details are shown in the drawings. Care should be taken to have a tight beveled joint between the director and the deflector. Build this type only where a Wing or a V Deflector will not accomplish the desired result. The work and the material will be much less.

A Y Deflector is, in reality, a pair of wing deflectors. A wing deflector, though, must always have the director, the lower part of the wing, at an angle as shown in the wing deflector on page 339. If this angle is not accomplished, the digging and eddying power will be lost.

Y DEFLECTOR

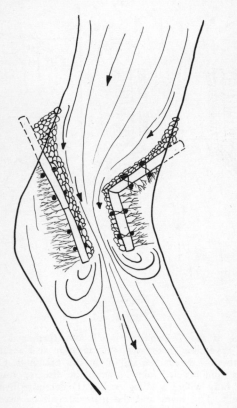

FIGURE 117.

Method of using Y Deflector to direct current around bend to prevent erosion as well as to speed up the current. Note the variation in the length of logs used.

BOOM COVER

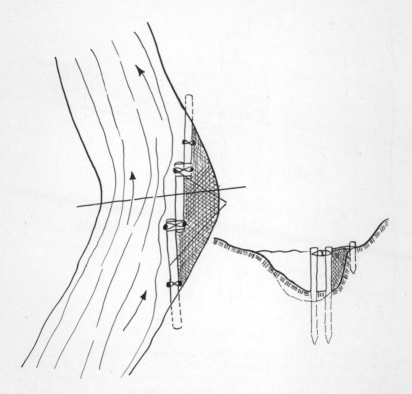

FIGURE 118.

The boom cover is designed to prevent erosion of banks on sharp bends, to provide shelter for the fish, to create a hole and to direct the current into the desired channel. The boom cover should be well filled with short logs and stumps. The poles and brush, and the brush mat cross-wired to hold it in place are shown in the drawing. The logs should be over-lapped and wired together and to the stakes. Stakes should be used on the inside and outside opposite each flap to support the boom. This structure will eventually be filled with sediment carried down by the stream and will form a solid "river bank."

BANK COVER

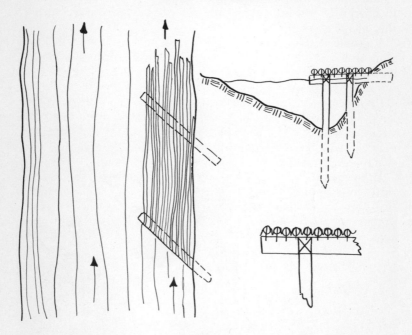

FIGURE 119.

To improve a stream successfully, cover must be provided in addition to new spawning beds, food and cooler water. Any type of shelter will help prevent the loss of trout by predators both from the water and air. Shelters can be provided by the use of various types of cover such as alders, dogwood or man-made cover.

The bank cover is generally used and has proved the most satisfactory. It consists of a frame covered with saplings as shown in the drawing. The frame must be of rigid construction and the upstream end of the saplings are to be wired to the frame. These should not be used in extremely fast water, rapids or in very shallow water. It is desirable that a bank cover be placed above, opposite or below every deflector.

These covers should be built at a 45 degree angle or less to the bank to prevent the lodging of debris or ice jams which would tend to destroy the structure or defeat its usefulness. Slant the cover slightly into the upstream current. Then all floating stuff will skid over it and not "hang up."

The construction of these covers will be noted in the drawing.

STREAMSIDE PLANTING CAN HELP OR HURT

You can surely reduce the temperature of a trout stream several degrees by planting trees along the banks for shade. But where would you plant trees? And what trees would you plant?

These are two questions I must know before I can place you in charge of my stream improvement crews when we turn to this phase of our work.

I assume that by reading this far in the book you will know more or less about water, the trout and the fisherman. If you plant wisely, the water, the fish and the anglers will praise you. Plant wrongly and they will condemn you.

Consider the fisherman's viewpoint first. In the event you have planted hundreds of tiny willows every place along the stream banks, within a few seasons the angler cannot throw a fly without being entangled in the branches overhead. Then you'll mourn.

Who would think that those willow cuttings, no thicker than your thumb, would grow such wide-spreading branches that they would meet and form a cover over the entire stream?

Fig. 120—A boom cover such as this protects a stream from claybank washing and a sandy bank from erosion. It sifts the sand in suspension under the boom cover so that eventually the cover is as solid as the bank itself.

"Let the fishermen go hang", you say. "See how I have shaded this stream. Note that I have reduced the temperature almost 5 degrees. See what welcome shade I have given the trout." Then you wait for the appointment I shall not give you.

Not until you have learned to work closer with nature can I place you in charge of this most important aspect of stream improvement.

In your heedless planting of willows you have not only created hazards over the stream for the fishermen, you have also brought hardship to the trout and the food they eat.

Too much shade is not good for a stream. Your knowledge of transparency tells you that the sun is responsible for practically all fish food. By closing off the sun's rays with the tree trunks and wide-spreading branches you have shut off the sun's power to grow the slime—the algae—which all fish food depends upon.

You have not allowed the water to offer a supermarket to the trout. You have only made a hotel which will have few guests, no matter how comfortable you have made the rooms as far as temperature is concerned.

To provide a complete home, your hotel must have food, too, and you cannot obtain it if you plant willows so close to the shore that their branches spread over the entire stream. It is far better to set willows back too remote from the bank than too close.

Whether you plant willows, cedar, spruce and other coniferous trees, or hardwoods, look first at the mature trees. When full grown their branches may spread over 60 feet all around the trunk. Surely then, small trees should be planted no closer to the bank than 30 feet. Even then the time will come when their shadows will shade the stream all day long, but the high sun can get in enough work to grow food for the fish.

It is a good idea to study the prevailing winds in your area from May to September, or to get this information from your nearest local weather station. If the prevailing winds are from the southwest it is best to plant trees on the west side of the stream. This enables the morning sun to get at the stream to raise fish food, but the afternoon rays will be shaded by the trees, helping keep the water temperature down. Here, in the shade on the west bank after 4 o'clock in the afternoon, the mayfly nymphs will leave their bottom homes and come up to hatch in the not so bright waters. All along this side of the stream the trout will be feeding and the anglers will be fishing.

It's a case of "ring around the rosy". The morning sun will grow more food for more nymphs for more trout to eat for more fishermen to catch in the cooled waters you have created by your "prevailing winds" planting. And not to be overlooked is the fact that these winds will also blow good food from the trees into the stream, everything from ants to caterpillars, thus supplementing the water-raised food of the trout.

Knowing what to plant should be easy for you, so easy you may yet land that supervising job.

Go to nature for the answer. Look along the stream banks and observe which trees are doing best there. You can, of course, always fall back upon willows but this stream will be here for centuries and we like to plant trees which are natural to its area, if we possibly can.

After deciding what trees you believe should be planted, go to your County Agricultural Agent for further consultation. Bring him a sample of the various soils and he will test them for you. Get his opinion and follow the advice of this trained man. He will give you pamphlets or tell you where they may be obtained. Consult your area forester if you have one.

When you have done this, come back to me and I shall be glad to give you the job at an excellent salary—your pay will be five more trout each day you go fishing. One at a time, fellows! Don't rush, I'll have a job for each of you in this streamside planting department for we are "awfully short of help".

Fifteen years ago I was in a little village where I talked with the fishermen. When I showed them how—but never mind now. Surely there must be another village, town or city where there is an organization called a Rod and Gun Club.

Maybe, I said maybe, the members can be persuaded to bestir themselves long enough to plant a few trees now and then to help themselves to help themselves to more trout. Remember, though, I said "maybe".

The paper mills and lumber companies might help if we all agree upon a sound tree planting program for our streams. Some of my friends have refused to "clear cut" along roads and around lakes. I am sure that many will aid the fishermen by leaving some standing timber for shade along stream banks.

CHAPTER XXIII

Lake Improvement Is
a Modern Necessity

THE YEAR WAS 1900. Back in the wilderness Bill Spivis, a venturesome fellow, bought a 40 on a lake. While he owned only the 40 acres, the land around the entire shoreline was his to use, for no one bothered to come that far for fishing. The buggy would be worn out and the old mare would be exhausted before the fishermen got that far.

Bill wasn't so "looney", though, even if his only company was the loons. Bill and his family had sole use of the lake at that time. He proceeded to develop his land. He felled the dead trees, cut up the down stuff and thinned out the timber so the remainder would have better opportunity for growth.

Then he proceeded to clean up the shoreline at his cabin, along with several hundred feet on either side of his dock so the youngsters could wade and swim to their hearts' content. He let the waterlogged materials dry, and every once in awhile the family would have a glorious bonfire, using the stuff he cut off the land and the waterlogged timbers he had removed from the lake to dry. Bill could go out any place along the shore and take fish among the downtrees and waterlogged brush that still remained untouched in the lake.

Then came the automobiles. Bill wasn't alone with his family any more. He sold off some of his 40 and bought some more land, and some more, and kept on selling until most of the lake frontage was occupied by cottage owners. Each cleaned up his shoreline and land, just as Bill had done years before in the vicinity of his cabin. There were more bonfires, and then came more nice wading in the renovated beaches.

Somehow, the fishing fell off. The blunt nose minnows which used to paste their eggs under the waterlogged stuff in the

357

FIG. 121.–Fish Food On One Stick Of Wood.

You can see the dozens of caddis houses on this waterlogged stick no larger than the man's coat sleeve. You cannot see the dozens of freshwater shrimp, clambering mayfly nymphs or the damsel and dragon fly nymphs that were there when I lifted and returned the stick to the water. Fish food galore!

358

lake began to dwindle in numbers. With the advent of the beach-combing cottagers they had fewer places to spawn. And when the blunt nose minnows declined, the bass became scarcer, since minnows were their chief source of food.

Before long Bill's neighbors began to complain that the fishing was getting worse and worse. Even Bill, in spite of the loyalty he held for his "development", admitted it privately to his wife, but to no one else.

Bill thought nothing of it when an offshore wind felled two big trees into the lake during one summer's evening, but a year later he was delighted when he took a fish from the submerged tangle. Then he caught another. Every once in awhile when his wife would remark how nice it would be to have a mess of fish for a change, Bill would unobtrusively go to his private water timber and perform. In spite of his fishing success, he never woke up to the fact that he and his friends had, with no malice aforethought, helped kill the fishing in the lake by removing the same kind of cover that was now proving so effective.

How easily he could have rehabilitated his *soft* water lake with the aid of his neighbors, if only he had known more about the water, fish and the cover they needed to furnish good fishing year after year!

If a cottage owner, instead of burning the brush he cuts on his land, will tie it up into a bundle and sink it in the lake, he will be restoring some cover there. If he drags a large tree into the water, sinks a deadhead, or puts a few slabs in the water for blunt nose minnows to paste their eggs under, he'll bring back some of the fish food for the bass.

When I tested the waters of some of the lakes in the East, I found most of them *very soft* to *soft*, and with little cover in the water. I was shocked! How readily the shoreline land owners could improve their fishing with just a little concerted effort of a few inspired workers.

Just one little branch no thicker than half your little finger will furnish enough ALL YEAR food for one nymph of the mayfly or caddis fly. The small snails will crawl along it, too, eating the algae which the sun grows on the underwater branch. If that is true, and I'll stake my life on it, just think what a hundred branches will do for a lake, or a thousand branches, a dozen logs, and a half dozen trees and stumps! See Figure 121.

Tie some wire around one small bunch of brush, put a stone in the center of it for weight, and sink the brush in the lake a few feet off shore. Next year, after it has become thoroughly

359

waterlogged, lift it up and examine it. The fish food on and in the bundle will amaze you. The little fish you see dashing away will surprise you, too, and now and then the large fish you catch there will delight you. One bundle of brush!

If you really want to go into lake improvement on a larger scale, drop one of each of the types of devices shown on the next few pages in the lake on which your cottage is located. I'll guarantee that before the next year is over you'll become an ecologist. Not only that, but if you work with your area biologist for an hour or two, you will become a conchologist, entomologist, aquatic botanist, aquatic biologist and ichthyologist as well because you'll be observing snails, insects, plants, water and fish. And, who knows but that you might send your son to college to become a limnologist and earn the degree that every fisherman would be proud to possess. Limnology embraces all this and more.

Before undertaking any intensive lake improvement work of your own, or hiring it done, I would suggest that you turn back to Chapter II in this book to make sure you have fixed in your mind the necessary information concerning colors of water. That little white plate I talk about MUST be used to tell you where to place the devises you build for a lake.

Look at the large brush refuge in Figure 122. Imagine all that work, and then sinking it too deeply for the sun's rays to shine upon it and grow all the fish food which can potentially be raised upon it if the sun can get down to it. Or if it is a bundle of loose brush or some stumps that you have sunk too deeply, that labor would be lost, too.

The white plate tells you where and how far down the sun will glow the algae on every twig, branch and trunk in the water. If you sink a refuge, log, stump or sapling tangle three feet below the surface in *dark brown* water you lose every bit of its effectiveness. Should you sink it in 15 feet of *tan* water, it would likewise be useless. In *clear* and *very clear* water, however, it would do wonderful work at that depth.

Never sink a device in too shallow water. Boats will hit it; the ice push will tear it to pieces and your labor will be for naught. There is no need for placing a refuge in a lake which has the maximum of good fish and cover. The trouble with that lake may be too many fish, and only intensive angling would be the best method to "improve" that water.

Before you decide to build spawning boxes, you should make a complete circuit of the lake to determine whether they really are necessary. The smallmouth bass will use every spawning box you sink, but if at least 25 per cent of the lake's beach already has good spawning gravel they would not be needed if the gravel shows at a water depth of five feet and continues in the shallower water towards the shoreline. If there are no natural spawning beds in a lake, the artificial spawning boxes are excellent, no matter what its quality, from *very soft* to *hard*.

When you build your sapling tangles, get the saplings from clumps of maple, oak or any other cluster of wood except white birch and hemlock that isn't peeled. Both underwater insects and fish shun the white-barked sticks, and the birch rots quickly in water. They shun hemlock because the bark, in lake or stream, poisons the water.

Don't cut down the entire clump of saplings as you gather tangle material on your land. Cut out the crooked saplings and leave one or two of the straight ones to continue their growth. Eventually these will grow into good "sticks of timber", for they will no longer have to compete for light and air with the saplings which have been culled. Where any poor timber is shutting off the light and air of a better tree, use that for the sapling tangles, too, or for the brush refuge if it is large enough. All this is practicing "timber stand improvement" as well as lake improvement.

Minnow spawning devices are a great aid in boosting the minnow population in a lake, and thereby enhancing the food supply for game fish. The day after placing minnow spawners in a lake, I have picked them up and found some literally painted with the eggs of blunt nose minnows. In my files are letters from owners of summer houses and resorts telling me their lakes were fished out, but once my crews built and installed minnow spawners and stocked the waters with blunt nose minnows and bass, the fish multiplied to such an extent that the "fished out" waters soon were continuously productive. Like Bill Spivis, these lake frontage owners had cut up every tree lying in the lake, removing the natural spawning places for the blunt nose and fat head minnows.

Set your minnow spawners in water as shallow as you dare, but have due regard for wading youngsters, swimmers, boats and ice. Take no chances on having them shoved ashore. Blunt nose minnows like water from two to three feet in depth but they will use the boards of the spawning devices at three to five feet. Four feet will be the best all around depth to prevent the ice from working them ashore and boats from striking them.

In 1934 Doctors Birge and Juday of the University of Wisconsin told me that for experimental purposes they had put in three tons of hydrated lime to the acre of water in Weber Lake near their summer laboratory in Northeastern Wisconsin. This *very clear, very soft* seepage lake is 45 feet deep and 40 acres in area. I tested it for several years and found that the increased fertility held quite constant. The lake was poisoned about 15 years later and now yields rainbow trout. It must now be stocked each year, but Birge and Juday showed us that acid lakes can be helped appreciably through these first water fertilizer experiments in the United States.

In Crystal Lake, about one mile from Weber, the water was not fertilized. It is twice as deep and twice as large as Weber Lake, and is 10 feet better in transparency. The water is *softer*, 2.0 ppm CO_2 compared with 3.0 ppm in Weber Lake.

Dr. Juday asked that we build no refuges in Weber Lake as they might throw off the true results of the fertilizer experiment. He said he and Birge did not intend to experiment with Crystal Lake and that they thought it would be a good idea to sink lake structures there. I would be less than frank if I didn't admit here that I naturally felt quite proud when these noted scientists told me that after all their intensive years of research on water, I was the first in Wisconsin to put their scientific findings in use for the fishermen.

My crews constructed and sank many structures in Crystal Lake. Within three years the anglers reported catching many more bass than before. To me this was strong evidence that sandy-bottomed, *soft* water lakes, barren of cover and fish food, can be helped immensely with refuges, minnow spawners and bass spawning boxes. I saw this demonstrated over and over in the sand-lined kettle lakes throughout Wisconsin. In *hard* water lakes with no good cover, the same good results were obtained.

Some day the Boy Scouts and other youth organizations will learn from their instructors how to improve lakes and streams. If these fine young lads start improving the waters, what a good fishing future they will bring to themselves and their children.

No fisherman need ever consider himself "broke" as long as he has the true wealth of the woods and waters at his disposal. May you have many birthdays, but never grow too old to fish.

362

Prepare the frame for brush piling by lacing long saplings lengthwise of the frame. Weave or lace the saplings eight or ten inches apart. Begin with a butt of a sapling, pull it under and over the cross pieces until it rests firmly on the end piece. Continue until you have the frame laced, first a butt, then a tip of a sapling resting on the end pieces. This forms a mat for brush piling, preventing your load from dragging under the frame.

Now pile brush lengthwise of the frame, alternating tips with butts to keep a fairly level layer. Pile to a height of 15 inches

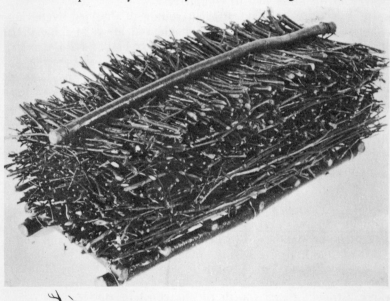

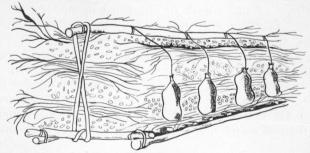

Fig. 122.—Brush Refuge.
Construction and photographs by William O'Gara in figures 122 to 126 inclusive.

and see to it that no butts or tips extend beyond the ends or sides of the frame.

The second layer is cross piled with shorter brush to the same height—15 inches. A third course, or layer, of lengthwise piling, a fourth of crosswise piling, a fifth of lengthwise piling and a sixth, or last, of cross piling. This last top layer, being cross piled, will help the binding pole bind the brush firmly.

Now cut a binding pole about the same size as one of the side frame pieces—16 feet in length. Place binding pole on center, top. Cramp the end down tightly and wire as shown. Wire the other end the same way to complete.

In all lengthwise piling, prevent rolling of the load by having all brush a trifle higher on the outside and lower at the center. In all crosswise piling, see that the ends are higher and the slope, if any, must be towards the center.

It is understood that all end piling does not extend beyond the ends of the frame. All side piling should be in line with the sides of the frame. Make a neat, square job so that the work will be good on all four sides, but have the tips make all the small refuges you can achieve. Never cut the tips off the branches, for a perfectly square solid "box" is a refuge for no fish or fish food. The sun's rays will not penetrate it to grow the algae for the nymphs, snails and small clams.

Sink these every 300 feet around the lake in water deep enough to have a clearance for ice and boats of at least four feet, at the lake's lowest level. Six or eight bags filled with sand should sink them, or boulders, if handy, can be wired on the frame ends.

I had hundreds of husky young men to build and handle these big refuges. You, your wife and children can build them, too, but reduce them to the size you can sink easily. Two or three refuges of one fourth to one third of the size we made will prove excellent for food and cover. Build one first to find what size you can handle conveniently.

Never, under any circumstances, place anything on the ice and expect the melting ice to sink it right there. An early spring blow may carry it ashore or take it out so far that it will sink too deeply to be of any use for the fish. If ice cutting is too much for you to handle for the sinking of your structures, reduce their size and tow them out in the spring, summer or autumn.

I started this work in Wisconsin in 1934. When we examined the brush refuges in 1936, after sinking several hundred of them, the result was amazing. The great quantity of fish food reared

364

in each refuge, the many fish which fed there and the large number which used them for shelter, made us very proud of our work. You'll have many criticisms, just as I had, but grin to yourself and "take it". The results will reward you and that will be compensation enough.

MINNOW SPAWNER

Fig. 123.—Minnow Spawner. (See next page)

Three five-foot pieces of split poplar, oak, pine, cedar or other material which may be available should be nailed together as illustrated. Nail two rounds of timber on the bottom slab to prevent sinking in the sand as much as possible. Planks or boards picked up along the shore line, or purchased slabs are ideal, of course, but seldom available.

Split the timber in five-foot lengths or shorter. If in five-foot lengths, the size of the timber may be two and one-half to eight inches in diameter. Three-, four- or six-foot sticks which may be found on the beach or left over from constructing other improvements are often used.

The spawners can be anchored by wiring rocks, of sufficient size, to sink them. The most practical manner of sinking is with stakes. Two stakes are necessary. Drive the stakes opposite one another at the inside of the V or hub. Before the stakes disappear under the surface in driving, wire them from one to the other. In the driving, the stakes will pull the wire down on the spawner, and anchor it firmly to the bottom. Then saw the stakes off underwater if they are too long. They should be level with the spawners.

The FLAT SURFACES must face the bottom. Minnows spawn on the flat under-surfaces of these spawning wheels, not on the top. In the spring, the underpart of the spawners are colored with the spawn of those species of minnows which must have flat surfaces for reproduction. For the best results the spawners should be sunk in three to four feet of water, although five feet will not be too deep in *clear* water. Do not place the spawners or any other improvement devices in front of cottages where bathers will stumble over them.

The most efficient number to each large brush refuge is 25 minnow spawners. Here, too, you can reduce the size, thus reducing the number of rocks you will need to sink them or smaller stakes to hold them.

You will be pleasantly surprised to see the great number of eggs pasted on the underside of these spawners. The blunt-nose minnows, *Hyborhynchus notatus*, will literally paint their eggs there. The fat head or black head minnow, *Pimphales promelas*, does the same but the blunt-nose grows to four inches while the fat head runs about three inches. I have seen many a "poor" lake become a "rich" lake because the game fish then grew fast there.

366

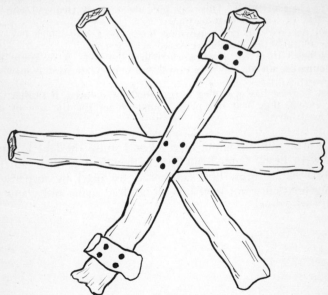

FIG. 123. Minnow Spawner.

BASS SPAWNING BOX

FIGURE 124

Bass spawning boxes are made of poplar, pine, cedar, oak or any other material which will hold gravel season after season.

The size should be no smaller than two and one-half feet in width and three feet in length. Completed, they should be not lower than 16 to 20 inches high, including the bottoms, to prevent them from sinking too far in the silt. Build five for each large brush refuge you place in the lake.

Split the poplar so that you may have a fairly smooth box inside, like the illustration. Finish the corners with half or quarter rounds and fit the timbers closely. This will prevent the gravel from being lost in carrying or in the fanning of the nest.

In filling the box with gravel, mix the top six inches with one-fourth to one-fifth of sand. In order to keep the bass from attacking one another while nesting, place these boxes not less than 25 feet apart, in approximately five feet of water. This will give them about two and one-half to three feet of ice and boat clearance.

It is not necessary to build spawning boxes for a lake which has one-fourth or more of its shoreline covered with gravel.

Do not build these for river work, unless the river is so sandy that the deflectors cannot dig down to gravel and thus create natural spawning beds.

The size of these bass spawning boxes cannot be reduced. If smaller than the size shown, they will not permit ample room for the size of nest the bass must have.

I am a little dubious about marl lakes. I study the lake in June. If I see firm nests, fanned out by the bass and panfish and the eggs are eyed, bright, not smothered by marl in suspension, spawning boxes are not necessary. The dead snails and clams do the work of gravel.

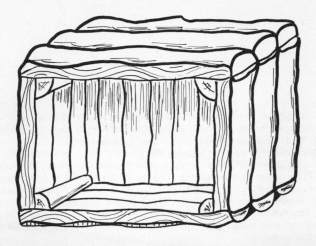

Fig. 124.—Bass Spawning Box.

SAPLING TANGLES

FIGURE 125.

These tangles are made of oak, alder, maple or other saplings or branches two to three inches at the butt. Build them 32 to 36 inches high and 10, 12 to 18 feet long, depending upon the available material.

Lay three six- to ten-inch logs on the ground for a work bench, crosswise, so you may pull your binding wire under and over the tangle to tighten. Place eight or ten saplings lengthwise on the logs. Another course of eight to ten saplings is placed upon the first course. Stagger these ends as much as possible to leave many openings for the fish.

Three "spreaders" are now placed on top of the two courses, crosswise. Place one on the center and the other two about three feet on either side of the center.

Two more sapling courses are laid lengthwise similar to the courses below the spreaders. Three more spreaders are now placed exactly above the three lower spreaders. As these are to be used as handles for carrying the tangles, they should extend about a foot on each side, not cut off flush with the tangle like the lower spreaders should be. The extension handles can be sawed off before cutting the ice and save two feet of ice cutting.

Now pile two more courses of sapling tangles on top of the spreader handles. Pull your No. 9 soft black iron wire tightly around the tangle as shown in the illustration, making it about two and one-half feet in width when completed. Build five for each large brush refuge constructed.

Make all the small openings possible to provide refuge for small fish only and to enable the sun to work in the openings to grow algae for the insects. The more crooked and staggered the tangle, the more desirable. Do not stack the saplings evenly, like cordwood, or you defeat the purpose for which the tangles are intended.

Sink with sand bags in about five or six feet of water.

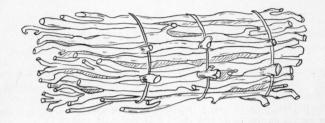

FIG. 125.—Sapling Tangle.

FRAME FOR BRUSH REFUGE

FIGURE 126.

Materials necessary: No. 9 black, soft iron wire, one and one-half inch staples, 40D nails, claw hammer, double bitted ax, side cutting pliers, one-man cross cut saw.

Oak, poplar, pine or other timber, except white birch, with a minimum of six inches at the butt, and three and one-half inches at the top should be used for side pieces. Fifteen foot lengths are the most practicable. All knots should be made smooth for easy dragging.

The sides of the frame should be braced with seven cross pieces as shown. The center brace and the two end braces should be six feet, six inches long. These should be wired and nailed as shown in the illustration. Drive a one and one-quarter-inch staple where the wires are to cross, pull the first complete turn through the eye of the staple, tighten with claw of hammer and drive the staple home. Then twist the wire upon itself and complete the X wiring as shown.

While the two end braces and the center cross brace should be a minimum of three and one-half inches in diameter, the remaining four braces need not be under two and one-half inches. Nail these four braces as shown, but do not wire them. All braces should be six feet, six inches long to allow for a three-inch overlap on the side frames. This is necessary to good brush piling.

When completed, the side pieces should be six feet apart, overall, as shown, and 15 feet long. It is best to build the frame with the butt opposite a top, as illustrated.

Where you have no help to handle such a large refuge, cut the size of the frame and the amount of brush to one that you can handle nicely.

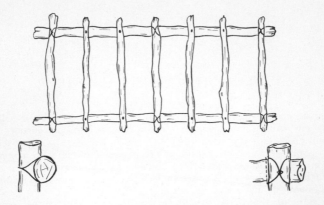

FIG. 126.—Frame-Brush Refuge.
Brush refuge frame laced with brush to hold upper layers of cross piling.

APPENDIX

Some of the Waters of the United States and Canada

THE FISHERMAN WILL REALIZE the significance of my water tests. Take Canyon Lake in Arizona, for instance. The parts per million of bound carbon dioxide reads 65.0 ppm. CO_2. This shows that the pH will be *hard* water. Immediately the fisherman who uses the chemical information outlined in Chapter IV will know that this is a lake very rich in lime content.

He multiplies the reading, 65.0, by 50 and arrives at the figure of 3250 pounds of fish and fish food to the acre of water. He labels the lake a *hard* water lake which is rich in fish food and therefore should abound in fish life. Having read Chapters II to VIII he will be able to recognize the factors which limit, or increase the food production. When he fishes the lake, his acquired knowledge of water should enable him to form his own pattern as to the method of fishing it, or any other body of water he may meet up with in his travels.

UNITED STATES WATERS

ARIZONA

Canyon Lake	65.0	*Hard*
Carl Pleasant Lake	90.0	*Hard*
Lake Mead—Hoover Dam	58.0	*Hard*
Roosevelt Lake	70.0	*Hard*
Saguaro Lake	62.0	*Hard*
Colorado River	60.0	*Hard*
Salt River	71.0	*Hard*

ARKANSAS

Current River	71.0	*Hard*
Neosho (Grand) River	32.0	*Hard*
St. Francis River	22.0	*Medium Hard*

CALIFORNIA

Lake Tahoe	17.5	*Medium*
Patrick Creek	29.0	*Medium Hard*
Smith River	20.0	*Medium*
Klamath River	34.0	*Hard*
Eel River	44.0	*Hard*
Russian River	49.0	*Hard*

COLORADO

Prospect Lake	6.5	*Soft*
Gunnison River	39.0	*Hard*
Arkansas River	20.0	*Medium*
South Platte River (Middle Fork)	86.0	*Hard*
South Platte River	21.0	*Medium Hard*

CONNECTICUT

Rogers Lake	6.2	*Soft*

FLORIDA

Florida claims more lakes than any state in the Union, 30,000, I believe. Her waters run from *very soft* to *hard.*

Alligator (Big) Lake	7.0	*Soft*
Apopka Lake	56.0	*Hard*
Dora Lake	39.0	*Hard*
Eustis Lake	30.0	*Hard*
Isabella Lake	9.0	*Soft*
Jeffrey Lake	3.0	*Very Soft*
Lochloosa Lake	10.0	*Soft*
Okeechobee Lake	63.0	*Hard*
Silver Springs	72.0	*Hard*
Thopekaliga Lake	9.0	*Soft*
Tsala Apopka Lake	27.0	*Medium Hard*
Everglades, Canal (Tamiami Trail)	79.0	*Hard*
Crystal River	36.0	*Hard*
Homasassa River & Springs	52.0	*Hard*
Ochlooknee River	8.0	*Soft*
St. Johns River	28.0	*Medium Hard*
Suwanee River near Gulf	66.0	*Hard*
Withlacoochee River	55.0	*Hard*

GEORGIA

Suwanee River at source	2.0	*Very Soft*
Okefenokee Swamp	2.0	*Very Soft*

IDAHO

Pend de Orielles Lake (Ponderay)	34.0	*Hard*
Couer de Alene Lake	10.0	*Soft*
Spokane River	10.0	*Soft*

ILLINOIS

Illinois River	68.0	*Hard*
Mississippi River	49.0	*Hard*
Ohio River	39.0	*Hard*

376

KENTUCKY
Reelfoot Lake .... 45.0   *Hard*

MAINE
Bigwood Lake .... 8.0   *Soft*
Mose Holden Pond .... 7.0   *Soft*
Long Pond .... 6.5   *Soft*
Moosehead Lake .... 5.0   *Very Soft*
Mooselookmeguntic Lake .... 5.0   *Very Soft*
Sebago Lake .... 5.0   *Very Soft*
Rangely Lakes .... 4.5   *Very Soft*

MASSACHUSETTS
Great South Pond .... 4.0   *Very Soft*
Billington's Sea Lake .... 5.0   *Very Soft*
Plymouth Rock Trout Ponds .... 4.0   *Very Soft*

MARYLAND
Pauxtent River .... 9.0   *Soft*

MICHIGAN
Michigan, with her thousands of lakes and thousands of miles of streams has slightly less than Minnesota and Wisconsin lakes. Her lakes run from *very soft* water to *hard* water, just as do Minnesota and Wisconsin. Michigan leads though in her trout streams and trout fishing over Minnesota or Wisconsin in stream mileage and numbers of brook, brown and rainbow trout. New York's famous Au Sable River and branches test from *very soft* to *soft* water (see N. Y. tests). Michigan's famous Au Sable River shows:

Au Sable—North and South Branches .... 60.0   *Hard*
East Branch .... 65.0   *Hard*
Main Au Sable River .... 65.0   *Hard*

Thus, it runs from six to over 15 times richer in lime content than New York's Au Sable River. Practically all of Michigan's streams run from *medium hard* to *hard* in the lower peninsula of Michigan. In the Upper Peninsula of Michigan, at my old home town of Gladstone, here is the test for Little Bay de Noc, famous for walleyed pike and Bass.

Little Bay de Noc (Noquette) .... 54.5   *Hard*
The trout streams:
The Escanaba River .... 43.5   *Hard*
The Days River, The Whitefish River, The Rapid River, and the Haymeadow River all test about .... 60.0   *Hard*
Ontonagon River (near Watersmeet) .... 35.0   *Hard*

The Fox, near Manistique, The Chocolay near Marquette and dozens of others in the U. P. are all *medium* to *hard* water streams.

MINNESOTA

Minnesota, with her 10,000 lakes from *very soft* to *hard* waters, offers every type of fishing. Minnesota does not equal Wisconsin in her muskie fishing and does not rank with either Michigan or Wisconsin in trout fishing streams, but her 1500 more lakes than either Michigan or Wisconsin give her equal rank with either of those states for fishermen.

Here are some of her trout streams from Duluth to Pigeon River on the North Shore of Lake Superior:

Cascade River	23.0	Medium Hard
Baptism River	17.0	Medium
Gooseberry River	29.0	Medium Hard
Reservation River	20.0	Medium
Temperance River	10.0	Soft

MISSOURI
Current River	71.0	Hard
Black River	45.0	Hard
Eleven Points River	67.0	Hard
Little North Fork	98.0	Hard
Long Creek	61.0	Hard
St. Francis River	22.0	Medium Hard
White River	51.0	Hard
Big Springs	79.0	Hard
Lake Taneycomo	52.0	Hard
Norfork L.	69.0	Hard

MONTANA
West Gallatin River	57.0	Hard
Clark Fork	48.0	Hard

NEW HAMPSHIRE
Joe's Pond	18.0	Medium
Webster Lake	3.5	Very Soft
Winnepesaukee Lake	4.5	Very Soft
Androscoggin River	4.0	Very Soft
Ammonoosuc River	5.0	Very Soft
Ottauquechee River	9.0	Very Soft

NEW JERSEY
Great Egg Harbor River	3.0	Very Soft
Babcock Creek	2.0	Very Soft

NEW MEXICO
Pecos River	67.0	Hard
Rio Grande River	90.0	Hard
Carlsbad Cavern Pool	134.0	Hard

NEW YORK

Canadice Lake	13.7	Medium
Canandaigua Lake	47.5	Hard
Seneca Lake	43.5	Hard
Cayuga Lake	43.5	Hard
Lake Placid	4.0	Very Soft
Eagle Lake	13.0	Medium
Kiamesha Lake	7.0	Soft
Au Sable River	10.0	Soft
Au Sable East Branch	7.0	Soft
Au Sable West Branch	3.5	Very Soft
Neversink River	5.0	Very Soft
Beaverkill River	4.0	Very Soft
Mongaup River	5.0	Very Soft
Willowemoc River	5.0	Very Soft
Delaware River	4.0	Very Soft
Niagara Falls	39.0	Hard
Thousand Islands (St. Lawrence River)	42.0	Hard

OKLAHOMA

Canadian River	86.0	Hard
Cimarron River	102.0	Hard

OREGON

Crater Lake	12.5	Medium
Multonomah Falls	13.0	Medium
Applegate River	39.0	Hard
Columbia River	33.0	Hard
Deschutes River	27.0	Medium Hard
Hood River	15.0	Medium
Illinois River	26.0	Medium Hard
Rogue River	18.0	Medium
Sandy River	14.0	Medium
Willamette River	15.0	Medium
Umpqua R. N. Branch	15.0	Medium
Umpqua R. S. Branch	31.0	Hard

PENNSYLVANIA

Wallenpaupack Lake	6.0	Soft
Dryberry River	11.0	Medium
Bushkill River	3.5	Very Soft
Shohola River	3.0	Very Soft
Susquehanna River*	18.0	Medium
Juniata River*	40.0	Hard
Conodoguinet Creek*	85.0	Hard
Yellow Breeches Creek*	46.0	Hard
Big Spring*	64.0	Hard
Letort*	95.0	Hard
Boiling Springs*	47.0	Hard

Samples from last seven waters* were supplied by Charles K. Fox for my analysis.

RHODE ISLAND
Hamilton Pond .... 7.0 *Soft*

SOUTH DAKOTA
Missouri River .... 60.0 *Hard*

TEXAS
Brazos River .... 50.0 *Hard*
Colorado River .... 69.5 *Hard*
Rio Grande River .... 90.0 *Hard*
San Berhard River .... 9.0 *Soft*
Lake Austin .... 66.0 *Hard*

TENNESSEE
Reelfoot Lake .... 45.0 *Hard*

UTAH
Salt Lake .... 118.0 *Hard*
Utah Lake .... 150.0 *Hard*
Jordan River .... 90.0 *Hard*
Virgin River, North Fork .... 95.0 *Hard*
Weber Creek .... 69.0 *Hard*

VERMONT
Moose River .... 4.0 *Very Soft*
Connecticut River .... 4.0 *Very Soft*
Winoski Pond .... 26.0 *Medium Hard*
Lake Champlain .... 22.0 *Medium Hard*

VIRGINIA
Bull Run River .... 5.0 *Very Soft*
Hughes River .... 4.0 *Very Soft*
Rapidan River .... 10.0 *Soft*
Rappahanock River .... 9.0 *Soft*
Robinson River .... 5.0 *Very Soft*
Wilderness Run .... 9.0 *Soft*

WASHINGTON
Crescent Lake .... 26.0 *Medium Hard*
Black Lake .... 12.0 *Medium*
Liberty Lake .... 11.0 *Medium*
Spirit Lake .... 16.0 *Medium*
Bogacheil River .... 26.0 *Medium Hard*
Chehalis River .... 14.0 *Medium*
Cowlitz River .... 15.0 *Medium*
Hoh River .... 14.0 *Medium*
Humptulips River .... 16.0 *Medium*
Lewis River, North Fork .... 12.0 *Medium*
Columbia River .... 33.0 *Hard*
Newaukum River .... 13.0 *Medium*
Skagit River .... 15.0 *Medium*
Skookum Chuck .... 16.0 *Medium*
Toutle River .... 16.0 *Medium*
Washougal River .... 7.0 *Soft*
Wind River .... 14.0 *Medium*
White Salmon River .... 14.0 *Medium*

WISCONSIN

Wisconsin's 8,500, or more, lakes range from *very soft* waters to *hard* water. All fresh water fish from muskies to pan fish are plentiful, but Wisconsin ranks first of all the states in muskie fishing in her northern belt, Eagle River to the Indian Head area.

Wisconsin's Largest Lake:

Lake Winnebago	90.0	*Hard*

Wisconsin's trout streams are all *medium*, *medium hard* and *hard* waters and her thousands of miles of rich waters have brook, brown and rainbow trout. They run from 20 to more than 60.0 ppm CO_2. Her famous Brule River, in its 60 mile course averages 28.0 ppm CO_2.   *Medium Hard*

Brule River	28.0	*Hard*
Clam River	30.0	*Hard*
Des Moines or Sucker Lake	30.0	*Hard*
Round Lake	31.0	*Hard*

WYOMING

Bear River	50.0	*Hard*
Bear Creek	18.0	*Medium*
Boulder River	8.0	*Soft*
Hoback River	62.0	*Hard*
Lake Creek	93.0	*Hard*
Laramie River	41.0	*Hard*
Green River	39.0	*Hard*
Medicine Bow River	39.0	*Hard*
North Platte River	30.0	*Hard*
Pass Creek	90.0	*Hard*
Powder River	60.0	*Hard*
Ten Sleep River	23.0	*Medium Hard*
Shoshone River	26.0	*Medium Hard*
Wind River	30.0	*Hard*
Sandy River	18.0	*Medium*
New Fork, R. E. Branch	18.0	*Medium*
Snake River	29.0	*Medium Hard*
Jackson Lake	27.0	*Medium Hard*
Jenny Lake	9.0	*Soft*

NOTE. Data on additional states became available after press work had started. This information is listed on page 384.

YELLOWSTONE PARK

Firehole River	58.0	*Hard*
Madison River	43.0	*Hard*
Yellowstone River	16.0	*Medium*
South Twin Lake	26.0	*Medium Hard*
Old Faithful Geyser	78.0	*Hard*

MISSOURI RIVER

At Chamberlin, S. D.	60.0	*Hard*

MISSISSIPPI RIVER

At Fountain City, Wis.	52.0	*Hard*
At Cairo, Ill.	49.0	*Hard*
At Hayti, Mo.	50.0	*Hard*
At Baton Rouge, La.	45.0	*Hard*

THE GREAT LAKES

Lake Superior Average	21.0	*Medium Hard*
Lake Huron—North	24.0	*Medium Hard*
Lake Michigan	34.0	*Hard*
Lake Erie	39.0	*Hard*
Lake Ontario	42.0	*Hard*

GULF OF MEXICO

At Key Largo, Fla.	69.0	*Hard*
At Key West, Fla.	54.0	*Hard*
Near Pensacola, Fla.	53.0	*Hard*
Near Gulfport, Miss.	37.0	*Hard*

ATLANTIC OCEAN

At Bar Harbor, Me.	50.0	*Hard*
Atlantic City, N. J.	49.0	*Hard*
Marineland, Fla.	57.0	*Hard*
The Keys at Craig, Fla.	56.0	*Hard*

PACIFIC OCEAN

Discovery Passage (Tyee Club) Canada	49.0	*Hard*
La Push, Wash.	50.5	*Hard*
Below Long Beach, Calif.	51.0	*Hard*

CANADIAN WATERS

We who live near or along the Canadian border, think of Canada as American rather than Canadian. One could spend a lifetime testing the waters in the United States and never finish the job. So could he in Canada with her vast acreage of lakes and miles of streams.

The Province of British Columbia alone, would hold all of Texas, Michigan and the New England states. Ontario, still larger, would cover Texas, Minnesota and Wisconsin. The Province of Quebec would have room for all of Ontario, with the State of Texas thrown in. Canada's waters, like ours in the United States, are vast and varied from Newfoundland to the Yukon.

ALBERTA

Lake Louise	39.0	Hard
Lake Moraine	31.0	Hard

BRITISH COLUMBIA

Kamloops Lake	22.0	Medium Hard
Kootenay Lake	38.0	Hard
Paul Lake	73.0	Hard
Shuswap Lake, East	20.0	Medium Hard
Shuswap Lake, West	15.0	Medium
Columbia River at headwaters	56.0	Hard
Columbia River at Boat Encampment	33.0	Hard
Columbia River, The Dalles in Washington and Oregon, U. S. A.	33.0	Hard
Fraser River	30.0	Hard
Thompson River	18.0	Medium

VANCOUVER ISLAND, B. C.

Campbell Lake	10.0	Soft
Brewster Lake	5.0	Very Soft
Gosling Lake	10.0	Soft
Mohun Lake	6.0	Soft
Campbell River	10.0	Soft
Cowichan River	11.0	Medium
Quinsam River	20.0	Medium

ONTARIO

Lukinto Lake	50.0	Hard
Lake Nipigon	37.0	Hard
Gravel River	50.0	Hard
Jackfish River	34.0	Hard
Nipigon River	37.0	Hard
Lake Superior at Rossport	20.0	Medium

QUEBEC
Trois River .... 13.0 *Medium*
St. Lawrence River, City of Quebec .... 38.0 *Hard*

	pH	
Catfish River*	7.1	*Medium*
Tomasine River *	6.8	*Soft*
Old Woman Creek*	7.7	*Hard*
Desert Lake*	6.7	*Soft*
Irish Lake*	7.4	*Medium*
Gatinea Lake*	7.0	*Medium*
Lac Bas*	7.2	*Medium*
Loyal Lake*	6.7	*Soft*

The last eight waters* were tested by a friend of mine using a pH set only.

_____

The following data was recorded by Sid Gordon directly prior to the time *How To Fish From Top To Bottom* went to press:

INDIANA
French Lick Springs Pluto Water	125.0	*Hard*
Lost River	61.0	*Hard*
White River, West Fork	62.0	*Hard*
Wabash River	90.0	*Hard*

ILLINOIS
Bloomington Lake	65.0	*Hard*
Twin Lakes	68.0	*Hard*
Vermilion Lake	59.0	*Hard*
Illinois River	60.0	*Hard*
Kickapoo Creek	128.0	*Hard*
Sangamon River	72.0	*Hard*
Vermilion River	114.0	*Hard*

KENTUCKY
Kentucky River	42.0	*Hard*
Licking River	23.0	*Medium Hard*
Little Sandy River	34.0	*Hard*
Triplett Creek	15.0	*Medium*

MARYLAND
Middle Creek	20.0	*Medium*
Tuscarora River	42.0	*Hard*

OHIO
Lake Milton	29.0	*Medium Hard*

WEST VIRGINIA
Gauley River	12.0	*Medium*
Greenbrier River	27.0	*Medium Hard*
Howards Creek	35.0	*Hard*
Jackson River	53.0	*Hard*
New River	26.0	*Medium Hard*
Potomac River	47.0	*Hard*